AMERICA'S CHRISTIAN HISTORY

AMERICAN VISION

The mission of American Vision, Inc. is to publish and distribute books that lead individuals toward:

- A personal faith in the one true God: Father, Son, and Holy Spirit

- A lifestyle of practical discipleship

- A worldview that is consistent with the historic Christian faith

- An ability to apply the Bible to all of life

© 1993, 1995 American Vision, Inc. All rights reserved.
Published February 1993, First Edition.
Published February 1995, Second Edition.
Reprinted October 1995, 1996, 2000, 2003
Reprinted August 2005 with additions.
Printed in the United States of America.

AMERICAN VISION, INC.
3150-A Florence Rd, SW
Suite 2
Powder Springs, GA 30127
www.AmericanVision.org • 1-800-628-9460

Cover: *The Baptism of Pocahontas at Jamestown, Viginia (1613)* by John G. Chapman. (See Appendix H for complete image of painting and identification of subjects.)

Library of Congress Cataloging-in-Publication Data

DeMar, Gary.
    America's Christian History: The Untold Story/Gary DeMar—2nd ed.
    Includes bibliographical references and index.
    ISBN 0-915815-17-6 Hardbound
    1.History 2.Religion (Christianity) 3.Church/State

America's
Christian
History

Gary DeMar

American Vision Inc.
Powder Springs, Georgia

CONTENTS

CONTENTS

CONTENTS

INTRODUCTION

AMERICA'S CHRISTIAN HISTORY: FACT OR FICTION?

I believe no one can read the history of our country without realizing that the Good Book and the spirit of the Savior have from the beginning been our guiding geniuses.... Whether we look to the first charter of Virginia... or to the Charter of New England...or to the Charter of Massachusetts Bay...or to the Fundamental Orders of Connecticut...the same objective is present: A Christian land governed by Christian principles....

I believe the entire Bill of Rights came into being because of the knowledge our forefathers had of the Bible and their belief in it: freedom of belief, of expression, of assembly, of petition, the dignity of the individual, the sanctity of the home, equal justice under law, and the reservation of powers to the people....

I like to believe we are living today in the spirit of the Christian religion. I like also to believe that as long as we do so, no great harm can come to our country.

—Former Chief Justice Earl Warren,
addressing the annual prayer breakfast
of the International Council of
Christian Leadership, 1954[1]

WHEN KIRK FORDICE (1934-2004), FORMER GOVERNOR OF MISSISSIPPI, stated that "America is a Christian nation,"[2] the response from those opposed to this self-evident historical truth bordered on the hysterical: "There is a fine line between anti-Semitism and ignorance," said Rabbi Steven Engel, who leads Mississippi's largest Jewish congregation. "The governor has no tolerance at all to diversity—religious or racial," said state Rep. Ed Blackmon. "Unworthy of any governor elected to represent a diverse and pluralistic constituency," wrote Anti-Defamation League leaders.[3]

I wonder how atheists would have responded if Gov. Fordice had stated that we are "endowed by our Creator with certain inalienable rights"? Would they have claimed that the Declaration of Independence is "intolerant" of atheists and evolutionists?

The governor's controversial remarks landed him on CNN. His comments are perceptive and irrefutable. He stated simply:

> Christianity is the predominant religion in America. We all know that's an incontrovertible fact. The media always refer to the Jewish state of Israel. They talk about the Muslim country of Saudi Arabia, of Iran, of Iraq. We all talk about the Hindu nation of India. America is not a nothing country. It's a Christian Country.[4]

Fordice went on to cite "surveys noting that 86 percent of Americans consider themselves Christian, but praised America's ethnic diversity. 'It's the true melting pot of the world,' he said. 'That's the strength of our country, and the strength certainly is not enhanced by denying simple facts that Christianity is the predominate religion.'"[5]

History is on the side of Governor Fordice. "Protestant Christianity has been our established religion in almost every sense of that phrase.... The establishment of Protestant Christianity was one not only of law but also, and far more importantly, of culture. Protestant Christianity supplied the nation with its 'system of values.'"[6] This statement of historical fact, inscribed into law by the United States Supreme Court and echoed by presidents and governors for more than two centuries, is being weighed on the scales of modern-day secular presuppositions and the normless ideals of "multiculturalism" and "pluralism." By these standards, we should expect the claim of America's Christian heritage to be found wanting. There are, however, other standards which today's social critics ignore.

> In 1931 the U.S. Supreme Court noted that the United States is a Christian nation. In a mid-Atlantic summit with British Prime Minister Winston Churchill in the darkest hours of World War II, President Roosevelt—who had described the United States as "the lasting concord between men and nations, founded on the principles of Christianity"—asked the crew of an American warship to join him in a rousing chorus of the hymn "Onward, Christian Soldiers."
>
> In 1947, writing to Pope Pius XII, President Truman said flatly, "This is a Christian nation."
>
> Nobody argued with any of them.[7]

Roosevelt and Truman would be forced into a debate if they uttered such statements today in the highly charged atmosphere of Political Correctness that is sweeping across our nation. So would former presidents

Woodrow Wilson and Jimmy Carter. In his famous address, "The Bible and Progress," delivered in Denver on May 7, 1911, Woodrow Wilson told his audience that "America was born a Christian nation. America was born to exemplify that devotion to the elements of righteousness which are derived from the revelations of Holy Scripture."[8] Presidential candidate Jimmy Carter told reporters in June of 1976 that "We have a responsibility to try to shape government so that it does exemplify the will of God."[9]

Woodrow Wilson stated emphatically that "America was born a Christian nation."

A great deal of the editorial savagery leveled against Governor Fordice could have been alleviated if the historical record had been studied. But even this would not have been enough. Facts are not the problem. There is a decided bias against things Christian. Religion is fine, say the secularists, as long as it remains "Socially irrelevant, even if privately engaging."[10] Mixing religion and politics is the ultimate social *faux pas*.[11] But this has not always been the case.

What It Is Not

The proposal that America is a Christian nation does not mean that *every* American is now or ever was a Christian. Moreover, it does not mean that either the Church or the State should force people to profess belief in Christianity or attend religious services. Furthermore, a belief in a Christian America does not mean that non-Christians, and for that matter, dissenting Christians, cannot hold contrary opinions in a climate of a general Christian consensus.

Christianity *presupposes* that there are people who are not Christians. There is no ethnic, ecclesiastical, or national right to the Christian religion. The Great Commission is a command for Christians to work for the discipleship of nations (Matt. 28:18–20). Even though others of competing religious traditions might be horrified at such a thought, evangelism is a fundamental part of the Christian worldview.

What is the discipleship process? *Proclamation* coupled with *persuasion*. Forcing people to embrace Christ is foreign to the Christian worldview. In addition, there is nothing in the Christian worldview that gives the State authority to coerce non-Christians to profess Christ. Christianity is a religion of the heart. "Our best lead here is David Riesman's phrase 'inner directed.'"[12] There can be no change in a person unless the Holy Spirit does His sovereign work of regeneration. Regeneration is not the work of man, the Church, or the State. The Christian's duty is to proclaim the redemptive message of the cross and to "contend earnestly for the faith which was once for all delivered to the saints" (Jude 3).

Having said this, the State is duty bound to protect Christians and the Church as they carry out their God-ordained mission (Rom. 13:1–4; 1 Tim. 2:1–2). This was the view of John Witherspoon (1723–1794), a Presbyterian minister, president of the College of New Jersey (1768–93), a delegate to the Continental Congress (1776–1782), the only clergyman to sign the Declaration of Independence, and a member of the New Jersey state legislature (1783, 1789). As the College of New Jersey's chief lecturer, Witherspoon touched the lives of nearly 500 graduates. Eleven percent of them became presidents of colleges. Nearly one-sixth of the 55 participants in the national Constitutional Convention of 1787 were Princeton graduates.

As both a statesman and a clergyman, Witherspoon had a profound effect on the development of the early colonies.

James Madison, known as the "father of the Constitution," was his most notable student. Witherspoon taught a vice president, 21 senators,

29 representatives, 56 state legislators, and 33 judges, three of whom became members of the United States Supreme Court.[13] Witherspoon called on the civil magistrate to supply "protection and security" for the various Christian sects while it remained neutral to their ecclesiastical constitutions.[14]

It would be unreasonable for Christians *not* to work for a legal and civil system that would be more protective of things expressly Christian. This means electing to civil office supporters of the Christian faith. Christians believe that a nation is blessed, blessed for everyone, "whose God is the Lord" (Psalm 33:12).

> Witherspoon and most American political thinkers believed that society was antecedent to government; that is, social institutions, rooted in the family, village life, and voluntary associations, existed prior to government and took precedent over it. In practical terms, this meant that the commanding position of Christianity in American *Society* would allow religion to flourish as long as the civil government did nothing to interfere with it. That Americans were a Protestant Christian people was taken for granted by Witherspoon and most of his generation.[15]

The early constitutional framers, similar in perspective as Witherspoon, were convinced that there was an intrinsic connection between morality and good government. In practical terms this means that non-Christians are not exempt from God's moral law. An atheist, for example, cannot appeal to his atheism and freely live as an ethical anarchist. While the State certainly has no jurisdiction over his beliefs, it does have something to say about how he acts. This moral and civil authority remains an irritant for many in our day. All people, however, answer to some standard of behavior. The question is this: In a religiously diverse society, what ethical standard should the civil magistrate use to make moral judgments about civil activity? This question is the essence of the debate about a "Christian America."

What It Is

It's one thing to claim that there is no evidence of a Christian America and prove it. It's another thing to fabricate history to suit one's entrenched presuppositions. An honest study of America's past will show that a majority of Americans shared a common religion and ethic. America's earliest founders were self-professing Christians and their founding documents expressed a belief in a Christian worldview. John Winthrop's

5

sermon aboard the *Arbella* in 1630 is one piece of evidence supporting this historical truth.

> For the persons, we are a Company professing ourselves fellow members of Christ....
>
> For the work we have in hand, it is by a mutual consent through a special overruling providence, and a more than an ordinary approbation of the Churches of Christ to seek out a place of Cohabitation and Consortship under a due form of Government both civil and ecclesiastical....[16]

John Winthrop described the group of Puritans who formed Massachusetts Bay Colony as "a Company professing ourselves fellow members of Christ."

It is important to point out that Winthrop believed that the Christian religion goes beyond its application to the individual in regeneration and personal holy living, and that it is perfectly suited for both civil and ecclesiastical concerns. From Winthrop's perspective, if theft was wrong for the individual and his family, it was equally wrong in business, Church, and State. The same ethical principles applied in all relationships, including the civil sphere.

Freedom and liberty, ideals cherished by all Americans, were rooted in a biblical moral order. Liberty was not license. Freedom was not the right always to do what one pleased.

> For Winthrop, success was much more explicitly tied to the creation of a certain kind of ethical community than it is for most Americans today. His idea of freedom differs from ours in a similar way. He decried what he called "natural liberty," which is the freedom to do whatever one wants, evil as well as good. True freedom—what he called "moral"

freedom, "in reference to the covenant between God and man"—is a liberty "to that only which is good, just and honest." "This liberty," he said, "you are to stand for with the hazard of your lives."[17]

Winthrop's definition of liberty is far from the modern meaning of liberty. As it is usually defined today, liberty is freedom *from* moral restraints. One is not truly free, according to the contemporary use of the term, if one is bound by any moral code.

A Christian Commonwealth

America cannot be rightly understood without first understanding that the early settlers established what can be best described as a "Christian Commonwealth." Winthrop appealed to God's "Commandments, Ordinances, and Laws" as the philosophical and moral foundation of this early social experiment. Such a society was to be biblically centered. Of this there is no question. No other choice was possible: "Therefore, let us choose life," Winthrop declared, "that we, and our Seed, may live; by obeying his voice, and cleaving to him for he is our life, and prosperity [Deut. 30:19b–20a]."

The ethical system adopted by Americans and embedded in their social order rested on the bedrock of a biblical moral order. This is the essence of the Christian America claim. To say it another way, the Bible served as the ethical foundation for the young Republic, even for those who did not profess the Christian religion. "Not all the founders acknowledged a formal faith, but it was significant that their view of man had a deeply religious foundation. Rights were 'God-given'; man was 'endowed by his Creator'; there were 'natural laws' and 'natural rights'; freedom was related to the 'sacredness' of man. The development of a free man was not divorced from the idea of moral man, any more than religious man could be separated from moral man."[18] Freedom was not opposed to law.

A Foreigner's View

In 1831 the French social philosopher Alexis de Tocqueville landed in America to observe the new nation and her institutions. Tocqueville's work was published in two parts in 1835 and 1840 as *Democracy in America*, "the most comprehensive and penetrating analysis of the relationship between character and society in America that has ever been written."[19] His observations on the ethical justification of America are revealing and worthy of study.

The sects that exist in the United States are innumerable. They all differ in respect to the worship which is due to the Creator; but they all agree in respect to the duties which are due from man to man. Each sect adores the Deity in its own peculiar manner, *but all sects preach the same moral law* in the name of God.... Moreover, all the sects of the United States are comprised within the great unity of Christianity, and *Christian morality is everywhere the same.*

It may fairly be believed that a certain number of Americans pursue a peculiar form of worship from habit more than from conviction. In the United States the sovereign authority is religious, and consequently hypocrisy must be common; *but there is no country in the world where the Christian religion retains a greater influence over the souls of men than in America.*[20]

Two-hundred years after John Winthrop's sermon aboard the *Arabella,* Tocqueville continued to find in America "an ostensible respect for Christian morality and virtue."[21] This is the substance of a working definition of "Christian America"—the sharing of common moral values that have been shaped with reference to the Bible. "The biblical model of a 'city on a hill,'" to use Winthrop's phrase, "was the relevant goal for political action. Puritan divines called for the establishment of a 'Holy Community,' governed according to standards derived from Christian principles of morality and justice."[22]

Alexis de Tocqueville: "All the sects of the United States are comprised within the great unity of Christianity, and Christian morality is everywhere the same."

The Great Reversal

One only has to look at what laws have been overturned in recent years to prove that Americans once shared a Christian ethic. Consider the legalization of abortion and sodomy. One of the arguments used to push for legalization of these moral evils is that laws prohibiting the practices "have their roots in religious doctrines—fundamentalist Protestant, Mormon, Roman Catholic."[23] The support of anti-abortion legislation because the Bible forbids abortion would mean enacting "laws that impose such doctrines on the people as a whole."[24] It is because the prohibition against abortion is found in the Bible, so the reasoning seems to go, that abortion *must be legalized*. The same would be true of homosexuality, adultery, and bestiality.

Citing another example, school sex-education programs supporting abstinence as *the* way of guaranteeing protection against pregnancy and the deadly AIDS virus are criticized and often opposed because abstinence rests on religious presuppositions.[25] The Bible is also against rape, incest, and assault. Should these deeds be legalized because they are prohibited by laws found in the Bible? Are all laws suspect because they are based on religious presuppositions? Our nation is paying a high price for such perverse logic. "Woe to those who call evil good, and good evil; who substitute darkness for light and light for darkness; who substitute bitter for sweet, and sweet for bitter!" (Isa. 5:20).

Still in Search of Christian America

A number of scholars discount the historical evidence of a Christian America by defining the concept out of existence. Here is a representative example of this methodology: "Some commendable examples of Christian principles and practices can be found in America's origins. But since such principles and practices seldom appeared in anything like pure forms, claims about America's Christian origins should be carefully qualified. If the colonial or revolutionary past is to be used as a model, it must be done selectively."[26] This argument erects an impossible standard. It is like saying that a Church is not Christian because there are hypocrites among its members. No one is maintaining that America was heaven on earth. Christian Americans were as "pure" as their biblical counterparts in their personal, social, and civil behavior. In a word, they were sinners.

The historical record is available for all to see. America's Christian history is a fact. It is not honest to redefine history or tamper with the historical record just so that people of differing opinions are not offended. It was America's moral choice that made this nation the envy of the world and a haven for the oppressed.

The Supreme Court Has Spoken

In 1892 the United States Supreme Court determined, in the case of *The Church of the Holy Trinity vs. United States*, that America was a

9

Christian nation from its earliest days. After examining a full range of historical documents, Associate Justice David J. Brewer concluded that Americans are "a religious people. This is historically true. From the discovery of this continent to the present hour, there is a single voice making this affirmation." Beginning with Ferdinand and Isabella's commission to Christopher Columbus—"by the grace of God" and "by God's assistance"—to make a voyage "to some of the continents and islands in the oceans" to a survey of then current state constitutions, the court concluded:

David J. Brewer, Associate Justice of the U.S. Supreme Court, surveyed the historical evidence of America's founding and concluded, "This is a Christian nation."

There is no dissonance in these declarations. There is a universal language pervading them all, having one meaning; they affirm and reaffirm that this is a religious nation. These are not individual sayings, declarations of private persons: they are organic utterances; they speak the voice of the entire people.

If we pass beyond these matters to a view of American life as expressed by its laws, its business, its customs and its society, we find everywhere a clear recognition of the same truth. Among other matters note the following: The form of oath universally prevailing, concluding with an appeal to the Almighty; the custom of opening sessions of all deliberative bodies and most conventions with prayer; the prefatory words of all wills, "In the name of God, amen"; the laws respecting the observance of the Sabbath, with the general cessation of all secular business, and the closing of courts, legislatures, and other similar public assemblies on that day; the churches and church organizations which abound in every city, town and hamlet; the multitude of charitable organizations existing everywhere under

Christian auspices; the gigantic missionary associations, with general support, and aiming to establish Christian missions in every quarter of the globe. These, and many other matters which might be noticed, add a volume of unofficial declarations to the mass of organic utterances that this is a Christian nation.[27]

In 1931, Supreme Court Justice George Sutherland reviewed the 1892 decision and reaffirmed that Americans are a "Christian people." As late as 1952, even the liberal Supreme Court Justice William O. Douglas declared that "we are a religious people and our institutions presuppose a Supreme Being."

In 1931, Supreme Court Justice George Sutherland reviewed the Supreme Court's 1892 decision and reaffirmed that Americans are a "Christian people."

David Brewer and the *Holy Trinity* Case

It seems, however, that not even a decision from the Supreme Court is enough to convince some people of the Christian nation thesis. Representatives of Americans United for Separation of Church and State dispute the significance of the Supreme Court's 1892 *Holy Trinity v. United States* decision authored by Justice David Brewer (1837–1910). They claim that the *Trinity* decision is a "legal anomaly that has been cited by the court only once since then." They further dismiss its significance by asserting that "the opinion of one obscure Supreme Court justice does not amount to an official decree that the United States is a Christian nation." Americans United claims that five years later, in an unrelated case, Brewer seemed to "step away from" his 1892 decision.[28]

While Americans United believes that two Supreme Court acknowledgments (1892 and 1931) are not enough to substantiate the claim that America was founded as a Christian nation, supposedly a single statement in the 1797 Treaty of Tripoli which declares that "[T]he Government of the United States is not, in any sense, founded on the Christian religion...," is enough to debunk the Christian nation claim.[29] Why is a single obscure treaty enough evidence to *disprove* the notion that America is a Christian nation but two Supreme Court rulings are not enough evidence to *prove* America was founded as a Christian nation?

Americans United does not tell people that the 1797 Treaty with a Muslim nation was written to assure its rulers that the United States would not force the people of Tripoli to embrace Christianity. In addition, in 1805 the treaty was revised and did not include the language stating that "the Government of the United States is not, in any sense, founded on the Christian religion." (See chapter 8 of *America's Christian History* for a detailed study of the historical background and significance of the Treaty of Tripoli.)

As was stated, Americans United claims that David Brewer "seemed to step away" from the 1892 *Trinity* case when he ruled in favor of a New Orleans city ordinance allowing prostitution in one zone in the city. Supposedly a group of Methodist ministers argued that the ordinance encouraged prostitution, and cited the *Trinity* decision as evidence that such activity is inconsistent with Christianity "which the Supreme Court of the United States says is the foundation of our government and the civilization which it has produced...." Americans United claims that "Brewer completely ignored the church's religious argument and upheld the New Orleans law."[30] Americans United offers no documentation for its claim (see Appendix D).

In addition, how does Americans United explain Brewer's *The United States: A Christian Nation*, a series of lectures that was published in book form in 1905 while he was still a member of our nation's highest court?[31] In it, Brewer reiterates the history behind the 1892 *Trinity* case and states clearly that America was founded as a Christian nation, as the following citations indicate:

- "This republic is classified among the Christian nations of the world" (13).

- "In the case of Holy Trinity Church *vs.* United States, 143 U.S. 471, that court, after mentioning various circumstances, add, 'these and many other matters which might be noticed, add a volume of unofficial declarations to the mass of organic utterances that this is a Christian nation'" (13).

12

- "[W]e constantly speak of this republic as a Christian nation—in fact, as the leading Christian nation in the world. This popular use of the term certainly has significance. It is not a mere creation of the imagination. It is not a term of derision but has a substantial basis—one which justifies its use" (13–14). Brewer then spends twenty-six pages convincingly supporting his claim with historical evidence.

- "In no charter or constitution is there anything to even suggest that any other than the Christian is the religion of this country. In none of them is Mohammed or Confucius or Buddha in any manner noticed. In none of them is Judaism recognized other than by way of toleration of its special creed. While the separation of church and state is often affirmed, there is nowhere a repudiation of Christianity as one of the institutions as well as benedictions of society. In short, there is no charter or constitution that is either infidel, agnostic, or anti-Christian. Wherever there is a declaration in favor of any religion it is of the Christian" (24).

- "You will have noticed that I have presented no doubtful facts. Nothing has been stated which is debatable. The quotations from charters are in the archives of the several States; the laws are on the statute books; judicial opinions are taken from the official reports; statistics from the census publications. In short, no evidence has been presented which is open to question" (29).

- "I could show how largely our laws and customs are based upon the laws of Moses and the teachings of Christ; how constantly the Bible is appealed to as the guide of life and the authority in questions of morals" (29).

- "This is a Christian nation..." (30).

A study of Brewer's judicial career could hardly lead anyone to conclude that he was an "obscure Supreme Court justice." He is "obscure" only to those who reject "his Puritan sense of character and obligation."[32]

What About Now?

Can America now be called a Christian nation? While the majority of Americans tenuously hold on to the remnants of a biblical moral order, there is no doubt that the memory is fading quickly. The shift in America's moral foundation has taken place. Just as there is overwhelming evidence that America was founded as a Christian nation, there is ample evidence that there is a conscious effort to abandon that heritage in our education and legal systems.

> The Bible, already banned in some schools, legislatures and graduation ceremonies, is becoming increasingly unwelcome in the nation's courtrooms.
>
> In the past 13 months [of 1991–1992], two state supreme courts ruled that it is no longer acceptable for prosecutors to attempt to obtain death-penalty sentences by reading biblical-scriptures to jurors.[33]

Soon after the defeat of George Bush in the 1992 election, a group of "centrist" Republicans met to outline a strategy to bring the party back to what they considered to be the "mainstream." How would they accomplish this? "Our purpose," Representative Tom Campbell of California said, "is to exclude issues of morality and conscience as litmus tests of being a Republican."[34] Of course, no one is saying that a person cannot be a Republican if he or she does not agree with the platform of the party. The same is true of Democrats. The issue is values. What does the party stand for? Morality is essential in developing social policy. Certain causes, for example protection of the unborn, are rooted in the conviction that those who cannot defend themselves should expect protection from those who are able to fight for them. Here is one Republican's evaluation of the new centrist Republican Party:

> Representative Tom Campbell of California announced the formation of the Republican Majority Coalition by declaring, "We are inclusive, not exclusive." He and his co-founders want to build a party that steers clear of controversies about "values." They vow to avoid vexing moral quandaries, from abortion to the teaching of ethics in schools.
>
> These make-nice Republicans have taken up the mantle of the Laodiceans, whom the Book of Revelation says were "neither cold nor hot...[but] lukewarm." Yet like the Laodiceans, they invite contempt. Having given up the chance to define themselves by principles, they can define themselves only by dollars-and-cents promises. At best, they can create cover for libertarians in the Republican fold.[35]

EMANCIPATOR—*EXTRA*.

NEW-YORK, SEPTEMBER 2, 1839.

American Anti-Slavery Almanac for 1840.

The seven cuts following, are selected from thirteen, which may be found in the Anti-Slavery Almanac for 1840. They represent well-authenticated facts, and illustrate in various ways, the cruelties daily inflicted upon three millions of native born Americans, by their fellow-countrymen! A brief explanation follows each cut.

The peculiar "Domestic Institutions of our Southern brethren."

Selling a Mother from her Child.   *Mothers with young Children at work in the field.*

A Woman chained to a Girl, and a Man in irons at work in the field.   *"They can't take care of themselves"; explained in an interesting article.*

Slavery with dogs and guns. A Slave drowned.   *Scenery of the Northern States in executing the law.*

Even though abolitionist newspapers such as the *Emancipator* used propaganda to further their cause, both sides of the slavery debate formed their arguments based on moral considerations.

I wonder how Representative Campbell's desire to "exclude issues of morality and conscience" would have gone over with slaves in the 1860s or blacks in the 1960s. The slavery issue in Kansas was an ethical issue that called the Republican Party into existence in 1854. "The pronouncement that slavery was a moral, social and political evil was coupled with denunciation of the Kansas-Nebraska legislation and the Fugitive Slave law."[36] The Republican Party came to power in 1861 with Abraham Lincoln as president. Those who started the Republican Party did so in terms of "morality and conscience."

Not to be outdone, after the 1994 mid-term election, Jesse Jackson equated the efforts of the Christian Coalition with Nazi Germany. In comments reported in the December 3, 1994, issue of the *Chicago Sun-Times*, Jackson alleged that "the Christian Coalition was a strong force in Germany.... It laid down a suitable scientific, theological rationale for the tragedy in Germany." Contrary to Jackson's revisionism, Christianity was an enemy of Nazism.

According to the late William L. Shirer, author of *The Rise and Fall of the Third Reich*, "the Nazi regime intended eventually to destroy Christianity in Germany...and substitute the old paganism of the early tribal Germanic gods and the new paganism of the Nazi extremists."[37] Martin Bormann, "one of the men closest to Hitler, said publicly in 1941, 'National Socialism and Christianity are irreconcilable.'"[38] George L. Mosse, author of *Nazi Culture*, quotes from Bormann's "National Socialist and Christian Concepts Incompatible" speech where Bormann states, "We can do without Christianity." He went on to say:

> The Christian Churches build upon the ignorance of men and strive to keep large portions of the people in ignorance because only in this way can the Christian Churches maintain their power. On the other hand, National Socialism [Nazism] is based on scientific foundations. Christianity's immutable principles, which were laid down almost two thousand years ago, have increasingly stiffened into life-alien dogmas. National Socialism [Nazism], however, if it wants to fulfill its task further, must always guide itself according to the newest data of scientific searches.[39]

This is why Shirer could write in *The Nightmare Years*, "We know now what Hitler envisioned for the German Christians: the utter suppression of their religion."[40] With this historical context in mind, Jackson's rhetoric sounds frighteningly familiar and sinister.

Even with the steady secularization of law in America, remnants of the Christian moral order remain. It is this remnant that maintains societal stability. Biblical law of the Old and New Testaments is essential for the development and maintenance of a free and just society. The survival and stability of our nation depends on how faithful Americans will be in retaining what is left of these ethical absolutes.

Notes

1. Quoted in Jim Nelson Black, *When Nations Die: Ten Warning Signs of a Culture in Crisis* (Wheaton, IL: Tyndale House Publishers, 1994), 253.
2. *U.S. News & World Report* (November 30, 1992), 21.
3. Quoted in Robert Davis, "Mississippi Governor's 'Christian Nation' Remark Sparks Furor," *USA Today* (November 19, 1992), 2A.
4. "Mississippi Governor Criticized for 'Christian Nation' Remark," *Dallas/Fort Worth Heritage* (January 1993), 14. Quoted in John W. Whitehead, *Religious Apartheid: The Separation of Religion from American Public Life* (Chicago, IL: Moody Press, 1994), 149.
5. "Mississippi Governor Criticized for 'Christian Nation' Remark," 14.
6. Terry Eastland, "In Defense of Religious America," *Commentary: A Monthly Publication of the American Jewish Committee* (June 1981), 39–41.
7. Larry Witham, "'Christian Nation' Now Fighting Words," *The Washington Times* (November 23, 1992), A1.
8. *The Papers of Woodrow Wilson*, ed. Arthur S. Link, 57 vols. (Princeton, NJ: Princeton University Press, 1966), 23:12–20. Quoted in Richard V. Pierard and Robert D. Linder, *Civil Religion and the Presidency* (Grand Rapids, MI: Academie/Zondervan, 1988), 153.
9. Richard G. Hutcheson, Jr., *God in the White House: How Religion Has Changed the Modern Presidency* (New York: Macmillan, 1988), 1.
10. Os Guinness, *The Gravedigger File: Papers on the Subversion of the Modern Church* (Downers Grove, IL: InterVarsity Press, 1983), 79.
11. Michael Gartner, "Religion and politics just don't mix," *USA Today* (October 4, 1994), 11A and James W. Watkins, "A try to wrap politics in religion," *The Plain Dealer* (October 5, 1994), 11B.
12. Crane Brinton, *A History of Western Morals* (New York: Harcourt, Brace and Company, 1959), 223.
13. John Willson, "John Witherspoon and the Presbyterian Constitution," *We The People: Essays on the Major Documents of the American Founding* (Hillsdale, MI: Hillsdale College Press, 1994), 3.

14. Willson, "John Witherspoon and the Presbyterian Constitution," 23.

15. Willson, "John Witherspoon and the Presbyterian Constitution," 24.

16. John Winthrop (1588–1649), "A Model of Christian Charity," (1630), quoted in Mark A. Noll, ed., *Eerdmans' Handbook to Christianity in America* (Grand Rapids, MI: Eerdmans, 1983), 38.

17. Robert N. Bellah, *et al.*, *Habits of the Heart: Individualism and Commitment in American Life* (Berkeley, CA: University of California Press, 1985), 29.

18. Norman Cousins, *'In God We Trust': The Religious Beliefs and Ideas of the American Founding Fathers* (New York: Harper & Brothers, 1958), 10.

19. Robert N. Bellah, *Habits of the Heart*, viii.

20. Alexis de Tocqueville, *Democracy in America*, 2 vols. (New York: Alfred A. Knopf, 1945), 1:303. Emphasis added.

21. Tocqueville, *Democracy in America*, 1:305.

22. A. James Reichley, *Religion in American Public Life* (Washington, DC: The Brookings Institution, 1985), 55.

23. Barbara S. Mosbacher and Robert M. Pennoyer, "Republicans Must Change Abortion Plank," Letter to the Editor, *New York Times* (May 4, 1992), A14.

24. Mosbacher and Pennoyer, "Republicans Must Change Abortion Plank," A14.

25. Andrea Stone, "Abstinence Push at Center Stage in Sex-Ed Debate," *USA Today* (May 8, 1992), 10A.

26. George M. Marsden, "Were American Origins 'Christian'?" *Eerdmans' Handbook to Christianity in America*, 151.

27. *Church of the Holy Trinity v. United States*. Argued and submitted January 7, 1892. Decided February 29, 1892. Justice Brewer delivered the opinion of the court.

28. From a booklet titled *In 1962 Madalyn Murray O'Hair Kicked God, the Bible and Prayer Out of School* (Silver Spring, MD: Americans United for Separation of Church and State, n.d.), 10–11.

29. *In 1962 Madalyn Murray O'Hair Kicked God, the Bible and Prayer Out of School*, 8–9.

30. *In 1962 Madalyn Murray O'Hair Kicked God, the Bible and Prayer Out of School*, 9.

31. David J. Brewer, *The United States: A Christian Nation* (Powder Springs, GA: American Vision, [1905] 1996).

32. Kermit L. Hall, "David J. Brewer," in Leonard W. Levy, ed., *Encyclopedia of the American Constitution*, 2 vols. (New York: Macmillan, 1986), 1:153.

33. Valerie Richardson, "Bible put on book blacklist by courtrooms in two states," *Washington Times* (December 17, 1992).

34. Quoted in Ernie Freda, "GOP moderates search for mainstream," *Atlanta Constitution* (December 16, 1992), A8.

35. Tony Snow, "The Great Giveaway Game," *New York Times* (December 22, 1992), A13.

36. Edgar E. Robinson, "Republican Party (U.S.)," *Encyclopedia Britannica*, 24 vols. (Chicago, IL: Encyclopedia Britannica, Inc., 1961), 19:201–202.

37. William L. Shirer, *The Rise and Fall of the Third Reich* (New York: Simon and Schuster, 1960), 240.

38. Shirer, *Rise and Fall of the Third Reich*, 240.

39. Martin Bormann, "National Socialist and Christian Concepts Incompatible" in George L. Moss, *Nazi Culture* (New York: Grosset & Dunlap, 1968), 244.

40. William L. Shirer, *The Nightmare Years: 1930–1940* (Boston: Little, Brown and Company, 1984), 156.

CHAPTER 1

CENSORING THE PAST

THERE IS A LOT OF TALK TODAY ABOUT CENSORSHIP. RECENT ART EXHIBITS, funded by tax dollars and promoted by the National Endowment for the Arts, have come under severe attack. Many Americans rightly criticize these exhibits as inappropriate, certainly for viewing, but most assuredly for government support and funding. Museums, government-funded artists, Hollywood activists, homosexual groups, and the government-funded NEA (National Endowment for the Arts)[1] are crying "censorship" over such protests.

In the 1990's, Rev. Donald Wildmon and his American Family Association targeted Waldenbooks, a subsidiary of K-Mart, for selling pornography. Harry Hoffman, president of Waldenbooks at the time, said that Wildmon and others like him "want to censor and stop the sales of constitutionally protected publications they deem objectionable."[2]

Protests against pornography and government-funded art are not acts of censorship. Censorship is a mandate by the civil government that prohibits the publication, sale, or distribution of material it deems to be politically harmful to its own interests. As civil libertarian Nat Hentoff describes censorship, "Legally, censorship in violation of the First Amendment can only take place when an agent or agency of the state—a public school principal, a congressman, a President—suppresses speech."[3]

In constitutional terms, it is not considered censorship for a government to refuse to pay for objectionable material. In the case of pornographic "art," the protestors are only asking that their tax money not be used to fund the offensive material. Rev. Wildmon was not asking the government to prohibit Waldenbooks from selling *Playboy* and *Penthouse;* he was only calling on concerned citizens to stop doing business with K-Mart and its subsidiaries.[4] He wanted the same freedoms that the pornographers claimed only belonged to their industry. Wildmon writes: "We don't want K-Mart, *Playboy* and *Penthouse* drawing the line for the rest of us. The First Amendment belongs to all Americans, not just to pornographers."[5]

The Censorship Bandwagon

Literature of all types has been scrutinized by numerous groups from different ends of the political and religious spectrum. Those on the political left have denounced classic works like Charles Dickens' *Oliver Twist* as being "anti-semitic." William Shakespeare's *King Lear* has been condemned as "sexist." *Tom Sawyer*, Mark Twain's coming-of-age classic, has suffered a double blow with denouncements of "racism" and "sexism." Beatrix Potter's *Peter Rabbit* and *Benjamin Bunny* have been criticized "because they are about 'middle-class rabbits.'"[6]

In 1988, librarians in Cobb County, Georgia, wanted to remove *Nancy Drew* and the *Hardy Boys* from the library shelves. The librarians cited lack of shelf space as the reason for the exclusion of the popular mystery series. Mary Louis Rheay, director of the Cobb County Library System, tells a different story, saying that "series books are poorly written and do not meet library standards for book selection."[7] In 1994, the library board in Wellesley, Massachusetts, voted 5 to 1 to keep *Playboy* on the shelves. The board said the magazine, like all its material, is protected by free speech provisions. "There is something in the library to offend everyone," librarian Anne Reynolds said. "We cannot be in the position of censoring everything. Those days are gone." Trustee Carol Gleason, who voted to remove the magazine, said, "If minors cannot buy the magazine in a store, why should they be able to obtain it in the library?"[8]

Who Draws the Line?

An *ad hoc* public school committee supported the removal of books by Dr. James Dobson, a Christian psychologist, from the library of the Early Childhood Family Education Program of the Mankato, Minnesota, school system. They were removed because the staff "disagreed with Dobson's views on child discipline, which includes an endorsement of spanking, and because of the religious nature of his philosophy."[9]

Donated books are often refused by libraries because of religious content. *The Closing of the American Heart*, written by Dr. Ronald H. Nash, was donated to the Haggard Library in Plano, Texas, by a group of concerned citizens. Nash is a former professor of religion and philosophy at Western Kentucky University who presently teaches at Reformed Theological Seminary in Orlando, Florida. He has also served as an advisor to the United States Civil Rights Commission. Why was his book refused? Certainly not because of his academic and professional credentials. Book donations had to pass the library's evaluation criteria.[10] *Closing of the American Heart* did not pass because of its Christian perspective.

Each year People for the American Way (PAW), a liberal political advocacy group, publishes a report on censorship and "book banning." Most of the books which are brought into question deal with occultic themes, promiscuous sexual content, and advocacy of homosexuality. Most of the protestors are parents who send their children to government controlled (public) schools. PAW considers such parental concern over what children read "attacks on the freedom to learn."[11] What PAW does not tell its unsuspecting audience is that incidents of so-called censorship are negligible compared to the number of schools and libraries in existence. For example, the most challenged book, *Scary Stories to Tell in the Dark,* "was challenged only 7 times out of 84,000 public schools and never removed." In fact, Kristi Harrick, press secretary for the Family Research Council, reports that "none of the most challenged books were censored."[12]

Eric Buehrer, a former public-school teacher and president of Gateways to Better Education in Lake Forest, California, states that "PAW has confused the issues of material selection and censorship. What used to be called discernment is now called censorship."[13] Why is it called "censorship" when parents apply standards for book selection but called "meeting library standards" when a librarian evaluates a book?

Judgments are constantly made as to what children should read and what books should appear on library shelves. As we've seen, librarians appeal to "library standards" when selecting books. There is nothing wrong with having "standards."

Unfortunately, these "library standards" are neither applied consistently in libraries and schools nor always reported in the same way by the press.[14] It seems that when concerned Christian parents voice objections to the content of books, they are said to be censors. But when books with Christian themes are refused by libraries or when teachers are denied the right to read a Bible silently during a reading period,[15] we learn that the rejection is based upon the religious nature of the literature. Rarely are such actions by libraries and schools said to be "censorship" by even the strongest opponents of book banning.

Will the Real Censors Please Stand Up

It is instructive how one segment of our society screams "censorship" every time its views are questioned, but when Christians claim "censorship" of the facts of history, they are ignored by the guardians of the First Amendment.

Liberal media coverage of world events is just one example of the anti-Christian bias of mainstream contemporary society. Consider journalistic coverage of events in Eastern Europe. Rev. Laszlo Tokes, the Hungarian pastor who sparked the Romanian Revolution, stated that "Eastern Europe is not just in a political revolution but a religious renaissance." How many people read in their local newspapers or saw on the evening news that Rev. Tokes believed he had been saved from execution through "divine intervention"? Explicitly Christian themes are regularly excluded from news articles: "References to 'Jesus,' the 'Christian spirit,' and Czechoslovakia's role as the 'spiritual crossroads of Europe' were omitted from excerpts of President Vaclav Havel's New Year's Day address. *The New York Times, The Washington Post,* and *Newsweek* were among the sinful censors."[16]

None of these examples should surprise the informed Christian. The present educational establishment, to cite just one group, has been obscuring the past so that our children have no way of comparing the facts of history with the distorted version promoted by biased secular historians.

Censorship at Work in the Classroom

Public school textbooks are fertile ground for the seeds of willful historical deception. Paul C. Vitz, professor of psychology at New York University, spent months of careful analysis of sixty textbooks used in elementary schools across the country. The study was sponsored by the National Institute on Education. The texts were examined in terms of their references to religion, either directly or indirectly. "In grades 1 through 4 these books introduce the child to U.S. society—to family life, community activities, ordinary economic transactions, and some history. *None of the books covering grades 1 through 4 contain one word referring to any religious activity in contemporary American life.*"[17] Dr. Vitz offers an example of how this translates into the real world of classroom instruction:

> Some particular examples of the bias against religion are significant. One social studies book has thirty pages on the Pilgrims, including the first Thanksgiving. But there is not one word (or image) that referred to religion as even a part of the Pilgrims' life. One mother whose son is in a class using this book wrote me to say that he came home and told her that "Thanksgiving was when the Pilgrims gave thanks to the Indians." The mother called the principal of this suburban New York City school to point out that Thanksgiving was when the Pilgrims thanked God. The principal responded by saying "that was her opinion"—the schools could only teach what was in the books![18]

In 1986 school children in Seattle, Washington, were given a large dose of revisionist history in the booklet *Teaching about Thanksgiving*. The children were told that "the Pilgrims were narrow-minded bigots who survived initially only with the Indian's help, but turned on them when their help wasn't needed anymore." The Pilgrims "had something up their sleeves other than friendship when they invited the Indians to a Thanksgiving feast, and it was the Indians who ended up bringing most of the food, anyway."[19] The booklet has obvious biases and is filled with historical inaccuracies. For example, supposedly Increase Mather preached a sermon in 1623 where he reportedly "gave special thanks to God for the plague of smallpox which had wiped out the majority of Wampanoag Indians, praising God for destroying 'chiefly young men and children, the very seeds of increase, thus clearing the forests for a better growth.'"[20] This sermon could not have been preached by Increase Mather, at least not in 1623, because he was not born until 1639.

Secular history texts regularly delete the religious core of the Pilgrims' lives.

The rewriting of history has even reached the pages of the Sunday comics. A story recently appeared about "Squanto and the First Thanksgiving." As all children know, Squanto was a great help to the Pilgrims. But was Squanto so much of a help that the first Thanksgiving was given in his honor? According to the author of the Squanto column, we learn that "the Pilgrims so appreciated Squanto's generosity that they had a great feast to show their thanks."[21] William Bradford, governor of Plymouth and the colony's first historian, continually makes reference to "the Lord Who never fails," "God's blessing," and "the Providence of God," in times of both plenty and want.[22] How uncharacteristic it would have been for the Plymouth settlers to ignore thanking God during a time of harvest. Edward Winslow, in his important chronicle of the history of Plymouth, reports the following eyewitness account of the colony's thanksgiving celebration:

Our harvest being gotten in, our governor sent four men out fowling, that so we might, after a special manner, rejoice together after we had gathered the fruit of our labors. They four in one day killed as much fowl as, with a little help beside, served the company almost a week. At which time, among other recreations, we exercised our arms, many of the Indians coming among us, and among the rest their greatest king, Massasoit, with some ninety men, whom for three days we entertained and feasted; and they went out and killed five deer, which they brought to the plantation, and bestowed on our governor, and upon the captain and others. And although it be not always so plentiful as it was at this time with us, *yet by the goodness of God* we are so far from want, that we often wish you partakers of our plenty.[23]

Squanto was an example of God's providential care of the Pilgrims. He taught them how to farm in the New World and led them on trading expeditions.

There is no doubt that these early Christian settlers thanked the "Indians" in general and Squanto in particular for their generosity in supplying venison to supplement the Pilgrims' meager Thanksgiving rations. As the historical record shows, however, thanksgiving was ultimately made to God. "Governor Bradford, with one eye on divine Providence, proclaimed a day of thanksgiving to God, and with the other eye on the local political situation, extended an invitation to neighboring Indians to share in the harvest feast…. This 'first Thanksgiving' was a feast called to suit the needs of the hour, which were to celebrate the harvest, thank the Lord for His goodness, and regale and impress the Indians."[24] (See Appendix A for a historical survey of Thanksgiving.)

The Pilgrim Edward Winslow expressed thanks that, despite their hardships, "by the goodness of God we are so far from want."

Censorship through Creative Editing

Dr. Vitz is not the only person to uncover the way public school texts minimize the role that Christianity played in the founding of our nation. Consider how a teacher's guide for the high school history text *Triumph of the American Nation*, published in 1986, omits material from the Mayflower Compact without informing the teacher that the document has been edited. Students in discussing the document are left with an incomplete understanding of what motivated these early founders *because they do not have all the facts.* The Mayflower Compact is depicted solely as a political document with its more striking religious elements deleted. Here is the document as presented by the textbook company. The **bold face** portions are missing from the textbook version:

In the name of God, Amen. We whose names are underwritten, **the loyal subjects of our dread sovereign lord, King James, by the grace of God, of Great Britain, France, and Ireland, King, Defender of the Faith, etc.,** having undertaken **for the glory of God and advancement of the Christian faith and honor of our king and country,** a voyage to plant the first colony in the northern parts of Virginia, do **by these presents** solemnly and in the presence of God, and one another, covenant and combine ourselves together into a civil body politic….[25]

These brave men and women had more on their minds than political freedom. Missionary zeal and the advancement of the Christian faith were their primary motivations as they risked life and property to carve out a new home in an uncertain wilderness.

The Mayflower Compact was signed on November 21, 1620, as the *Mayflower* rocked at anchor in Provincetown Harbor, Massachusetts.

The critics of America's early Christian origins have steadily removed such references from textbooks and have created a tense legal environment that frightens many teachers from even raising evidence contradicting the censored texts. Will a member of the ACLU threaten legal action against a teacher who decides to cite original source material to support a view that differs from the historical perspective of the textbook?

Hollywood History

The entertainment industry has entered the field of creative editing in an animated version of the story of Pocahontas, the Native American woman who pleaded with her father to spare the life of John Smith. Pocahontas later became a Christian and married another colonist, John Rolfe. But this episode will all be deleted from an animated retelling of the story. Kendall Hamilton of *Newsweek* offers the following report on the newly designed and politically correct Pocahontas:

The film's P.C. prospects are…helped by the exclusion of Pocahontas's potentially, er, problematic later years, in which she was kidnapped by settlers and, after converting to Christianity, married one of her captors. Male-domination fantasy! Subversion of morally superior indigenous culture! Well, maybe, but [Producer James] Pentecost says such considerations weren't a factor: "We didn't really sidestep any of it for any reason other than this was the most direct way to tell the story and the clearest." Pass the peace pipe.[26]

Pocahontas's conversion and baptism were carefully edited from Disney's animated version of her story.

While this might be the *official* explanation from Disney, my guess is that the studio was pressured by Native Americans to hide Pocahontas's "mistake" of rejecting her native religion.

William Holmes McGuffey's Eclectic Readers

A study of the historical record reveals that religion played a major role in the development of the public school curriculum. "Textbooks referred to God without embarrassment, and public schools considered one of their major tasks to be the development of character through the teaching of religion. For example, the *New England Primer* opened with religious admonitions followed by the Lord's Prayer, the Apostles' Creed, the Ten Commandments, and the names of the books of the Bible."[27]

The most widely used textbook series in public schools from 1836 to 1920 were William Holmes McGuffey's *Eclectic Readers*. More than 120 million *Readers* were sold during this period. The *Readers* stressed religion and its relationship to morality without protests from the courts that the use of religious material in schools was somehow constitutionally objectionable. In an introduction for a reissue of the *Fifth Reader,* historian Henry Steele Commager writes:

What was the nature of the morality that permeated the *Readers?* It was deeply religious, and…religion then meant a Protestant Christianity…. The world of the *McGuffeys* was a world where no one questioned the truths of the Bible or their relevance to everyday contact…. The *Readers*, therefore, are filled with stories from the Bible, and tributes to its truth and beauty.[28]

William Holmes McGuffey wrote a series of reading textbooks that stressed religion and morality. His books were the most widely used textbooks in public schools from 1836 to 1920.

Competing textbooks of the same era contained varying amounts of biblical material, but *McGuffeys* contained the greatest amount—"more than three times as much as any other text of the period."[29] Subsequent editions of the *Readers*—1857 and 1879—showed a reduction in the amount of material devoted to biblical themes. Even so, the 1879 edition contained the Sermon on the Mount, two selections from the Book of Psalms, the Lord's Prayer, the story of the death of Absalom (2 Samuel 18), and Paul's speech on the Areopagus (Acts 17). The Bible was still referred to as "'the Book of God,' 'a source of inspiration,' 'an important basis for life,' and was cited in support of particular moral issues."[30]

Antiseptic Texts

Since the nineteenth century, secularists have been gradually chipping away at the historical record, denying the impact Christianity has had on the development of the moral character of the United States. In 1898 Bishop Charles Galloway delivered a series of messages in the Chapel at Emory College in Georgia. In his messages he noted that "books on the making of our nation have been written, and are the texts in our colleges, in which the Christian religion, as a social and civil factor, has only scant or apologetic mention. This is either a fatal oversight or a deliberate purpose, and both alike to be deplored and condemned. A nation ashamed of its ancestry will be despised by its posterity."[31]

The 1980s saw an even greater expurgation of the impact the Christian religion has had on our nation. So much so that even People for the American Way had to acknowledge that religion is often overlooked in history textbooks: "Religion is simply not treated as a significant element in American life—it is not portrayed as an integrated part of the American value system or as something that is important to individual Americans."[32] A 1994 study of history textbooks commissioned by the federal government and drafted by the National Center for History in the Schools at UCLA concluded that religion "was foolishly purged from many recent textbooks."[33] In 1990, Warren A. Nord of the University of North Carolina wrote:

What cannot be doubted is that our ways of thinking about nature, morality, art, and society were once (and for many people still are) fundamentally religious, and still today in our highly secular world it is difficult even for the non-religious to extricate themselves entirely from the webs of influence and meaning provided by our religious past.... To understand history and (historical) literature one must understand a great deal about religion: on this all agree. Consequently, the relative absence of religion from history textbooks is deeply troubling.[34]

The removal of the topic of religion from textbooks is not always motivated by a desire to slam Christianity. Textbook publishers fear special interest groups that scrutinize the material for any infraction, whether it be religious, racial, sexual, or ethnic. For example, "the 1990 Houghton Mifflin elementary series first made special efforts to include material (and in state hearings received savage criticism from militant Jews, Muslims, and fundamentalist Christians)."[35] The easiest way to placate these diverse groups is to remove all discussion of the topic. This deletion of material is either outright censorship or else a reluctance to fight ideological wars, but whatever the case, failure to deal factually with the past distorts a student's historical perspective. This has happened to such an extent that even when religious themes are covered "their treatments are uniformly antiseptic and abstract."[36]

Notes

1. Miriam Horn with Andy Plattner, "Should Congress censor art?," *U.S. News and World Report* (September 25, 1989), 22, 24; Bo Emerson, "Civil War over Censorship: Morality is the Issue on Battlefield of Culture," *Atlanta Journal/Constitution* (July 25, 1990), D1; and "Four artists to NEA: Who are you to judge?," *The Atlanta Constitution* (March 19, 1991), B6.

2. Harry Hoffman, "Protect the Right to Buy and Sell Books," *USA Today* (April 25, 1990), 10A.

3. Nat Hentoff, *Free Speech for Me—But Not for Thee: How the American Left and Right Relentlessly Censor Each Other* (New York: HarperCollins, 1992), 2.

4. Those who promote liberal causes are not opposed to boycotts of companies and products they deem objectionable from their perspective. Ultra-liberal leftist groups promote "Working Assets Long Distance Service" as a way of funding radical groups such as Planned Parenthood, Greenpeace, Rainforest Action Network, and over 100 other action groups. One of their tactics is the promotion of "boycotts and buycotts." See Cathy Lynn Grossman, "Boycotting is popular resort for activists," *USA Today* (October 11, 1994), 4D.

5. Donald C. Wildmon, "Protect the Right to Boycott Pornography," *USA Today* (April 25, 1990), 10A. See Ben Shapiro, Porn Generation: How Social Liberalism is Corrupting Our Future (Washington, D.C.: Regnery, 2005).

6. Joseph W. Grigg, "'Peter Rabbit' banned from London schools," *Atlanta Journal/Constitution* (April 7, 1988), 1A.

7. Peggie R. Elgin, "Hardy Boys banned from Cobb libraries," *Marietta Daily Journal* (January 13, 1988), 1A.

8. "Residents want 'Playboy' out of library," *Marietta Daily Journal* (October 18, 1994), 4A.

9. Willmar Thorkelson, "Book Ban Considered," *Washington Post* (September 1, 1990).

10. Reported in "Texas Report," a supplement to the *Christian American* (July/August 1992).

11. PAW evaluation reported in Andrew Mollison, "Group says efforts to ban schoolbooks focus on alleged satanic, occult content," *Atlanta Constitution* (August 29, 1991), A11.

12. "PAW Cries Censor-Wolf: Attempt to Keep Parents Out of Schools, Says FRC," Family Research Council Press Release (August 31, 1994), 1.

13. Quoted in "The great 'censorship' hoax," *Citizen* (September 19, 1994), 8.

14. David Shaw, "Abortion Bias Seeps Into News," reprinted from *Los Angeles Times* (July 1–4, 1990) and Al Knight, "School races turn nasty," *Denver Post* (October 10, 1993), 1D and 5D. Knight writes: "The term religious right, in the hands of PFAW and other groups, has become one of the most elastic political labels in memory. It is routinely stretched to include nearly anyone who might be motivated either by conservative or by religious or moral concerns" (1D).

15. John W. Whitehead, *The Rights of Religious Persons in Public Education: A Complete Resource for Knowing and Exercising Your Rights in Public Education*, rev. ed. (Wheaton, IL: Crossway Books, [1991] 1994), 112–13.

16. Barbara Reynolds, "Religion is Greatest Story Ever Missed," *USA Today* (March 16, 1990), 13A.

17. Paul C. Vitz, *Censorship: Evidence of Bias in Our Children's Textbooks* (Ann Arbor, MI: Servant Books, 1986), 1. Emphasis added.

18. Vitz, *Censorship*, 3.

19. As reported in Carey Quan Gelernter, "The Real Thanksgiving," *Seattle Post-Intelligencer* (November 23, 1986), L1.

20. As reported in Gelernter, "The Real Thanksgiving," L2.

21. "Squanto and the First Thanksgiving," Rabbit Ears, *Atlanta Journal/Constitution* (November 27, 1994).

22. William Bradford, *Bradford's History of the Plymouth Settlement: 1608–1650*, original manuscript entitled *Of Plymouth Plantation* rendered into modern English by Harold Paget (Portland, OR: American Heritage Ministries, [1909] 1988)

23. Edward Winslow, *How the Pilgrim Fathers Lived*, 2:116. Emphasis added. *CD Sourcebook of American History* (Mesa, AR: Candlelight Publishing, 1992). Also see *Mourt's Relation: A Journal of the Pilgrims of Plymouth*, ed. Jordan D. Fiore (Plymouth, MA: Plymouth Rock Foundation, [1622] 1985), 67–69.

24. Diana Karter Appelbaum, *Thanksgiving: An American Holiday, An American History* (New York: Facts on File Publications, 1984), 9.

25. This editing was exposed in *Education Update*, Heritage Foundation, 10:3 (Summer 1987). Quoted in Robert P. Dugan, *Winning the New Civil War: Recapturing America's Values* (Portland, OR: Multnomah Press, 1991), 149–50.

26. Kendall Hamilton, "No Red Faces, They Hope," *Newsweek* (November 21, 1994), 61.

27. Whitehead, *The Rights of Religious Persons in Public Education*, 41–42.

28. Henry Steele Commager, "Preface," *McGuffey's Fifth Eclectic Reader*. Quoted in Whitehead, *The Rights of Religious Persons in Public Education*, 42.

29. John H. Westerhoff, III, "The Struggle for a Common Culture: Biblical Images in Nineteenth-Century Schoolbooks," *The Bible in American Education*, eds. David L. Barr and Nicholas Piediscalzi (Philadelphia, PA: Fortress Press, 1982), 32.

30. Westerhoff, "The Struggle for a Common Culture: Biblical Images in Nineteenth-Century Schoolbooks," 28.

31. Charles B. Galloway, *Christianity and the American Commonwealth; or, The Influence of Christianity in Making This Nation* (Powder Springs, GA: American Vision [1898] 2005), 5.

32. O. L. Davis, Jr., et al., *Looking at History: A Review of Major U.S. History Textbooks* (1986), 3. Quoted in Joan Delfattore, *What Johnny Shouldn't Read: Textbook Censorship in America* (New Haven, CT: Yale University Press, 1992), 85.

33. This is also the conclusion of the editorial writers of the *Marietta Daily Journal:* "History needing revision" (October 30, 1994), 2D. *The National Standards for United States History* has called for the restoration of the role religion played in the founding of America while pushing a "politically correct" agenda in nearly everything else. See Lynne V. Cheney, "The End of History," *Wall Street Journal* (October 20, 1994), A24.

34. Warren A. Nord, "Taking Religion Seriously," *Social Education*, vol. 54, no. 9 (September 1990), 287. Quoted in *History Textbooks: A Standard and Guide, 1994–95 Edition* (New York: American Textbook Council, 1994), 32.

35. *History Textbooks: A Standard and Guide, 1994–95 Edition*, 32.

36. *History Textbooks: A Standard and Guide, 1994–95 Edition*, 33.

CHAPTER 2

LESSONS FROM THE PAST

SOMEONE WHO CLAIMS SOVEREIGNTY ALSO EXPECTS HIS SUBJECTS TO LIVE in his realm in terms of his law and name. Sovereignty, therefore, is inevitably connected to control. The denial of one sovereign assumes the sovereignty of another. If God is denied as the only true and independent sovereign, man will usurp this claim. Denying God as sovereign does not eliminate the reality of sovereignty. Sovereignty is only transferred. For example, when Jerusalem was plundered by Nebuchadnezzar's army, Nebuchadnezzar was determined to seize the Israelites' allegiance. Young male Israelites were brought to Babylon "to enter the king's personal service," that is, to further the kingdom of Babylon (Daniel 1:5). Nebuchadnezzar tried to change their worldview through government-controlled education. He ordered Ashpenaz, the chief of his officials, "to teach them the literature and language of the Chaldeans" (1:4).

To symbolize the change in sovereignty, the Babylonians gave new names to the sons of Judah. The names Daniel, Hananiah, Mishael, and Azariah reflected the majesty and sovereignty of the God of Israel. The suffixes of these names either use the general name for God (*el*) or God's personal name (*yah*). Daniel means *God is my judge*. Hananiah can be rendered *Jehovah has favored*. Mishael can be translated *Who is what God is?* Azariah means *Jehovah has helped*. In each case, Babylonian names that reflected the attributes of the Babylonian gods, Marduk and Nebo, were given to the quartet. Similar tactics have been followed by other equally repressive regimes.

Marxism and Education

The Marxist worldview, as put forth by Karl Marx and implemented by Nikoli Lenin, also had aspirations of dominion. Education had to be centralized. The State would become the educator, the new parent. Lenin saw the value in monopolizing education and bringing it under the exclusive control of the State. He believed that time was on his side. The old order would pass away along with its outdated ideas regarding religion, family, and education. The process for change, however, had to begin with the children. The sooner they could be taken from their parents the sooner the reprogramming could take place.

Hananiah, Mishael, and Azariah were given Babylonian names in order to force their allegiance to Babylonian rule. Even under persecution, however, they remained loyal to God.

Karl Marx promoted a worldview in which the State was elevated to deity. He knew that through a monopolized State education system he would be able to capture the younger generations.

In his *Principles of Communism* (1847), Friedrich Engels advocated the "education of all children, as soon as they are old enough to dispense with maternal care, in national institutions and at the charge of the nation."[1] To make it easier for parents to make the decision to turn the education of their children over to the State, they were offered "free education for all children in public schools" as well as food, clothing and school supplies.[2] The State, of course, would assume all costs. These policies drastically changed the family and social structure of the nation.

> We are bringing the women into the social economy, into legislation and government....We are establishing communal kitchens...infant asylums...educational institutions of all kinds. In short, we are seriously carrying out the demand of our program for the transference of the economic and educational function of the separate household to society....The children are brought up under more favourable conditions than at home....[3]

Education was centralized under communism. The functions of the "separate household" were transferred "to society." Mothers were encouraged to enter the work force in ever greater numbers. This allowed the State to care for the children in "educational institutions of all kinds." Propaganda was the order of the day. History was rewritten to serve the interests of the State, and competing educational institutions were shut down.

Nazism and Education

Adolf Hitler understood that by manipulating the minds of the youth through education he could implement his vision of a new world order, a secular millennial reign where man would rule according to Nazi truth. Hitler would use the power of the State to accomplish his goals. All competing educational establishments would be eliminated.

Adolf Hitler understood that by manipulating the minds of the youth he could implement his vision of a new world order.

In *Mein Kampf* Hitler stressed "the importance of winning over and then training the youth in the service 'of a new national state.'"[4] Hitler used education and the authority and power of the State to accomplish his goal. He knew that by controlling the educational establishment he could push through any worldview he desired. He believed that time was on his side to shape the minds of the young. Hitler understood that the direction of the nation would be determined by the ideology of the younger generation.

> "When an opponent declares, 'I will not come over to your side,'" he said in a speech on November 6, 1933, "I calmly say, 'Your child belongs to us already....What are you? You will pass on. Your descendants, however, now stand in the new camp. In a short time they will know nothing else but this new community.'" And on May 1, 1937, [Hitler] declared, "This new Reich will give its youth to no one, but will itself take youth and give to youth its own education and its own upbringing."[5]

Educational control was taken away from the parents and local authorities and "every person in the teaching profession, from kindergarten through the universities, was compelled to join the National Socialist

Teachers' League which, by law, was held 'responsible for the execution of the ideological and political co-ordination of all the teachers in accordance with the National Socialist doctrine.'"[6] Hitler demanded that the State be supported "without reservation" and that teachers take an oath to "be loyal and obedient to Adolf Hitler."[7] The Nazi educational worldview was comprehensive. Hitler's goal was to remake the social and moral climate in the image of the Nazi worldview. "In Germany there was Nazi truth, a Nazi political truth, a Nazi economic truth, a Nazi social truth, a Nazi religious truth, to which all institutions had to subscribe or be banished."[8] All who opposed Hitler's worldview met with loss of job, position, or life.

Socialism and Education

Twentieth-century socialist regimes have followed a similar path. Education's purpose, in the words of former Swedish Minister of Education Ingvar Carlsson, "is to produce a well adjusted, good member of society. It teaches people to respect the consensus, and not sabotage it."[9] Ideally, the Socialist educational system aimed to turn out good civil servants devoted to the interests of the State. A complete break with the past had to be made in order to accomplish this goal. "It is a truism that to change people it is desirable to cut off the past. In the Swedish schools, the study of history has been truncated and the emphasis laid on the development of the Swedish Labour movement....[T]he European heritage and the classical background have been dismissed, and an atmosphere created in which only recent decades appear to count."[10] For Sweden, "Nothing matters before 1932," the year in which the Social Democrats came to power.[11]

> Of course, the anti-historical bias of younger intellectuals is a universal phenomenon, at least in the West. What is distinctive about Sweden is that this bias is, if not exactly shared, at least encouraged and exploited by authority.[12]

The State has monopolized education in Sweden. Teachers have no independence and are bound by the methods and contents of the lessons provided by the Schools Directorate. "Textbooks are severely controlled. They must be approved by a State commission, subordinate to the Directorate, and they may not be used without approval."[13] The content of the textbooks must conform to the official policies of the State. Criticism of Swedish social policies is not permitted. The goal is to eradicate reactionary tendencies. For example, at a 1969 party congress,

Prime Minister Olof Palme quoted a passage from a certain textbook that displayed a non-socialist viewpoint. "That book," he said, "had not been investigated by the textbooks commission."[14] He was implying that if it had been investigated it would not have been adopted by the committee and would not have gotten into the hands of students.

Government education in America aims to develop good civil servants devoted to the interests of the State.

Socialism, at least in the Swedish model, views contact with the past a risk. A reference point for evaluating current trends is lost. As one critic of the Swedish education system observed, "Scrapping historical knowledge deprives pupils of the instrument for criticizing society here and now. And perhaps that is the intended effect."[15] The result is that "Sweden has been dechristianized more efficiently than any other country, Russia not excepted."[16]

Sweden has been able to condition the people by controlling every facet of a child's education. Competition from private schools is nearly non-existent. Pre-school training is designed to cut children off from their social and historical heritage. The "School," in the words of Ingvar Carlsson, "is the spearhead of Socialism."[17] How has Sweden accomplished this goal?

In the attainment of these goals, great care has been devoted to severing intellectual roots. The general curtailment of history has been one method. Within this, there has been included the more refined concept of cutting Swedish links with Western Europe. Whatever the public justification for such a step, the consequence has turned out to be a cultural vacuum, and it is such a state that mass conditioning is really effective.[18]

Creating a vacuum by erasing the past and the nation's identification with it is a necessary step in reconditioning the people to accept a new worldview.

Humanism and Education

Not only has the classroom become the conductor for socialism, but it has also been used to propagate a humanist worldview. The word "humanism" means different things to different people. Humanism, however, should not be confused with the *humanities* or *humanitarianism*. Over time the definition of "humanist" has changed meaning. Scholars who studied literature, art, and music were often described as humanists. Those who performed acts of kindness and worked for social reform were also termed humanists.

The path of humanist education leads children to skepticism and eventually atheism.

The modern definition of humanism is the belief that all of life begins and ends with man. "Humanism," in the words of Francis Schaeffer, "is the placing of Man at the center of all things and making him the measure of all things."[19] To distinguish the older usage of "humanist"—and its relationship to the humanities and humanitarianism—from the modern philosophy of humanism, the term "secular humanism" was coined. *Secular humanism* emphasizes the autonomy of the individual and the primacy of the intellect. Man can solve the problems of society through his own efforts, especially through education and technology.[20]

Reliance upon the ultimacy of *reason* instead of *revelation* is the order of the day for secular humanists. The ultimate goal of this naturalistic worldview is to remove God from the picture altogether and attempt to create society based on non-Christian presuppositions.[21] The classroom has become the laboratory where the secularist worldview has been formulated. Here is a prominent humanist educator explaining the humanist goal to reshape the minds of students to adopt a worldview where God is systematically removed:

> I am convinced that the battle for humankind's future must be waged and won in the public school classroom by teachers who correctly perceive their role as the proselytizers of a new faith: a religion of humanity that recognizes and respects the spark of what theologians call divinity in every human being. These teachers must embody the same selfless dedication as the most rabid fundamentalist preachers, for they will be ministers of another sort, utilizing a classroom instead of a pulpit to convey humanist values in whatever subject they teach, regardless of the educational level—preschool day care or large state university. The classroom must and will become an arena of conflict between the old and the new—the rotting corpse of Christianity, together with all its adjacent evils and misery, and the new faith of humanism, resplendent in its promise of a world in which the never-realized Christian ideal of "love thy neighbor" will be finally achieved.[22]

Charles Darwin hoped to set man free from the shackles of religion through his theory of evolution. Instead, he devalued man to mere animal, at best.

The goals of the humanists are clear and forthright. They hide nothing and demand everything. The humanist agenda has been relentless in its efforts to remake man and the world in the image of autonomous man. There is no compromise or lack of vision. The humanist worldview is comprehensive. Humanist thinkers have made a concerted and planned effort to work for an ideological monopoly in the areas of education, law, and religion. Unfortunately, many Christians believe that an arena of neutrality exists where humanists and Christians can discuss issues based on an "objective" study of the facts. This is an impossibility.

Once people undermine the authority of the Bible, they will quickly find themselves with no moral ground to stand on.

Down the Same Path?

Most Americans have turned over the education of their children to the State and the National Education Association, which is "the largest union in all of America"[23] and highly partisan. The airwaves and newspapers are filled with educational "experts" who claim that they know what's true and best for America's children. It is time that we learn the truth for ourselves so that we will not be tempted one day by a golden-throated dictator.

The first step in immunizing ourselves against the propaganda of those who deny our nation's Christian heritage is to look into the facts, many of which have been systematically obscured. The State-mandated academic community has an agenda to establish a worldview which has little need for the ethical values of the Bible. In addition, over-zealous and ill-informed government officials are purging our nation of its religious heritage. Consider these examples:

- The Pennsylvania Supreme Court threw out a sentence of a murderer who killed a 70-year-old woman with an ax, on the grounds that the prosecutor had unlawfully cited biblical law to the jury in his summation urging the death penalty.

- In Decatur, Illinois, a primary-school teacher discovered the word "God" in a phonics textbook and ordered her class of seven-year-olds to strike it out, saying that it is against the law to mention God in the public school. (I wonder if the school cafeteria accepts money that has "In God We Trust" stamped on it? Do the children pledge allegiance to the flag citing the phrase "one nation under God"?)

- The town of Oak Park, Illinois, blocked a private Catholic hospital from erecting a cross on its own smokestack because, city councilors say, some local residents would be offended.[24]

- The Federal appeals court in Chicago declared that the city seal of Zion, Illinois, was unconstitutional. The seal displays the design Zion's evangelical founder selected, a banner with the words "God Reigns" surrounded by images of a dove, a cross, a sword, and a crown.

- A painting of a crucifixion scene that has hung on the wall of an auditorium in upstate New York for twenty five years was ordered to be taken down by a Federal judge in Syracuse.[25]

- A federal judge in Grand Rapids, Michigan, ordered a public school to remove a portrait of Jesus that had been displayed in a hall for thirty years.[26]

- A public school teacher was ordered by his principal to remove from view of his students the Bible he kept on his desk and read silently at recess.[27]

- A war memorial to University of Virginia law students killed in the Civil War was removed from the law school's hallway (after being there for many years) because it contained a message that was overtly religious.[28]

- In Idaho, the ACLU has sued to remove religious references from public monuments and memorials.

- In New York, a prison guard was fired because he wore the cross he had inherited from his father under his shirt while he was on duty.

- In Illinois, the valentines of elementary school children were censored when the public school teacher discovered Christian tracts included in some of the sealed envelopes.[29]

CHRISTMAS
29 USA
Elisabetta Sirani, 1663
National Museum of Women in the Arts

- The United States Postal Service began the 1994 holiday season by announcing that stamps depicting the Virgin Mary and the Christ Child would no longer adorn Christmas stamps. The new seasonal stamps were to feature a "Victorian-era angel,"

Santa Claus, and children with holiday gifts. After some protest the Postal Service rescinded the Herodian edict. This did not stop Postal Service officials from nixing the greeting "Merry Christmas," however. The new rule states: "Expressions 'Seasons Greetings' and 'Happy Holidays' must be used in lieu of 'Merry Christmas' or 'Happy Hanukkah.'...Avoid the appearance of favoring any particular religion or religion itself."[30] Of course, postal employees will still get Christmas day off *with pay*.

Rarely are such instances of "religious cleansing" seen as a threat to the religious liberties of Christians or a violation of the First Amendment to the Constitution. Neither are they regarded as official acts of censorship by those who cry "censorship" at the drop of a hat.

The Fallout of Rival Faiths

The prevailing godless ideology strives to remove the strictures of religion from socio-political thought. Humanists believe that a removal of Christianity from the public eye will allow a resurgence of the utopian dream that man can create a paradise independent of any higher law. History has played what seems to be a cruel joke on these optimistic humanists. "In the past sixty years there has been more brutality and obscurantism, more senseless conflicts, more of the past's heritage destroyed, more crass idolatry, more lies and hoaxes perpetuated, more people murdered or cast adrift as undesirable elements than in any other time in history; most of this in purportedly just causes for the advancement of mankind in general."[31]

When the once darling of the media, Aleksandr Solzhenitsyn, said, "Man has forgotten God, that is why this has happened," the intelligentsia dismissed his critique as "simplistic."[32] But Solzhenitsyn was not the first to make such a "simplistic" pronouncement. Arthur Koestler "casually remarked in his autobiography *Arrow In The Blue* that the place of God has been vacant in the West since the end of the eighteenth century."[33] The remarkable thing about Koestler's assessment is that he spent his entire life disdaining all traditional religion.[34]

When the God of the Christian religion is rejected as the sovereign ruler over the affairs of men, an idol, usually some man-made ideology, replaces Him as the new operating sovereign.[35] Jesse T. Peck, author of *The History of the Great Republic*, writes that "nations are like their gods. The ideas which a people entertain of the Supreme Power will mould their opinions and control their actions. In other words, the religion of a government will determine its character, and settle the question of its duration."[36] Even the skeptical philosopher Jean Jacques Rousseau admitted, "Never was a state founded that did not have religion for its basis."[37]

We are experiencing the fall-out of two rival faiths—Christianity, a worldview teaching that God is sovereign over all He has created, and secularism, a worldview teaching that man is sovereign over all that has evolved up to this moment in time.

Jesse Peck stated that "nations are like their gods. The ideas which a people entertain of the Supreme Power will mold their opinions and control their actions."

The issue is God or Man. According to humanism/secularism, man ought to control history. Humanism wants every vestige of Christianity expunged from the very nooks and crannies of life, even from the pages of history. There is a price to pay for the denial of God, as even the usually secular *Time* magazine admits:

> For God to be kept out of the classroom or out of America's public debate by nervous school administrators or overcautious politicians serves no one's interests. That restriction prevents people from drawing on this country's rich and diverse religious heritage for guidance, and it degrades the nation's moral discourse by placing a whole realm of theological reasoning out of bounds. The price of that sort of quarantine, at a time of moral dislocation, is—and has been—far too high.[38]

Don't expect America to fully embrace the founding religious principles any time soon. There are still those out there who want nothing to do with the past. Many believe "that the idea of a common Judeo-Christian tradition is, for the United States at least, already outmoded. 'What we need now to maintain social cohesion,' says Jonathan Sarna, professor of American Judaism at Brandeis University, 'is a new language of inclusion to encompass American Muslims, Buddhists and

Hindus.'"[39] What about including satanists and adherents of cults like voodoo and Santeria? And how do we know which religious principles to extract from these diverse offerings? We are left at square one. Our earliest founders encountered this dilemma centuries before. They resolved it by coming to a single conclusion—only the moral requirements outlined in the Bible can guarantee a nation's survival.

"False from Start to Finish"?

Both religious and political persecution motivated our forefathers to leave the shores of England and to start a "Christian Commonwealth" in the New World. "The purpose of the New England colonies was, with respect to church and state, twofold: First, to establish the true and free church, free of the *control of the state*, free to be a co-worker in terms of the Kingdom of God, to establish God's Zion on earth, second, to establish godly magistrates, i.e., a Christian state, magistrates as ordained by God."[40] Is there any historical evidence to support the claim that America was founded, not just on religious principles, but on standards of governance found in the Bible?

If we are to believe the critics of the "Christian America" thesis, the hypothesis is built on a "myth." Such is the opinion of journalist Jim Castelli:

> That myth—spread by TV preachers and other fundamentalists— holds that America was established as a Christian nation, that it has been led astray by "secular humanists" and that we must therefore return to America's roots by creating a new Christian nation ruled by Bible-based laws. This myth carries no eternal truth; it is false from start to finish.[41]

"False from start to finish"? That's a comprehensive and definite claim. Castelli does not leave any room for debate. According to his confident remarks, no matter how long and hard a person might look, he will find *no* evidence to support the opinion that "America was established as a Christian nation." Let's put Mr. Castelli's assertion to the test by surveying just *some* of the evidence to prove that America has a rich Christian heritage. The following chapters will provide solid documentation for a Christian America and will hopefully put to rest the claim that America was founded on religiously neutral ground.

Notes

1. Quoted in Francis Nigel Lee, *Communist Eschatology: A Christian Philosophical Analysis of the Post-Capitalistic Views of Marx, Engels and Lenin* (Nutley, NJ: The Craig Press, 1974), 351.
2. Lee, *Communist Eschatology*, 351.
3. Quoted in Lee, *Communist Eschatology*, 350.
4. William L. Shirer, *The Rise and Fall of the Third Reich* (New York, NY: Simon and Schuster, 1960), 248–49.
5. Shirer, *Rise and Fall of the Third Reich*, 249.
6. Shirer, *Rise and Fall of the Third Reich*, 249.
7. Shirer, *Rise and Fall of the Third Reich*, 249.
8. C. Gregg Singer, *From Rationalism to Irrationality: The Decline of the Western Mind from the Renaissance to the Present* (Phillipsburg, NJ: Presbyterian and Reformed, 1979), 28.
9. Quoted in Roland Huntford, *The New Totalitarians*, rev. ed. (New York: Stein and Day, [1972] 1975), 210–11.
10. Huntford, *The New Totalitarians*, 211.
11. Huntford, *The New Totalitarians*, 211.
12. Huntford, *The New Totalitarians*, 211.
13. Huntford, *The New Totalitarians*, 213.
14. Quoted in Huntford, *The New Totalitarians*, 213.
15. Quoted in Huntford, *The New Totalitarians*, 215.
16. Huntford, *The New Totalitarians*, 219.
17. Huntford, *The New Totalitarians*, 233.
18. Huntford, *The New Totalitarians*, 229.
19. Francis A. Schaeffer, *A Christian Manifesto* (1981), in *The Complete Works of Francis A. Schaeffer*, 5 vols. (Wheaton, IL: Crossway Books, 1982), 5:426.
20. See Gary Scott Smith, "Naturalistic Humanism," in *Building a Christian Worldview: God, Man, and Knowledge*, eds. Andrew Hoffecker and Gary Scott Smith (Phillipsburg, PA: Presbyterian and Reformed, 1986), 161–81.
21. See Gary DeMar, *War of the Worldviews: A Christian Defense Manual* (Atlanta, GA: American Vision, 1994).
22. John J. Dunphy, "A Religion for a New Age," *The Humanist* (January/February 1983), 26.
23. Mary Hatwood Futrell, "Report of the President," National Education Association of the United States, *Proceedings of the Sixty-Eighth Representative Assembly* (July 2–5, 1989) (Washington, DC: National Education Association, 1990), 7. Quoted in Thomas Sowell, *Inside American Education: The Decline, The Deception, The Dogmas* (New York: The Free Press, 1992), 247. Also see Peter Brimelow and Leslie Spencer, "The National Extortion Association?," *Forbes* (June 7, 1993).
24. These examples are cited in Nancy Gibbs, "America's Holy War," *Time* (December 9, 1991), 61.

25. Reported by Sam Howe Verhovek, "U.S. Judge Orders School to Remove Mural Depicting Crucifixion," *New York Times* (August 30, 1990), B1.

26. Reported in *Atlanta Constitution* (February 4, 1993), C3.

27. Linda Greenhouse, "Court to Hear Separation of Church and State Case," *The New York Times* (November 1, 1991), B9.

28. John W. Whitehead, *Religious Apartheid: The Separation of Religion from American Public Life* (Chicago, IL: Moody Press, 1994), 23.

29. Whitehead, *Religious Apartheid*, 156–57.

30. As reported by Joe Urschel, "Stamp out religion at Christmastime," *USA Today* (November 22, 1994), 11A and "Stamp out religion at Christmas—Part II," *USA Today* (December 2, 1994), 13A. Thelma James, affirmative action officer for Minnesota's state tax department, issued a staff memo that banned the "unwelcome greeting of Merry Christmas" via the department's electronic mail. ("'Merry Christmas' offensive, bureaucrat rules," *Atlanta Journal/Constitution* [December 11, 1994], A11).

31. Lloyd Billingsley, *The Generation that Knew Not Josef: A Critique of Marxism and the Religious Left* (Portland, OR: Multnomah, 1985), 24.

32. Billingsley, *The Generation that Knew Not Josef*, 24.

33. Billingsley, *The Generation that Knew Not Josef*, 24.

34. Arthur Koestler in Richard H. Crossman, ed., *The God that Failed* (Chicago, IL: Regnery Gateway, [1949] 1981), 15–75.

35. Herbert Schlossberg, *Idols for Destruction: Christian Faith and Its Confrontation with American Society* (Wheaton, IL: Crossway Books, [1983] 1993).

36. Jesse T. Peck, *The History of the Great Republic: Considered from a Christian-Standpoint* (New York: Broughton and Wyman, 1868), 320.

37. Quoted in Charles B. Galloway, *Christianity and the American Commonwealth; or, The Influence of Christianity in Making This Nation* (Nashville, TN: Publishing House of the Methodist Episcopal Church, 1898), 20.

38. Gibbs, "America's Holy War," 68.

39. Kenneth L. Woodward, "Losing Our Moral Umbrella," *Newsweek* (December 7, 1992), 60.

40. Rousas John Rushdoony, *This Independent Republic: Studies in the Nature and Meaning of American History* (Nutley, NJ: The Craig Press, 1964), 97–98.

41. Jim Castelli, "A Myth Keeps Living On," *Atlanta Journal* (July 4, 1984).

CHAPTER 3

CHRISTIAN COLONIES

O UR NATION BEGINS, NOT IN 1776, BUT MORE THAN ONE HUNDRED AND fifty years earlier. Thirteen colonies with independent governments and intact constitutions were in effect at the time the Declaration of Independence was drafted and signed. The political ideals of those who forged a more unified nation were not developed within a worldview vacuum. Since ideas have consequences, we should expect that the beliefs of the existing colonies would influence the future unified nation. Sadly, however, the truth about our once robust Christian heritage is being dismantled brick by brick.

Governor Kirk Fordice of Mississippi, for example, said that "the less we emphasize the Christian religion the further we fall into the abyss of poor character and chaos in the United States of America."[1] Governor Fordice should be praised for making such an unpopular statement in an era when things religious, especially if they are associated with the Christian religion, are denounced as being morally intrusive. Governor Carroll A. Campbell, Jr., of South Carolina added that a study of history shows that "the foundation of the country" was based on "a Judeo-Christian heritage."[2] The early colonies' reliance on God's providence is nothing more than a faded memory for most Americans. If we are ever to restore what is about to be lost, we will need to learn the truth about our nation's founding. A look at the earliest colonies is a good starting point.

First Charter of Virginia

All attempts by the English to establish colonies in America during the sixteenth century failed. These failures, however, did not deter later adventurers. The earliest efforts at colonization in the seventeenth century followed two main roads—the Jamestown Colony in Virginia (1607) and Plymouth Plantation in Massachusetts (1620). The London Company adequately planned and financed the expedition to establish the first permanent English colony in America at Jamestown. Like nearly all the colonial charters, the First Charter of Virginia emphasizes the Christian character of the purpose of the expedition:

We, greatly commending, and graciously accepting of, their desires for the furtherance of so noble a work, which may, by the providence of Almighty God, hereafter tend to the glory of His Divine Majesty, in propagating of the Christian religion to such people as yet live in darkness and miserable ignorance of the true knowledge and worship of God, and may in time bring the infidels and savages living in those parts to human civility and to a settled and quiet government, do, by these Our letters patent, graciously accept of, and agree to, their humble and well-intended desires.[3]

The First Charter of Virginia stated that the purpose of the colony was to spread "the Christian religion to such people as yet live in darkness and miserable ignorance of the true knowledge and worship of God."

While the expedition was well financed, those of the Virginia colony were not suitably prepared to handle the hardships that would confront them. Most of those who made the voyage were gentlemen adventurers. "There were no men with families. There were very few artisans, and none with any experience that would fit them to get a living out of the soil.... Of them Captain Smith said, 'A Hundred good workmen were worth a thousand such gallants.'"[4] Even so, their Christian faith saw them through periods of despair. The Rev. Robert Hunt—"an honest, religious, and courageous Divine," according to Captain John Smith—was chaplain of the expedition. Worship services began almost from the hour of landing in May of 1607. "There the first seed for English Christianity on the American continent was sown."[5]

The Jamestown colonists suffered great hardship. At a time when they were nearly out of food, with their original colony down to about fifty from the original 104, God provided a wise and effective leader: John Smith. Smith was a convinced that no society could flourish that ignored the biblical principle, If you don't work, neither will you eat. He also established good relations with the neighboring Indian tribes. One of the Jamestown survivors, William Simmonds, praised God that the Indians "brought such plenty of their fruits and provision that no man wanted."⁶ When Smith left Jamestown, the colony took a serious down turn. In fact, when the new governor of Jamestown, Lord de La Warr, arrived in 1610, the colony was on the verge of collapse. His first action was to organize a worship service and issue a biblical call for personal sacrifice and enterprise.

As governor of Jamestown, John Smith guided the colonists out of a grim "starving time," through his application of the principle, If you don't work, neither will you eat.

The marriage of John Rolfe and Pocahontas revealed the evangelical spirit of the colonists. Rolfe wrote of his desire to see Pocahontas become a Christian: "I will never cease until I have accomplished and brought to perfection so holy a work, in which I will daily pray God to bless me, to mine, and her eternal happiness."⁷ After a thorough study of the Virginia colonial period, B. F. Morris, in his voluminous *Christian Life and Character of the Civil Institutions of the United States*, concluded, "The Christian religion was the underlying basis and the pervading element of all the social and civil institutions of the Virginia colony."⁸

Massachusetts and the Mayflower Compact

In the early part of the seventeenth century, England was a country of religious intolerance. Ministers of the gospel were silenced, imprisoned, or exiled. In 1609, because of persecution, a group of Christians left their village in Scrooby, England, and went to the Netherlands, where they found a fair amount of religious tolerance. Led by their pastor, John

Robinson, this group settled in Leyden, Holland, where they formed an English Separatist Church.

After a few years the English transplants began to be concerned because their children were adopting the Dutch language and customs while losing sight of their English heritage. In addition, they wanted to live in a society which was thoroughly founded on the Bible, not simply a place where they would have the freedom to go to the church of their choice. These Separatists (Pilgrims) decided to go to the New World where they could live as Englishmen and in accordance with the Bible.

In September of 1620 the Pilgrims left England in the *Mayflower*.

Unable to finance the trip, the Separatists arranged financial support from a group of English businessmen. These businessmen were to receive any profits the colony made in its first seven years. The Pilgrims were also granted permission from the London group of the Virginia Company to settle in Virginia, north of Jamestown. Prior to their departure from Holland, Rev. Robinson called for a solemn fast and then delivered an embarkation sermon as a portion of the flock prepared to depart for American shores:

> I charge you, before God and his blessed angels, that you follow me no further than you have seen me follow the Lord Jesus Christ. The Lord has more truth yet to break forth out of his holy word. I cannot sufficiently bewail the condition of the reformed churches, who are come to a period in religion, and will go at present no further than the instruments of their reformation.—Luther and Calvin were great and shining lights in their times, yet they penetrated not into the whole

counsel of God.—I beseech you, remember it,—'tis an article of your church covenant,—that you be ready to receive whatever truth shall be made known to you from the written word of God.[9]

In September, 1620, the Pilgrims set sail from Plymouth, England, in a ship named the *Mayflower*. After more than two months at sea, the *Mayflower* reached the American shore but at a destination not specified by the original charter. The original charter had given the Pilgrim travelers the right to settle in the "northern parts of Virginia." The *Mayflower* had been drawn off course by stormy weather to a point that was north of the Virginia Company's jurisdiction. Need for a governing document forced the weary travelers to draft what has become known as the Mayflower Compact. The Compact was drafted and signed by forty-one adult males while aboard the *Mayflower* in Provincetown Harbor, Massachusetts, at the tip of Cape Cod, on November 21, 1620.[10] The Pilgrims did not settle there, but went on to Plymouth where they landed in late December of that same year.

By signing the Mayflower Compact, the Pilgrims agreed that the primary purpose of their new colony was "the Glory of God and advancement of the Christian Faith."

The Compact was to serve as a temporary legal "compact" for the arriving group of "saints and strangers." "By the terms of the so-called Mayflower Compact, the Pilgrims agreed to govern themselves until they could arrange for a charter of their own; they were never able to arrange for such a charter, and the Compact remained in force until their colony at Plymouth was absorbed in that of Massachusetts Bay in 1691."[11]

The preamble of the Mayflower Compact emphasizes religious themes and political loyalties which are reflected in later charters and state constitutions. The Compact reads in part:

> In the name of God, Amen.
>
> We, whose names are underwritten, the loyal subjects of our dread Sovereign Lord King James, by the Grace of God of Great Britain, France, and Ireland, King, Defender of the Faith, etc.
>
> Having undertaken for the Glory of God and advancement of the Christian Faith, and Honour of our King and Country, a Voyage to plant the First Colony in the Northern Parts of Virginia; do by these presents solemnly and mutually in the presence of God and one another, Covenant and Combine ourselves together into a Civil Body Politic, for our better ordering and preservation and furtherance of other ends aforesaid; and by virtue hereof do enact, constitute and frame such just and equal Laws, Ordinances, Acts, Constitutions and Offices, from time to time, as shall be thought most meet [suitable] and convenient for the general good of the Colony, unto which we promise all due submission and obedience.

These early settlers to the New World brought with them an old faith, that was rooted in "the name of God.... for the glory of God and advancement of the Christian faith." Those aboard the Mayflower believed that they were acting "in the presence of God" as they drafted what would later be called "the foundation stone of American liberty"[12] and the basis of representative government in the New World.

Plymouth Plantation

William Bradford (1590–1657), who followed John Carver as governor of Plymouth after Carver's death in 1621, also served as the colony's historian. In Book I of his *History of Plymouth Plantation*, Bradford chronicles the events that relate to the colony up to their landing at Plymouth in the winter of 1620. The remainder of the work completes the history of Plymouth up to 1650. As Bradford's work demonstrates, the Pilgrims were motivated by evangelism:

> Last and not least, they cherished a great hope and inward zeal of laying good foundations, or at least of making some way towards it, for the propagation and advance of the gospel of the kingdom of Christ in the remote parts of the world, even though they should be but stepping stones to others in the performance of so great a work.[13]

Plymouth was first a religious society, secondly an economic enterprise, and, last, a political commonwealth governed by biblical standards. The religious convictions of the Pilgrims were early expressed in the drafting of the Mayflower Compact.

Connecticut

Adriaen Black, a Dutch navigator, was the first European to explore the Connecticut region when he sailed up the Connecticut River in 1614. In 1633, when English colonists from Massachusetts Bay Colony became interested in the fertile Connecticut Valley, the Dutch tried to protect their claims by building a fort near what is now Hartford on land purchased from the Pequot Indians. Undaunted, the English responded by settling at Windsor in 1633, Wethersfield in 1634, and Hartford in 1635. They also founded additional communities along Island Sound.

John Davenport was one of the men who founded New Haven on "the rules which the Scriptures held forth to them."

New Haven was established by the Reverend John Davenport and Theophilus Eaton in 1638. It was at New Haven that the first general court convened in 1638 and enacted a body of laws. "After a day of fasting and prayer, they rested their first frame of government on a simple plantation covenant, that 'all of them would be ordered by the rules which the Scriptures held forth to them.'"[14] Under the guidance of Davenport, who became its pastor, and Eaton, who was annually elected its governor for twenty years until his death, the colony prospered and maintained its faithfulness to the Word of God. A year after the meeting of the general court, the colonists desired a more perfect form of government. A committee consisting of Davenport, Eaton, and five others, who made up what was known as "the seven Pillars," enacted a civil polity where God's Word was "established as the only rule in public affairs. Thus New Haven made the Bible its statute-book, and the elect its freemen."[15]

After a period of war with the Indians, the settlers of the western colony resolved to perfect its political institutions and to form a body politic by voluntary association. It was on January 14, 1639, that the Fundamental Orders of Connecticut, often called the world's first written constitution, was adopted at Hartford by the colonists. It was largely the work of Thomas Hooker, John Haynes, and Roger Ludlow. It reads in part:

> Forasmuch as it has pleased Almighty God by the wise disposition of His Divine Providence so to order and dispose of things that we the inhabitants and residents of Windsor, Hartford and Wethersfield and now cohabiting and dwelling in and upon the river Conectecotte [Connecticut] and the lands thereunto adjoining; and well knowing where a people are gathered together the Word of God requires that to maintain the peace and union of such a people there should be an orderly and decent government established according to God, to order and dispose of the affairs of all the people at all seasons as occasions shall require; do therefore associate and conjoin ourselves to be as one public State or Commonwealth, and do, for ourselves and our successors and such as shall be adjoined to us at any time hereafter, enter into combination and confederation together, to maintain and preserve the liberty and purity of the Gospel of our Lord Jesus which we now profess, as also the discipline of the churches, which according to the truth of the said Gospel is now practiced among us.[16]

The material that follows this preamble, similar to agreements in Rhode Island formed about the same time, is a body of laws. The provision of electing a governor is particularly interesting: "It is ordered...that no person be chosen governor above once in two years, and that the governor be always a member of some approved congregation...."

New England Confederation

The New England Confederation, put into effect on May 19, 1643, established a union of like-minded civil bodies. They shared a common understanding of limited civil government and the need to advance the cause of the gospel, a mission which they described as "to advance the Kingdom of God."

> We all came into these parts of America with one and the same end and aim, namely, *to advance the Kingdom of our Lord Jesus Christ and to*

enjoy the liberties of the Gospel in purity with peace.... The said United Colonies, for themselves and their posterities, do jointly and severally hereby enter into a firm and perpetual league of friendship and amity for offense and defense, mutual advice and succor upon all just occasions, both *for preserving and propagating the truth and liberties of the Gospel* and for their own mutual safety and welfare.[17]

The Bible was used as the standard for developing civil legislation. Civil rulers and courts were considered to be "ministers of God for the good of the people," to "have power to declare, publish, and establish, for the Plantations within their jurisdiction, the laws He hath made; and to make and repeal orders for smaller matters, not particularly determined in Scriptures, according to the more general rules of righteousness, and while they stand in force, to require execution of them."[18] The Christian religion was also protected from those who "shall go about to subvert or destroy the Christian faith or religion by broaching, publishing, or maintaining any dangerous error or heresy...."[19]

New Hampshire

The first settlements in New Hampshire were independent governments. Because they were unable to defend themselves against the Indians, they united with the colony of Massachusetts in 1641. This union continued until 1679 when New Hampshire was constituted a separate province. The Commission included the following:

> And, above all things we do by these presents, will, require, and command our said Council, to take all possible care for the discountenancing of vice, and encouraging of virtue and good living; and that by such examples, the infidel may be incited and desire to partake of the Christian religion; and for the greater ease and satisfaction of the said loving subjects in matters of religion, we do hereby require and command that liberty of conscience shall be allowed unto all Protestants.[20]

In 1680 laws were enacted to protect the Christian religion from those who would "wilfully presume to blaspheme the holy name of God the Father, Son and Holy Ghost, with direct, express, presumptuous or high-handed blasphemy, either by wilful or obstinate denying the true God, or his creation, or government of the world."[21]

New York

The history of New York demonstrates that this colony also strove to uphold the Christian religion, even at its founding by the Dutch when it was named New Netherlands. Under the Dutch West India Company, chartered in 1621, the Reformed Church was protected by law. Then, in 1664, when the English defeated the Dutch and seized control of the colony, renaming it New York, Christianity was still highly guarded. Under the royal grants of James, Duke of York and Albany, 1664 and 1674, the Church of England became the established church. In 1665, the colonial legislature of New York passed the following in reference to the Christian religion: "It is ordered that a church shall be built in each parish, capable of holding two hundred persons; that ministers of every church shall preach every Sunday, and pray for the king, queen, the Duke of York, and the royal family; and to marry persons after legal publication of license."[22] In 1673 each town was authorized to make laws against Sabbath breaking and other immoralities. The following preamble to a body of laws enacted in 1695 reveals its Christian character:

The Church was the center of society in the early colonies.

Whereas, the true and sincere worship of God, according to His holy will and commandments, is often profaned and neglected by many of the inhabitants and sojourners in this Province who do not keep holy the Lord's day, but in a disorderly manner accustom themselves to travel, laboring, working, shooting, fishing, sporting, playing, horse-racing, frequenting tippling-houses, and the using many other unlawful exercises and pastimes, upon the Lord's day, to the great scandal of the holy Christian faith,....[23]

In the area of education the Christian religion was to receive special emphasis. The day would begin with a child reading a "morning prayer" found "in the catechism." The day ended "with the Lord's prayer" and "by singing a psalm."[24]

Conclusion

A survey of all the colonies will lead any student of the era to conclude that they were founded on the religious precepts of Christianity. "Even in the fundamental law of the Province of Rhode Island, a Christian purpose is expressly stated and a particular form of Christianity (Protestantism) was required as a qualification for office."[25] As history attests, many of the religious provisions of early colonial legislation were later removed from both the legislative and judicial acts of the colonies. Remnants of these religious regulations, however, remained as the colonies developed into states.

Notes

1. Quoted in Richard L. Berke, "Religion Issue Stirs Noise in G.O.P. Governors' 'Tent,'" *New York Times* (November 18, 1992), A13.
2. Berke, "Religion Issue Stirs Noise in G.O.P. Governors' 'Tent,'" A13.
3. "First Charter of Virginia" (April 10, 1606), *Documents of American History*, ed. Henry Steel Commager, 6th ed. (New York: Appleton-Century-Crofts, 1958), 8.
4. Charles Lemuel Thompson, *The Religious Foundations of America: A Study in National Origins* (New York: Fleming H. Revell, 1917), 81–82.
5. Thompson, *The Religious Foundations of America*, 83.
6. Quoted in Paul S. Newman, *In God We Trust: America's Heritage of Faith* (Norwalk, CT: C.R. Gibson Co., 1974), 21.
7. Quoted in Mark A. Knoll, ed., *Eerdmans Handbook to Christianity in America* (Grand Rapids, MI: Eerdmans, 1983), 24.
8. B. F. Morris, *The Christian Life and Character of the Civil Institutions of the United States* (Philadelphia, PA: George W. Childs, 1864), 94.
9. George Bancroft, *History of the Colonization of the United States*, 10 vols. 4th ed. (Boston, MA: Charles C. Little and James Brown, 1837), 1:307.
10. The Pilgrims were still using the Julian Calendar which came into being in 46 B.C. The current Gregorian Calendar was developed in 1582, but England and the colonies did not use it until 1752. There is a difference of ten days between the two calendars. While the Mayflower Compact was signed on November 11, 1620, the Gregorian ten-day addition makes it the 21st.

11. Mortimer J. Adler, ed., "The Mayflower Compact," *Annals of America: 1493–1754*, 18 vols. (Chicago, IL: Encyclopedia Britannica, 1968), 1:64.

12. Frank R. Donovan, *The Mayflower Compact* (New York: Grosset & Dunlap, 1968), 12.

13. William Bradford, *Bradford's History of the Plymouth Settlement, 1608–1650*, rendered into modern English by Harold Paget (Portland, OR: American Heritage Ministries, [1909] 1988), 21. A copy of Bradford's account of the Mayflower Compact, from his manuscript *Of Plimoth Plantation*, can be found in *Mourt's Relation: A Journal of the Pilgrims of Plymouth*, ed. Jordan D. Fiore (Plymouth, MA: Plymouth Rock Foundation, [1841, 1865] 1985), between pages 10 and 11.

14. Bancroft, *History of the Colonization of the United States*, 1:403.

15. Bancroft, *History of the Colonization of the United States*, 1:404.

16. "Fundamental Orders of Connecticut" (January 14, 1639), *Documents*, 23.

17. "The New England Confederation" (May 19, 1643), *Documents*, 26. Emphasis added.

18. *Code of New Haven* (1656), 567. Quoted in Isaac A. Cornelison, *The Relation of Religion to Civil Government in the United States of America: A State without a Church, But Not without a Religion* (New York: Knickerbocker Press, 1895), 59.

19. *Code of New Haven*, 590. Quoted in Cornelison, *Relation of Religion to Civil Government in the United States of America*, 60.

20. *Provincial Papers*, 1:378. Quoted in Cornelison, *The Relation of Religion to Civil Government in the United States of America*, 41–42.

21. *Provincial Papers*, 1:363. Quoted in Cornelison, *Relation of Religion to Civil Government in the United States of America*, 42.

22. Quoted in Morris, *Christian Life and Character of the Civil Institutions of the United States*, 88.

23. Quoted in Cornelison, *Relation of Religion to Civil Government in the United States of America*, 67.

24. Quoted in Morris, *Christian Life and Character of the Civil Institutions of the United States*, 89.

25. Cornelison, *Relation of Religion to Civil Government in the United States of America*, 85.

CHAPTER 4

State Constitutions, Religious Oaths, and Biblical Law

L IKE THE COLONIAL CHARTERS, STATE CONSTITUTIONS LEADING UP TO THE revolutionary era express dependence on God for the maintenance of the civil polity.[1] Even though some of the state constitutions are not as evangelical as the colonial charters, they still maintain a solid Christian foundation for the development of laws. The charters expressed the goals of the colonies, one of which was to advance the Christian religion. Constitutions are governing documents designed to maintain an already established social and civil order, an order that was in this case decidedly Christian. In comparison to the federal Constitution, how religious were the pre-revolution state constitutions?

> On the one hand, many of the states take a more restricted view of religious freedom, limiting officeholders to "Christians" or to adherents of the "Protestant religion." Some states, notably the New England ones, also provide for public support of Protestant "teachers" and for legislative encouragement of attendance upon Protestant worship. On the other hand, many states specifically exclude any and all clergymen from holding any civil office.[2]

The federal Constitution makes only passing reference to religious issues, first by guaranteeing in the First Amendment that Congress has no authority either to establish or prohibit the free exercise of religion, and second by prohibiting a religious test for holding office at the federal level. A number of constitutional delegates believed that the new Constitution should not deal with issues related to religion. Such matters, so the argument goes, were considered best handled by the states. A study of the state constitutions will show that most Americans judged Christianity to be the standard by which civil government should perform its stated purpose. "Hence the men who have founded states on written constitutions have always resorted to religious sanctions to give practical power to their constitutions and to enforce the laws of the government."[3]

The Seal for the state of Rhode Island includes the motto "IN GOD WE HOPE."

Many of the states believed that, as more power was given over to a national government, religious issues were ignored. "The states, both before and after the adoption of the federal Constitution, took steps to fill the religious vacuum. State constitutions rang with religious language and proceeded to build on religious assumptions. Though accepting religious liberty as a given of the Revolution, these documents did not accept religious neutrality or indifference as a necessary consequence."[4]

State Constitutions

The federal government is a creation of the states. Powers not delegated to the national government through the Constitution remained with the states, including the subject of religion. The religious practices of the states as well as their constitutional provisions were not affected by the adoption of the federal Constitution. Evidence for this conclusion can be supported by a study of the state constitutions.[5]

Delaware (1776)
The Delaware constitution established the Christian religion while not elevating "one religious sect" in the "State in preference to another." A jurisdictional separation between church and state was maintained by prohibiting a "clergyman or preacher of the gospel, of any denomination" from "holding any civil office" in the state "while they continue in the exercise of the pastoral function." Delaware did require its office holders to subscribe to certain theological tenets, however:

> Article 22. Every person who shall be chosen a member of either house, or appointed to any office or place of trust...shall...also make and subscribe the following declaration, to wit:
> "I, _____, do profess faith in God the Father, and in Jesus Christ His only Son, and in the Holy Ghost, one God, blessed for evermore; and I do acknowledge the holy scriptures of the Old and New Testament to be given by divine inspiration."

Revisions to the Delaware constitution were made in 1792. The Preamble declares, "Through divine goodness all men have, by nature, the rights of worshipping and serving their Creator according to the dictates of their consciences." The people of Delaware are exhorted "to assemble together for the public worship of the Author of the universe," although not through compulsion by the state. In addition, "piety and morality" are to be "promoted." Like the federal Constitution, the 1792 Delaware constitution prohibits a "religious test" as a "qualification to any office, or public trust, under this State."

New Jersey (1776)

The earliest settlers in New Jersey were Puritans who came from the eastern end of Long Island, New York. They settled at Elizabethtown where the first colonial legislative assembly convened to transfer the chief features of New England laws to the statute book of New Jersey. The New Jersey constitution of 1776 stipulated that "no person shall ever...be deprived of the inestimable privilege of worshipping Almighty God in a manner agreeable to the dictates of his own conscience." A citizen of New Jersey would not be compelled by state law "to attend any place of worship, contrary to his own faith and judgment." Neither would he be "obliged to pay tithes, taxes, or any other rates, for the purpose of building or repairing any church or churches, places of worship, or for the maintenance of any minister or ministry."

These religious liberty provisions did not disestablish Protestant Christianity. They merely stated that the civil government could not establish "any one religious sect...in preference to another." The constitution did give Protestants special constitutional privileges in that "no Protestant inhabitant of this Colony shall be denied the enjoyment of any civil right, merely on account of his religious principles; but that all persons, professing a belief in the faith of any Protestant sect...shall be capable of being elected into any office or profit or trust, or being a member of either branch of the Legislature."

The following instructions from the legislature of New Jersey to its delegates in Congress in 1777 exemplifies the Christian sentiments of the men who directed the civil and military concerns of the Revolution:

> We hope you will habitually bear in mind that the success of the great cause in which the United States are engaged depends upon the favor and blessing of Almighty God; and therefore you will neglect nothing which is competent to the Assembly of the States for promoting *piety* and *good morals* among the people at large.[6]

New Jersey's history of Christian foundations goes back as far as 1683 with the drafting of the "Fundamental Constitution for the Province of East New Jersey." Religious liberty was upheld, and every civil magistrate was required to affirm this by law and swear a binding oath to Jesus Christ. Following this requirement we read: "Nor by this article is it intended that any under the notion of liberty shall allow themselves to avow atheism, irreligiousness, or to practice cursing, swearing, drunkenness, profaneness, whoring, adultery, murdering, or any kind of violence...."[7] Marriage was defined by "the law of God."[8]

Georgia (1777)

General James Oglethorpe (1696–1785) conceived a plan to provide a refuge for persecuted Protestants of Europe. On June 9, 1732, he was granted a charter by George II to establish a new colony.

James Oglethorpe, founder of Georgia, denounced slavery as "against the gospel and the fundamental law of England."

Oglethorpe named his colony Georgia. He was motivated primarily from strong Christian principles, which are evident in his denouncement of slavery. In London, in 1734, he praised Georgia for its anti-slavery policy:

Slavery, the misfortune, if not the dishonor, of other plantations, is absolutely proscribed. Let avarice defend it as it will, there is an honest reluctance in humanity against buying and selling, and regarding those of our species as our wealth and possessions.... The name of slavery is here unheard, and every inhabitant is free from unchosen masters and oppression.... Slavery is against the gospel as well as the fundamental law of England. We refused, as trustees, to make a law permitting such a horrid crime.[9]

Oglethorpe's words were not heeded. The "horrid crime" of slavery was soon introduced to Georgia. "In 1750 the law prohibiting slavery was repealed and Georgia became a slave-worked plantation colony like its neighbor, South Carolina."[10]

In keeping with the original charter which gave the colonists of Georgia "a liberty of conscience" to worship God, the 1777 Constitution retains its essential religious character. Article VI states that "The representatives shall be chosen out of the residents in each county...and they shall be of the Protestant religion." Article LVI declares that "All persons whatever shall have the free exercise of their religion; provided it be not repugnant to the peace and safety of the State." Like many of the state constitutions, the Georgia constitution prohibited clergymen from holding seats in the legislature. The 1789 constitution dropped the Protestant requirement.

Maryland (1776)

The Maryland colony started out under quite different religious circumstances, compared to the other colonies. The main difference was that, whereas most of the other colonies were settled by Protestant Christians, Maryland was founded as a Catholic colony. English Catholics first settled Maryland in 1634 under the direction of Cecilius Calvert, Lord Baltimore (1606–1675). Baltimore's proprietorship was often challenged and was eventually lost when Maryland became a royal colony in the late seventeenth century.

Cecelius Calvert founded
Maryland as a Catholic colony.

It cannot be disputed, however, that Maryland's civil government was dedicated to defending orthodox Christianity. Article XXXIII of its 1776 constitution declares, "All persons, professing the Christian religion, are equally entitled to protection in their religious liberty; wherefore no person ought by any law to be molested in his person or estate on account of his religious persuasion or profession, or for his religious practice; unless, under colour of religion, any man shall disturb the good order, peace and safety of the State." A general tax was collected "for the support of the Christian religion." Article XXXIV ordered "That no other test or qualification ought to be required...than such oath of support and fidelity to this State...and declaration of a belief in the Christian religion."

Massachusetts (1780)
Massachusetts has a long history of advancing and protecting the Christian religion. Its constitution of 1780 continues the state's Christian history by asserting that "It is the right as well as the duty of all men in society, publicly, and at stated seasons, to worship the SUPREME BEING, the great Creator and Preserver of the universe." After stating that the "governor shall be chosen annually," qualifications for holding office are next listed: "no person shall be eligible to this office, unless...he shall declare himself to be of the Christian religion." The following oath was also required: "I, _____, do declare, that I believe the Christian religion, and have firm persuasion of its truth."

New Hampshire (1784)

New Hampshire became a separate colony from Massachusetts in 1679. Because of its Puritan origins it shared The religious views of Massachusetts. The constitution of 1784 states:

> Part One, Article I, Section 5. Every individual has a natural and unalienable right to worship GOD according to the dictates of his own conscience, and reason; and no subject shall be hurt, molested, or restrained in his person, liberty or estate for worshipping GOD, in the manner and season most agreeable to the dictates of his own conscience, or for his religious profession, sentiments or persuasion; provided he doth not disturb the public peace, or disturb others, in their religious worship.

The constitution recognized that "morality and piety" are "rightly grounded on evangelical principles." State office holders—governor, senators, representatives, and members of Council—were required by law to be of the "protestant religion." New Hampshire's 1792 constitution, drafted after the full ratification of the United States Constitution in 1791, retained all the religious liberties as well as all the religious restrictions of the 1784 constitution. The national Constitution did not nullify the religious requirements of the individual states. The First Amendment to the Constitution states that "Congress shall make no law respecting an establishment of religion or prohibiting the free exercise thereof. . . ."

North Carolina (1776)

The French and Spanish were the first to explore the area of the Carolinas in the early sixteenth century. The English were the first to colonize the region. Sir Walter Raleigh led three expeditions to the area. The first permanent colony was founded about 1653 near Albemarle Sound by settlers from Virginia. In 1711 Carolina was divided into North Carolina and South Carolina. North Carolina became a royal colony in 1729.

Sir Walter Raleigh, the English courtier and navigator, led three expeditions to colonize North Carolina.

The 1776 constitution of North Carolina upholds religious freedom; Article XIX reads, "All men have a natural and unalienable right to worship God according to the dictates of their own consciences." Article XXXII is more specifically Christian in specifying the following qualifications for public officers in the state: "No person who shall deny the being of God, or the truth of the Protestant religion, or the divine authority of the Old or New Testaments, or who shall hold religious principles incompatible with the freedom and safety of the State, shall be capable of holding any office or place of trust or profit in the civil department within this State." This provision remained in effect until 1868 when "Protestant" was changed to "Christian."

South Carolina (1778)

James Underwood, a professor at the University of South Carolina Law School, has stated that South Carolina's constitution includes "provisions that are unconstitutional under the federal constitution."[11] These provisions, as of 1989, included the following:

- "No person shall be eligible to hold office of Governor who denies the existence of the Supreme Being."

- "No person who denies the existence of a Supreme Being shall hold any office under this constitution."

South Carolina's constitution reflects principles set forth in the 1778 version. Article XXXVIII of the 1778 constitution assures that "all persons and religious societies who acknowledge that there is one God, and a future state of rewards and punishments, and that God is publicly to be worshipped, shall be freely tolerated." In addition, the "Christian Protestant religion shall be deemed, and is hereby constituted and declared to be, the established religion of this State." While religious requirements were mandated by law for all who held political office, "No person shall, by law, be obliged to pay towards the maintenance and support of a religious worship that he does not freely join in, or has not voluntarily engaged in support."

Pennsylvania (1776)

Pennsylvania was founded by William Penn, a Quaker who had once been imprisoned for blasphemy. In his 1682 "Charter of Liberties," Penn cited the biblical origin of civil government, and maintained, citing 1 Timothy 1:9–10, that the law of God was made for the unrighteous. He went on to cite Romans 13:1–5: "This settles the divine right of government beyond exception, and that for two ends. First, to terrify evil doers; secondly, to cherish those that do well."[12]

In 1681 William Penn received the charter of Pennsylvania from King Charles I of England.

A 1705–06 act of the Pennsylvania legislature to regulate the number of members of the assembly required that to serve as a civil magistrate a person had to "also profess to believe in Jesus Christ, the saviour of the world" and take the following oath: "And I, _____, profess faith in God the Father and in Jesus Christ his eternal son, the true God, and in the Holy Spirit, one God blessed for evermore; and do acknowledge the Holy Scriptures of the Old and New Testament to be given by divine inspiration."[13]

The Pennsylvania constitution of 1776 declares that the legislature shall consist of "persons most noted for wisdom and virtue," and that every member should subscribe to the following:

I do believe in one God, the Creator and Governor of the universe, the Rewarder of the good and the Punisher of the wicked; and I acknowledge the Scriptures of the Old and New Testaments to be given by Divine inspiration.

Religious societies "incorporated for the advancement of religion or learning, or for other pious and charitable purposes, shall be encouraged and protected in the enjoyment of privileges, immunities and estates which they were accustomed to enjoy, or could of right have enjoyed, under the laws and former constitution of this state."

The 1790 constitution reaffirms the liberties established in 1776 and goes on to affirm "That no person, who acknowledges the being of God, and a future state of rewards and punishments, shall, on account of his religious sentiments, be disqualified to hold any office or place of trust or profit under this commonwealth."

Biblical Law Made a Part of American Law

Biblical law was the standard the states used to form civil legislation. A perfect example of this biblical foundation is in a Supreme Court ruling of the nineteenth century, dealing with a major tenet of Mormon belief, polygamy. The Supreme Court narrowly defined the legal protections of the First Amendment to exclude polygamy on the grounds that the practice was out of accord with the basic tenets of Christianity: "The organization of a community for the spread and practice of polygamy is, in a measure, a return to barbarism. It is contrary to the spirit of Christianity and the civilization which Christianity has produced in the Western world."[14] In the same year the Court declared that "Bigamy and polygamy are crimes by the laws of all civilized and Christian countries." The Court went on to assert, "Probably never before in the history of this country has it been seriously contended that the whole punitive power of the government, for acts recognized by the general consent of the Christian world in modern times as proper matters for prohibitory legislation, must be suspended in order that the tenets of a religious sect encouraging crime may be carried out without hindrance."[15]

Anti-sodomy laws were based on biblical law as were laws regulating marriage. Justice Warren Burger writes, "Condemnation of those practices is firmly rooted in Judeo-Christian moral and ethical standards."[16] All fifty states have had anti-sodomy laws on their books. Such laws were based on centuries of adherence to English Common Law which was based on the Bible.

At the turn of the nineteenth century, our nation's state and federal courts consistently declared that Christianity was the law of the land. The New York *Spectator* of August 23, 1831, relates the following story of a man who was denied the right to stand as a witness because he was an atheist:

> The Court of Common Pleas of Chester County (New York) a few days since rejected a witness who declared his disbelief in the existence of God. The presiding judge remarked, that he had not before been aware that there was a man living who did not believe in the existence of God; that this belief constituted the sanction of all testimony in a court of justice; and that he knew of no cause in a Christian country where a witness had been permitted to testify without such belief.[17]

Much has changed since 1831. In 1991 the Pennsylvania Supreme Court overturned the death sentence of a convicted murderer, saying he deserved a new resentencing hearing because the prosecutor quoted the Bible in closing arguments. Karl S. Chambers had been convicted of fatally beating 70-year-old Anna May Morris while robbing her of her Social Security money. District Attorney H. Stanley Rebert told the jurors, "Karl Chambers has taken a life. As the Bible says, 'And the murderer shall be put to death.'"[18]

The Pennsylvania Supreme Court ruled this argument out of order. Rebert's reaction to the ruling was to the point. "I don't know of any God-fearing prosecutor that has not used some scriptural or religious reference in arguing to a jury. God's law is the basis for Pennsylvania law and all law."[19]

It is ironic that the court ruled against an argument based on its application of the Bible, because in many (maybe most) courts, witnesses are required to swear an oath to tell the truth—an oath taken with a hand on the Bible. What if the prosecuting attorney had asserted that murder is wrong by making a reference to the Bible? Would the judge have ruled a mistrial? If there is no God, then there are no rules. Survival of the fittest prevails.

Notes

1. Benjamin Weiss, *God in American History: A Documentation of America's Religious Heritage* (Grand Rapids, MI: Zondervan, 1966), 155.
2. Edwin S. Gaustad, *Neither King Nor Prelate: Religion and the New Nation, 1776–1826* (Grand Rapids, MI: Eerdmans, 1993), 160.
3. B. F. Morris, *Christian Life and Character of the Civil Institutions of the United States, Developed in the Official and Historical Annals of the Republic* (Philadelphia, PA: George W. Childs, 1864), 83.
4. Gaustad, *Neither King Nor Prelate*, 114.

5. The material in this chapter can be found in a number of sources: Francis Newton Thorpe, *The Federal and State Constitutions, Colonial Charters, and Other Organic Laws of the States, Territories, and Colonies*, 7 vols. (Washington, DC: 1909) and W. Keith Kavenaugh, ed., *Foundations of Colonial America: A Documentary History*, 3 vols. (New York: Chelsea House, 1973). Edwin S. Gaustad's *Neither King Nor Prelate* includes material from the original state constitutions that reflect their Christian character.

6. Cited in Morris, *Christian Life and Character of the Civil Institutions of the United States*, 235.

7. "Fundamental Constitution for the Province of East New Jersey, 1683," in W. Keith Kavenaugh, ed., *Foundations of Colonial America*, 3 vols. (New York: Chelsea House, 1973), 2:1107.

8. "Fundamental Constitution for the Province of East New Jersey, 1683," in Kavenaugh, *Foundations of Colonial America*, 2:1108.

9. Quoted in Jesse T. Peck, *The History of the Great Republic, Considered from a Christian Stand-Point* (New York: Broughton and Wyman, 1868), 80.

10. Irwin Unger, *Instant American History: Through the Civil War and Reconstruction* (New York: Fawcett Columbine, 1994), 34.

11. Reported by Tom Strong, "S.C. Constitution labeled archaic," *Sun News* (Myrtle Beach, South Carolina) (July 9, 1989), 3D.

12. "Charter of Liberties and Frame of Government of Pennsylvania, April 25–May 5, 1682," in Kavenaugh, *Foundations of Colonial America*, 2:1134.

13. "Act to Ascertain the Number of Members of Assembly and to Regulate the Election, 1705–06," in Kavenaugh, *Foundations of Colonial America*, 2:1169.

14. *Church of Jesus Christ of Latter Day Saints* vs. *United States*, 136 U.S. 1, 49 (1890).

15. *Davis vs. Beason*, 133 U.S. 333, 341–342 (1890).

16. *Bowers vs. Hardwick*, 478 US 186, 92 L Ed 2d 140, 106 S. Ct 2841, 149 (1986).

17. Alexis de Tocqueville, *Democracy in America*, 2 vols. (New York: Alfred A. Knopf, [1834, 1840] 1960), 2:306.

18. "Court Rejects Bible," *Atlanta Constitution* (November 16, 1991), E6.

19. "Court Rejects Bible," E6. In 1824 the Pennsylvania Supreme Court held that: "Christianity, general Christianity, is, and always has been, a part of the common law of Pennsylvania." (*Updegraph vs. Commonwealth*, 11 Serg. and R. [Pa.] 394 [1824]).

CHAPTER 5

GOD AND THE CONSTITUTION

THE FIRST LEGISLATIVE ACT OF PENNSYLVANIA, PASSED AT CHESTER ON THE seventh of December in 1682, announced the following to be the goal of civil government: "Whereas the glory of Almighty God and the good of Mankind, is the reason and end of government, and therefore, government in itself is a venerable Ordinance of God," therefore, it is the purpose of civil government to "establish such laws as shall best preserve true Christian and Civil Liberty, in opposition to all Unchristian, Licentious, and unjust practices, (Whereby God may have his due, and Caesar his due, and the people their due), from tyranny and oppression...."[1]

B.F. Morris, author of the *Christian Life and Character of the Civil Institutions of the United States*, writes that "the frame of government which [William] Penn completed in 1682 for the government of Pennsylvania was derived from the Bible. He deduced from various passages 'the origination and descent of all human power from God; the divine right of government, and that for two ends, — first, to terrify evil doers; secondly, to cherish those who do well," a clear reference to the Apostle Paul's admonition of civil government's duties in Romans 13. Civil government, Penn said, "'seems to me to be a part of religion itself;' — 'a thing sacred in its institutions and ends.'"[2]

William Penn stated that the purpose of civil government is to "terrify evil doers and, secondly, to cherish those that do well."

George Bancroft, in his *History of the United States*, cites a portion of Penn's farewell address to the Pennsylvania colony: "You are come to a quiet land, and liberty and authority are in your hands. Rule for Him under whom the princes of this world will one day esteem it their honor to govern in their places."[3] Penn acknowledged biblical principles of delegated human authority and divine sovereignty (Romans 13:1). He expected the colonists to follow his pattern. The future of the colony, he believed, depended upon it.

Part of the Common Law

In the 1892 case of *Holy Trinity Church vs. United States*, the court made a survey of previous court decisions and then stated the basis of law in the state of Pennsylvania: "It is also said, and truly, that the Christian religion is a part of the common law of Pennsylvania (*Vidal v. Girard's Executors*)." Each of the thirteen original state constitutions established Christianity as the state-protected religion. Even today all fifty state constitutions express dependence on Almighty God for their preservation.[4] Therefore, the following summary of America's Christian heritage should not surprise us:

> Throughout its history our governments, national and state, have co-operated with religion and shown friendliness to it. God is invoked in the Declaration of Independence and in practically every state constitution. Sunday, the Christian Sabbath, is universally observed as a day of rest. The sessions of Congress and of the state legislatures are invariably opened with prayer, in Congress by chaplains who are employed by the Federal government. We have chaplains in our armed forces and in our penal institutions. Oaths in courts of law are administered through use of the Bible. Public officials take an oath of office ending with "so help me God." Religious institutions are tax exempt throughout the nation. Our pledge of allegiance declares that we are a nation "under God." Our national motto is "In God We Trust" and is inscribed on our currency and on some of our postage stamps.[5]

Did the religious character of the nation change judicially in 1787 when representatives from the colonies met in Philadelphia to draft a new national charter? Did the resulting Constitution make a formal break with the self-consciously Christian state constitutions?

A Constitutional Change

While the Constitution does not repudiate the Christian religion formally, it does imply its dismissal by not "acknowledging Almighty God as the source of all authority and power in civil government, the Lord

The Constitution did not repudiate the Christian foundations established by the state constitutions, but it did err by not acknowledging God as the source of all authority and power.

Jesus Christ as the ruler of all nations, and his revealed will as the supreme law of the land."[6] Historian Isaac A. Cornelison makes a similar observation when he writes that "very little is said in the Constitution on the subject of religion, and that what little is said is of a prohibitory character."[7] There are various theories as to why the Constitution makes no direct reference to God.

Religious Discord and States Rights

One theory to explain why the Constitution is virtually silent on religious issues is that there were so many different Christian denominations represented at the constitutional convention that the representatives were forced into religious neutrality. The Philadelphia convention was represented by numerous Christian sects: Congregationalist, Episcopalian, Dutch Reformed, Presbyterian, Quaker, Lutheran, Roman Catholic, Methodist, and Deist.[8] The Episcopalians predominated numerically. "James Madison tells us there was 'discord of religious opinions within the convention,' which undoubtedly kept theological controversy off the floor."[9] Some maintain that the proliferation of religious opinions among the delegates steered the convention away from including specific religious language in the Constitution.

Despite his unorthodox religious views, Benjamin Franklin stated belief in "one God, the Creator and Governor of the universe."

This argument breaks down somewhat when we analyze the environment of state constitutional conventions. The same religious discord was present at the state level, but this did not stop the states from clearly setting forth the basic precepts of Christianity as requirements for holding public office. For example, representatives to Philadelphia from Pennsylvania included the Deist Benjamin Franklin, the Episcopalian Robert Morris, the Roman Catholic Thomas FitzSimmons, and the Presbyterian Jared Ingersoll. Even with this religious diversity, every member of the Pennsylvania Legislature was required to subscribe to the following: "I do believe in one God, the Creator and Governor of the universe, the Rewarder of the good and the Punisher of the wicked; and I acknowledge the Scriptures of the Old and New Testaments to be given by Divine inspiration."

A variation of Madison's explanation is that the representatives wanted to guard the states from federal intrusion, preserving the authority of the states to establish their own religious parameters. Since the religious issue was already settled at the state level, there was no need for the federal government to meddle in an area in which the national government has no jurisdiction. The prohibition of a religious test "as a qualification to any office or public trust under the United States" applied only to *national* office holders: congressmen, senators, the president, and Supreme Court justices. States were free to apply their own test and oath, which they did.

Robert Morris was a leading Philadelphia merchant and banker and a member of the Continental Congress.

The First Amendment, which only addresses Congress, as well as the "no religious test" provision, "are expressly made to apply to the general government alone. They do not apply to the States. It may have been the intent in framing the Constitution to assign the matter of religion to the domain of the States, rather than to accomplish an elimination of all religious character from our civil institutions."[10] In his *Commentary on the Constitution of the United States*, Supreme Court Justice Joseph Story (1779-1845) writes, "Thus, the whole power over the subject of religion was left exclusively to the State governments, to be acted on according to their own sense of justice, and the State Constitutions."[11]

Story's *Commentary* clearly shows that the First Amendment was designed to prohibit the federal establishment of a national Church or the official preference of a particular Christian sect over all others. The First Amendment, according to Story, was not designed to disestablish the Christian religion at the state level:

> Probably, at the time of the adoption of the Constitution, and of the…[First Amendment], the general, if not the universal, sentiment in America was, that Christianity ought to receive encouragement from the State, so far as such encouragement was not incompatible with the private rights of conscience, and the freedom of religious worship. An attempt to level all religions, and to make it a matter of state policy to hold all in utter indifference, would have created universal disapprobation, if not universal indignation.[12]

While the national government garnished some new powers as a result of the ratification of the Constitution, denying the states jurisdiction over religious issues was not one of them. The Tenth Amendment supports this view: "The powers, not delegated to the United States by the Constitution, nor prohibited by it to the States, are reserved to the States, respectively, or to the people." In the Circuit Court of Tennessee, August 1, 1891, the Court said, "As a matter of fact they (the founders of our government) left the States the most absolute power on the subject, and any of them might, if they chose, establish a creed and a church and maintain them."[13]

Christianity Assumed

Another argument put forth to explain the Constitution's lack of explicit religious language "is that the Christian premises of the American Constitution and the people's reliance on the Christian deity were assumed by the framers, and thus explicit reference was unnecessary. 'The Bible,' argued Robert Baird, the trailblazing student of religion in America, 'does not begin with an argument to prove the existence of God, but assumes the fact, as one [of] the truth[s] of which it needs no attempt to establish.'"[14] Having said this, even Baird had to acknowledge his regret at the absence of "something more explicit on the subject…. Sure I am that, had the excellent men who framed the Constitution foreseen the inferences that have been drawn from the omission, they would have recognized, in a proper formula, the existence of God, and the truth and the importance of the Christian religion."[15] Baird wrote this in 1844! What would he say today?

"We Forgot"?

An apocryphal story has been floating around for some time that describes a chance meeting between a minister and Alexander Hamilton after the Philadelphia Convention had adjourned.[16] The minister asked Hamilton why "the Constitution has no recognition of God or the Christian religion." Hamilton is reported to have said, "we forgot it."[17] Hamilton's response is unlikely, considering the method he followed in the *Federalist Papers*.

> Indeed, Alexander Hamilton almost goes out of his way to ignore the Old Testament in his recital of the various republics and their history in "The Federalist," and in his list of republics Sparta, Athens, Rome and Carthage, as well as Venice and Holland, are all reviewed; but of Judaism there is no mention. In the list of the causes of war between competing States he never even mentions religion as a possible incitement…. It is not with his argument either in this or the following paper in "The Federalist" that we have especially to do, but with the striking fact that the republic's ablest group of statesmen, in defending the

Alexander Hamilton was the principle author of *The Federalist*, which is a collection of essays on the United States Constitution.

> proposed constitution in appeals to the widest public, and using skillfully every argument that would make the new document palatable to the greatest number of people, saw fit to ignore the whole subject of religion. It is not that it is attacked or made little of, but the fact that it is entirely ignored, that marks the entire disappearance of the Puritan theocratic idea…. Where a hundred years before every case, whether civil, political or criminal, was decided by a reference to the Old or New Testament, and that not alone

in Massachusetts, New Haven, Connecticut and Plymouth, but in Virginia and the Carolinas; in "The Federalist" the Bible and Christianity, as well as the clergy, are passed over as having no bearing upon the political issues being discussed.

Indeed, it is very striking to observe the authorities that have taken the place of Moses and the prophets. We find oftenest cited Montesquieu, Blackstone, Hume, with frequent indirect uses of Locke and Hobbes without use of their names; and especially used is Plutarch. The eighteenth-century conception of Greco-Roman Paganism has completely supplanted Puritanic Judaism.[18]

The constitutional framers' reliance on Roman and Greek models has been noticed by modern-day historians. It is no accident that they chose the word "Senate"—a Roman designation—for the national governing body. The worldview of these men was eclectic. They "read Aristotle, Plutarch, Herodotus, Thucydides, Virgil, Sallust, etc.—as well as the New Testament in Greek."[19]

The Founding Fathers believed that much wisdom could be gained through reading the works of Aristotle, although they confessed that the Christian system of morality was "the most benevolent and sublime."

An argument could be made, however, that these pagan authors were read discriminately in terms of an already constructed biblical worldview. The framers retained what was good and discarded what was bad in terms of biblical absolutes. Remember, it was Thomas Jefferson who wrote that Jesus Christ's "system of morality was the most benevolent and sublime...ever taught, and consequently more perfect than those of any of the ancient philosophers."[20] John Adams wrote, "The Christian Religion as I understand it is the best."[21]

A Political Document

Another argument for the Constitution's absence of references to God and the Christian religion is that it was formed directly for political, not for religious, objectives. This contention is plausible considering the existence of the state constitutions and an acknowledgment of only delegated powers granted to the newly formulated federal Constitution. Philip Schaff offers the following apologetic for the absence of references to Providence, the Creator, nature and nature's God, and the Supreme Being in terms of the document's secular purpose:

> The absence of the names of God and Christ, in a purely political and legal document, no more proves denial or irreverence than the absence of those names in a mathematical treatise, or the statutes of a bank or railroad corporation. The title "Holiness" does not make the Pope of Rome any holier than he is…. The book of Esther and the Song of Solomon are undoubtedly productions of devout worshippers of Jehovah; and yet the name of God does not occur once in them.[22]

The argument is that theology did not draw the delegates to Philadelphia in 1787. Instead, they came to debate the best practical form of civil government.

While the argument might seem credible, it does not stand up under scrutiny since, as William Lee Miller notes, existing "formal legal instruments—the state constitutions—often included substantive statements reflecting a collective piety."[23] The U.S. Constitution did not have to read like a theological treatise to acknowledge the sovereignty and providence of God over the affairs of the State.

An Imperfect Document

The most serious imperfections in the national Constitution are the absence of any direct reference to God and its failure to condemn slavery. As Christians we know that there is only one God-breathed (inspired) book: the Bible. All other books and writings are flawed. To maintain that the Constitution is an "inspired document" or that the framers were "inspired" is heretical. The framers were not "moved by the Holy Spirit" as if they "spoke from God" (2 Peter 1:20). Christians, therefore, should not despair if they find flaws in the Constitution. We should expect to find imperfections in a man-made document. Judging the Constitution, therefore, is every Christian's duty. Daniel Dorchester, in his comprehensive *Christianity in the United States*, makes this observation:

It seems unpardonable in a great constitutional compact, intended to bind together a people among whom the religious element had been so prominent, and whose history had been marked by religious heroism and remarkable providential interpositions, that the Almighty Ruler of the universe should not be acknowledged, not even directly alluded to, except in the date (*Anno Domini*) of the instrument. But this was in keeping with other acts of that convention, in which, during the entire session of about four months, prayer was not once offered; in the manifold perplexities of their deliberations never seeking wisdom from God. This was chiefly owing to the influence of French infidelity then tainting many of the leading minds of the nation. The unreligious mind of that time was misled by atheistical abstractions, discarding moral ideas and moral obligations in civil government, regarding it as a human composition, deriving its authority from the people and not from God. They followed the theory of Rousseau, according to which the foundation of all government is in a "social compact," and "the consent of the governed" was regarded as the source of civil obligation. They failed to see that such government must necessarily be weak and imperfect. Founded on the shifting sands of human caprice and passion, it could possess only a fluctuating authority, not ruling by the enduring power of moral obligations which press upon the conscience, and touch "a throne of order and law above the range of mere humanity."[24]

Dorchester was not alone in his assessment of the secularization of the Constitution. Luther Martin of Maryland, in a lengthy letter to the Speaker of the House of Delegates of Maryland, set forth his justification in leaving the convention and in refusing to sign the Constitution. He wrote: "The part of the system which provides that no religious test shall ever be required as a qualification to any office or public trust under the United States was adopted by a great majority of the Convention and without much debate." Martin saw the long-term implications of this stark and self-conscious omission. "There were some members so unfashionable as to think that a belief in the existence of a Deity and of a state of future rewards and punishments would be some security for the good conduct of our rulers, and that, in a Christian country, it would be at least decent to hold out some distinction between the professors of Christianity and downright infidelity or paganism."[25]

Martin's concerns were shared by a number of state legislatures. "The states which required test oaths thought the prohibition of such in the national government too liberal. There was also some opposition expressed because of the omission of reference to God." In addition, most of the states expressed criticism of the Constitution "due to the absence of sufficient specific guarantees of religious liberty as well as other fundamental freedoms."[26]

Luther Martin was wary of the absence of a religious test for public office.

At the time of the Constitution's ratification, a number of Christian organizations refused to support the newly formed political document because a specific reference to God was purposely omitted. Some objected because the Constitution did not recognize the Providence of God in the affairs of the colonies. "Two small Presbyterian bodies, the Associated Church and the Reformed Presbyterian Church, decided to abstain from voting [to ratify the Constitution] until the Constitution was so amended as to acknowledge the sovereignty of God and the subserviency of the state to the kingdom of Christ."[27]

The absence of a direct reference to God in the Constitution has played its hand in American politics and law. Only time will tell what further damage will be brought upon our Republic as we continue to rule in its absence.

Remnants of Religion

While our Constitution is seriously flawed in that it makes "We the people" the ultimate authority, our framers did not completely expunge Christianity from the framework of society. This was not the case in revolutionary France during its period of revolutionary change. The French revolutionaries were self-conscious about their efforts to turn France into a secular state. Throughout the nation a "campaign to de-christianize France spread like wildfire."[28] The dechristianization of the French Republic required a substitute religion. The leaders of the Paris

The French Revolution heralded the humanist declaration: "Liberty, Equality, Fraternity, or Death."

Commune demanded that the former metropolitan church of Notre Dame be reconsecrated as a "Temple of Reason." On November 10, 1793, a civic festival was held in the new temple, its facade bearing the words "To Philosophy." In Paris, the goddess Reason "was personified by an actress, Demoiselle Candeille, carried shoulder-high into the cathedral by men dressed in Roman costumes."[29] The Commune ordered that all churches be closed and converted into poor houses and schools. "Church bells were melted down and used to cast cannons."[30]

> Blatant infidelity precipitated that storm of pitiless fury. The National Assembly passed a resolution deliberately declaring "There is no God;" vacated the throne of Deity by simple resolution, abolished the Sabbath, unfrocked her ministers of religion, turned temples of spiritual worship into places of secular business, and enthroned a vile woman as the Goddess of Reason.[31]

The French revolutionaries pulled down many churches during their dechristianization campaign, including the Church of *St. Jean en Grève*.

The French Revolution replaced the God of Revelation with the Goddess of Reason, with disastrous results. Blood literally ran in the streets as day after day "enemies of the republic" met their death under the sharp blade of Madam Guillotine. "France, in its terrific revolution, saw the violent culmination of theoretical and practical infidelity."[32]

The French calendar was also changed. "At the suggestion of the deputy Romme, the Convention voted on 5 October 1793 to abolish the Christian calendar and introduce a republican calendar."[33] The founding

This depiction of Maximilien Robespierre guillotining the executioner describes the widespread slaughter of the French Revolution.

of the Republic on September 22, 1792, was the beginning of the new era. While the year still had twelve months, all were made thirty days long. "Weeks were replaced with periods of ten days (decades) so that the Christian Sunday would disappear...."[34]

The new French calendar hoped to destroy the old Christian order by making a break with the seven-day week established at Creation.

The New Republic went beyond this by changing place names that had "reference to a Christian past." In addition, "children were named after republican heroes such as Brutus and Cato, and observance of the new Revolutionary calendar, which abolished Sunday and Christian Feast days, was enforced."[35] The revisionist calendar was abandoned after twelve years.

Christian Continuity

The United States Constitution establishes continuity with the nation's Christian past by linking it with the Christian calendar. Article 1, section 7 recognizes Sunday as a day of rest. If the framers had wanted to strip every vestige of religion from the Constitution, why include a reference to an obvious religious observance? Sunday observance remained under constitutional protection at the federal and state levels for some time in the United States. As Supreme Court Justice David Brewer observes, the recognition of Sunday as a day of worship and rest is "a day peculiar to [the Christian] faith, and known to no other."[36]

The Constitution states that the drafting took place "in the year of our Lord one thousand seven hundred and Eighty seven." This phrasing is no doubt a convention of the times; however, the constitutional framers could have taken the direction of the French Revolutionaries and created a "new order of the ages" based on a new calendar if they had wanted to make a complete break with the Christian past.

The "new order" of France was based on the Laws of Man rather than the Laws of God.

Notes

1. *Charter to William Penn ..., and Duke of Yorke's Book of Laws* (Harrisburg, PA: 1879). The Preamble and Chapter I of the Great Law can be found in *Remember William Penn: 1644–1944* (Harrisburg, PA: The William Penn Tercentenary Committee, 1944), 85–86.

2. B.F. Morris, *The Christian Life and Character of the Civil Institutions of the United States* (Philadelphia, PA: George W. Childs, 1864), 83. Available from American Vision, 3150-A Florence Rd., Powder Springs, GA 30127.

3. George Bancroft, *History of the United States from the Discovery of the American Continent*, 10 vols., 15th ed. (Boston, MA: Little, Brown, and Co., 1855), 2:393.

4. Benjamin Weiss, *God in American History: A Documentation of America's Religious Heritage* (Grand Rapids, MI: Zondervan, 1966), 155.

5. Anson Phelps Stokes and Leo Pfeffer, *Church and State in the United States* (New York: Harper and Row, 1964), 102-103.

6. A portion of a preamble sponsored by Justice William Strong and the "National association to secure certain religious amendments to the Constitution." Cited by R. Kemp Morton, *God in the Constitution* (Nashville, TN: Cokesbury Press, 1933), 77.

7. Isaac A. Cornelison, *The Relation of Religion to Civil Government in the United States of America: A State Without a Church, but Not Without a Religion* (New York: G.P. Putnam's Sons, 1895), 92.

8. M.E. Bradford, *A Worthy Company: The Dramatic Story of the Men Who Founded Our Country* (Wheaton, IL: Crossway Books, [1982] 1988).

9. Morton, *God in the Constitution*, 71.

10. Cornelison, *Relation of Religion to Civil Government in the United States of America*, 94.

11. Joseph Story, *Commentary on the Constitution of the United States* (Boston, MA: Hilliard, Gray, and Co., 1833), 702-703. Story served as a justice of the United States Supreme Court from 1811 to 1845.

12. Joseph Story, *A Familiar Exposition of the Constitution of the United States* (Lake Bluff, IL: Regnery Gateway, [1859] 1986), 316.

13. *The Federal Reporter*, vol. 46, 912. Quoted in Cornelison, *Relation of Religion to Civil Government in the United States of America*, 95.

14. Daniel L. Dreisbach, "God and the Constitution: Reflections on Selected Nineteenth Century Commentaries on References to the Deity and the Christian Religion in the United States Constitution," 28. This paper is unpublished.

15. Robert Baird, *Religion in America; or, an Account of the Origin, Progress, Relation to the State, and Present Condition of the Evangelical Churches in the United States. With Notices of the Unevangelical Denominations* (New York: Harper & Brothers, 1844), 119. Quoted in Dreisbach, "God and the Constitution," 29.

16. In some accounts the minister is identified as the Rev. Dr. Miller, a distinguished professor at Princeton College (see Morris, *Christian Life and Character*, 248), and in others the minister is identified as Rev. Dr. John Rogers, an eminent chaplain of the War of Independence and Presbyterian clergyman (see Cornelison, *Relation of Religion to Civil Government in the United States of America*, 204).

17. George Duffield, Jr., *The God of Our Fathers*, An Historical Sermon, Preached in the Coates' Street Presbyterian Church, Philadelphia, on Fast Day, January 4, 1861 (Philadelphia, PA: T.B. Pugh, 1861), 15. See Morris, *Christian Life and Character*, 248. Further references can be found in Dreisbach, "God and the Constitution," 22, note 77.

18. Thomas Cuming Hall, *The Religious Background of American Culture* (Boston, MA: Little, Brown, and Company, 1930), 184–85.

19. Colin Campbell, "Our semi-pagan forebears," *Atlanta Constitution* (June 29, 1994), C6.

20. Quoted in F. Forrester Church, "The Gospel According to Thomas Jefferson," *The Jefferson Bible* (Boston: Beacon Press, 1989), 5.

21. John Adams to Horace Holley, July 22, 1818 in microfilm edition of *The Adams Papers* (Boston, 1954-57), reel 123. Quoted in Edwin S. Gaustad, *Neither King Nor Prelate: Religion and the New Nation, 1776-1826*, rev. ed. (Grand Rapids, MI: Eerdmans, [1987] 1993), 89.

22. Philip Schaff, *Church and State in the United States or The American Idea of Religious Liberty And Its Practical Effects* (New York: Charles Scribner's Sons, 1889), 40.

23. William Lee Miller, *The First Liberty: Religion and the American Republic* (New York: Alfred A. Knopf, 1986), 109.

24. Daniel Dorchester, *Christianity in the United States*, (New York: Phillips & Hunt, 1888), 563-64. For similar contemporary assessments, see John M. Murrin, "Religion and Politics in America from the First Settlements to the Civil War," *Religion and American Politics: From the Colonial Period to the 1980s*, ed. Mark A. Knoll (New York: Oxford University Press, 1990), 32-35, Gary DeMar, *God and Government: A Biblical and Historical Study* (Atlanta, GA: American Vision, [1982] 1990), 156-67, and Gary North, *Political Polytheism: The Myth of Pluralism* (Tyler, TX: Institute for Christian Economics, 1989).

25. Quoted in R. Kemp Morton, *God in the Constitution*, 79.

26. Robert T. Miller, "The Development in Constitutional Law of the Principles of Religious Liberty and Separation of Church and State," *Church and State in Scripture, History and Constitutional Law* (Waco, TX: Baylor University Press, 1958), 102.

27. Quoted in Morton, *God in the Constitution*, 72.

28. Walter Grab, *The French Revolution: The Beginning of Modern Democracy* (London: Bracken Books, 1989), 165.

29. Francis A. Schaeffer, *How Should We Then Live?* (1976) in *The Complete Works of Francis A. Schaeffer: A Christian Worldview*, 5 vols. (Wheaton, IL: Crossway Books, 1984), 5:122.

30. Grab, *The French Revolution*, 166. Robespierre considered the antichristianization campaign to be a political miscalculation. "At the beginning of December [1793], at Robespierre's suggestion, the Convention withdrew its anti-religious measures and restored the principle of religious freedom" (166-67).

31. Charles B. Galloway, *Christianity and the American Commonwealth; or, The Influence of Christianity in making This Nation* (Nashville, TN: Publishing House Methodist Episcopal Church, 1898), 25.

32. Jesse T. Peck, *The History of the Great Republic, Considered from a Christian Stand-Point* (New York: Broughton and Wyman, 1868), 321.

33. Grab, *The French Revolution*, 165. Also see "Marking Time: Different Ways to Count the Changing Seasons," *Did You Know? New Insight into the World that is Full of Astonishing Stories and Astounding Facts* (London: Reader's Digest, 1990), 267.

34. Grab, *The French Revolution*, 165.

35. Richard Cobb, gen. ed., *Voices of the French Revolution* (Topsfield, MA: Salem House Publishers, 1988), 202. Also see Simon Schama, *Citizens: A Chronicle of the French Revolution* (New York: Alfred A. Knopf, 1989), 771-80.

36. David J. Brewer, *The United States: A Christian Nation* (Philadelphia, PA: The John C. Winston Company, 1905), 26.

CHAPTER 6

COLONIAL EDUCATION

"O NE OF THE MOST USEFUL TOOLS IN THE QUEST FOR POWER IS THE EDUCATional system."[1] The implication of this statement is obvious: Whoever controls the educational system will set the goals for the nation, establish its religious values, and ultimately control the future. From Sparta and Athens to Geneva and Harvard, education has been the primary means of cultural transformation.

Christian educators learned how important education was for advancing Christian civilization. The Reformation of the sixteenth century stressed the reclamation of all of life, with education as an essential transforming force. Martin Luther in Germany (1483–1546) and John Calvin (1509–1564) in Geneva, Switzerland, did much to advance education as they worked to apply the Bible to every area of life. For these principal reformers, the outgrowth of the gospel included the redemption of all of life, not just the salvation of the soul.

Martin Luther set the fires of Reformation ablaze when he nailed the Ninety-five Theses on the Wittenberg church door in the year 1517.

The Academy of Geneva, Switzerland, founded by John Calvin in 1559, attracted students from all over Europe eager for an education that applied the Bible to all of life. The effects of the training at Geneva were far reaching: "It was not only the future of Geneva but that of other regions as well that was affected by the rise of the Geneva schools. The men who were to lead the advance of the Reformed Church in many lands were trained in Geneva classrooms, preached Geneva doctrines, and sang the Psalms to Geneva tunes."[2] Samuel Blumenfeld writes of the impact that Christian education had on the advancing reformation:

> Since the Protestant rebellion against Rome had arisen in part as a result of Biblical study and interpretation, it became obvious to Protestant leaders that if the Reform movement were to survive and flourish, widespread Biblical literacy, at all levels of society, would be absolutely necessary. The Bible was to be the moral and spiritual authority in every man's life, and therefore an intimate knowledge of it was imperative if a new Protestant social order were to take root.[3]

John Calvin emphasized that the Bible was the foundation of all society and all knowledge and the development of society.

In our own nation one of the first acts performed in the New World was the establishment of schools and colleges. The Virginia colony was the first to charter a college at Henrico, Virginia, in 1619, nineteen years before Harvard and seventy-four years before the College of William and Mary. Like all the colonial colleges, Henricus College was designed around the precepts of the Christian faith, "for the training and bringing up of infidels' children to the true knowledge of God and understanding of righteousness."[4] The New England colonial colleges were designed to further the gospel of Christ in all disciplines. The founders of these early educational institutions understood the relationship between a sound education based upon biblical absolutes and the future of the nation. Putting the Bible in the hands of the people was an essential step toward religious and political freedom. "From the very beginnings, the expressed purpose of colonial education had been to preserve society against barbarism, and, so far as possible, against sin. The inculcation of a saving truth was primarily the responsibility of the churches, but schools were necessary to protect the written means of revelation."[5]

A Colonial Curriculum

A young colonist's education in New England was provided by a very limited curriculum, consisting of three books in addition to the Bible: the *Hornbook*, the *New England Primer*, and the *Bay Psalm Book*. The *Hornbook* consisted of a single piece of parchment, covered with a transparent substance attached to a paddle-shaped piece of wood. The alphabet, the Lord's Prayer, and religious doctrines were written or printed on the parchment.

A typical *Hornbook*.

The *Bay Psalm Book* was the approved hymnal in the New England colonies, rendering the Psalms into verse.

In 1690 the first edition of the *New England Primer* appeared. By 1700 the *Primer* had replaced the *Hornbook* in a number of places. The

Primer expanded the religious themes by including the names of the Old and New Testament books, the Lord's Prayer, "An Alphabet of Lessons for Youth," the Apostles' Creed, the Ten Commandments, the Westminster Assembly Shorter Catechism, and John Cotton's (1584–1652) "Spiritual Milk for American Babes." The *Primer*, developed by Benjamin Harris, included an ingenious way to learn the alphabet while mastering basic biblical truths and lessons about life.

> A In Adam's Fall,
>   We sinned all
> B Thy Life to mend,
>   This **B**ook attend
> C The **C**at doth play,
>   And after slay

The *Primer* was later enlarged in 1777. Additional biblical material was added. The rhyming alphabet was updated and made more theological. For example, in the 1777 edition the letter **C** reads "Christ Crucified, For Sinners Died."

Higher Education in Colonial America

When Trinity University was endowed as Duke University in 1924, its bylaws stated: "The aims of Duke University are to assert a faith in the eternal union of knowledge and religion set forth in the teachings and character of Jesus Christ, the Son of God...."[6] A study of colonial colleges will show that the character of Duke's founding was nearly identical to those colleges started in the seventeenth century. As the following chart demonstrates, with the exception of the University of Pennsylvania (1755), all of the colonial schools began as distinctly Christian institutions. Unfortunately, Duke and its educational predecessors no longer hold to their original denominational affiliations or their religious affirmations.

Colonial Colleges and Religious Affiliation

Date	College	Colony	Affiliation
1636	Harvard	Massachusetts	Puritan
1693	William and Mary	Virginia	Anglican
1701	Yale	Connecticut	Congregational
1746	Princeton	New Jersey	Presbyterian
1754	King's College (Columbia)	New York	Anglican
1764	Brown	Rhode Island	Baptist
1766	Rutgers	New Jersey	Dutch Reformed
1769	Dartmouth	New Hampshire	Congregational

While most of the earliest colleges were established to train men for the gospel ministry, the curriculum was much more comprehensive than the study of divinity. "Regardless of the vocation for which a student was preparing, the colonial college sought to provide for him an education that was distinctly Christian."[7] The curriculum of Harvard, for example, emphasized the study of biblical languages, logic, divinity (theology), and skills in communication (public speaking and rhetoric). Churches expected their ministers to read the Scriptures in the original languages. "Although each of the three earliest colleges, Harvard, William and Mary, and Yale, was chartered by the established church in its colony, each also held a direct relationship to the state and served as the center for training civic as well as clerical leaders for its region."[8] For example, James Madison, considered to be the architect and "Father of the Constitution," studied under Rev. John Witherspoon at the College of New Jersey, a Presbyterian college now known as Princeton.

Harvard (Massachusetts)
John Eliot (1604–1690), the "Apostle to the Indians," first proposed a college for Massachusetts Bay in 1633. Eliot's desires were realized three years later in the founding of Harvard College. (Harvard was named after John Harvard who donated his library to the fledgling institution, and thus secured for himself a name in history.)

The founders of Harvard wanted the Christian legacy they brought with them from England to continue. One of the best ways to accomplish this was to train ministers, the primary educators in the colonies. The following explanation, taken from *New England's First Fruits* (1643), describes what led to the founding of Harvard College.

> After God had carried us safe to *New England* and we had builded our houses, provided necessaries for our liveli-hood, rear'd convenient places for God's worship, and settled the Civil Government: One of the next things we longed for and looked after was to advance *Learning* and perpetuate it to posterity; dreading to leave an illiterate ministry to the churches, when our present Ministers shall lie in the Dust.[9]

John Eliot (1604-1690) gathered a group of 3,600 Indians into fourteen self-governing communities that used the Bible as the standard for personal, family, and civil laws.

Fifty-two percent of the seventeenth-century Harvard graduates became ministers.[10] The Puritans, however, were strongly Calvinistic in their orientation in that they "did not distinguish sharply between secular and theological learning; and they believed that the collegiate education proper for a minister should be the same as for an educated layman. They expected that the early colleges would produce not only ministers but Christian gentlemen who would be civic leaders."[11]

While entry to Harvard required a thorough knowledge of Greek and Latin, a commitment to Jesus Christ and a belief that the Bible was the foundation for truth were even more essential. Harvard's "Rules and Precepts," adopted in 1646, included the following requirements:

> 2. Let every student be plainly instructed, and earnestly pressed to consider well, the main end of his life and studies is, to know

God and Jesus Christ which is eternal life (John 17:3) and therefore lay Christ at the bottom, as the only foundation of all sound knowledge and learning. And seeing the Lord only giveth wisdom, Let every one seriously set himself by prayer in secret to seek it of him, *Prov. 2:3.*

3. Every one shall so exercise himself in reading the Scriptures twice a day, that he shall be ready to give such an account of his proficiency therein, both in *Theoretical* observations of the language, and *Logic*, and in *Practical* and spiritual truths, as his Tutor shall require, according to his ability; seeing *the entrance of the word giveth light, it giveth understanding to the simple*, Psalm 119:130.

An early motto of Harvard was *Veritas Christo et Ecclesiae* (Truth for Christ and the Church). This motto has been abandoned in favor of the shortened *Veritas*—truth. Where the Bible says God's "word is truth" (John 17:17), Harvard now asserts that truth is relative. Harvard's founders had no such delusions. "Religion was so much a part of everyday learning in the early days of Harvard that for nearly two centuries no one thought of setting up a separate Divinity School. In the college, students gathered daily for prayer and readings from the Scripture. Hebrew as well as Greek were required subjects, because an educated person was expected to be able to read the Bible in the original tongues."[12]

"Let every student be plainly instructed, and earnestly pressed to consider well, the main end of his life and studies is, to know God and Jesus Christ which is eternal life (John 17:3) and therefore lay Christ at the bottom, as the only foundation of all sound knowledge and learning."

Harvard is now a place where Christianity is seen as an inhibitor of intellectual freedom. The following item appeared in the February 1993 issue of *Reason* magazine: "John Hinton thought he might find some spiritual sustenance at Harvard Divinity School. But in one class students were asked to talk about what they thought was central to Christianity. After listening to the discussion for several minutes, Hinton thought something important was being ignored, so he volunteered 'Jesus.' He was immediately derided by the others for being 'Christocentric.'"

Harvard is not content with the repudiation of its own Christian heritage. It now wants other schools to take the same path it took long ago—accepting the premise that Jesus is not "the only foundation of all sound knowledge and learning." Harvard, along with seven other leading universities, has scolded Westminster Schools, a Christian institution in Atlanta, Georgia, for maintaining an exclusive Christian faculty. The school's charter requires that faculty members profess a belief in Jesus Christ, and the school's value system is rooted in the Christian faith.[13] Harvard's founders would lament their institution's ideological disintegration and perhaps wonder if they had done the right thing in ever chartering the school.

Yale (Connecticut)

By the eighteenth century, a growing number of New England colonists believed that Harvard had drifted from its original course. Increase Mather, president of Harvard from 1685 to 1701, and his son Cotton Mather, had hoped they could prevent Harvard from moving away from its original

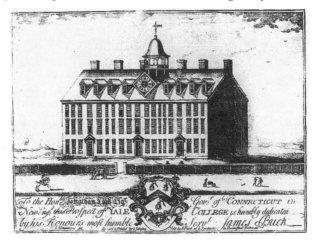

"Every student shall consider the main end of his study to wit to know God in Jesus Christ and answerably to lead a Godly, sober life."

Calvinist orientation. They failed. Harvard not only moved beyond Calvinism to Arminianism but drifted on to Unitarianism. To remedy these theological shortcomings, Yale College was established in 1701 in Connecticut. "The founders of Yale required the 'Westminster Confession to be diligently read in the Latin Tongue and well studyed [sic] by all the Schollars,' 'for the upholding of the Christian protestant Religion by a succession of Learned and Orthodox men.' The State of Connecticut in the Tale Charter of 1701 asserted its desire to support 'so necessary and Religious an undertaking.'"[14]

The founders of Yale yearned to return to the Christian foundation first laid at Harvard: "Yale in the early 1700s stated as its primary goal that 'every student shall consider the main end of his study to wit to know God in Jesus Christ and answerably to lead a Godly, sober life.'"[15] Yale demanded the same rigorous academic concentration as Harvard as well as a religious commitment to the cause of Christ and His Word: "All scholars shall live religious, godly, and blameless lives according to the rules of God's Word, diligently reading the Holy Scriptures, the fountain of light and truth; and constantly attend upon all the duties of religion, both in public and secret."[16] The Yale Charter of 1745 made it clear that the College, "Which has received the favourable benefactions of many liberal [generous] and piously disposed persons, and under the blessing of Almighty God has trained up many worthy persons for the service of God in the state as well as in the church."[17]

Cotton Mather supported the establishment of Yale University in order to preserve orthodox Christianity.

Like Harvard and all the other colonial schools, Yale has fallen on hard times theologically and morally. William F. Buckley, Jr., chronicled Yale's slide toward secularism and collectivism in 1951 with *God and Man at Yale*.[18] Buckley's exposé did little to stem the slide toward decadence.

"Harvard and Yale have assembled Curriculum Committees to explore course material on 'Gay, Lesbian, and Bisexual Studies.'"[19]

Columbia (New York)

An advertisement appeared in the *New York Mercury* on June 3, 1754, announcing the opening of King's College (Columbia University). The ad had been placed by Samuel Johnson (1696–1772), a graduate of Yale. In 1754 the theologian and philosopher accepted an invitation to become the first president of King's College, an office he held until 1763.

Samuel Johnson was the first president of King's College, which was later renamed Columbia University.

Similar to the requirements demanded by Harvard and Yale, King's College required a knowledge of Latin and Greek. Although the college was affiliated with the Anglican Church, the advertisement assured students and parents that "there is no intention to impose on the scholars the peculiar tenets of any particular sect of Christians, but to inculcate upon their tender minds the great principles of Christianity and morality in which true Christians of each denomination are generally agreed."[20] The advertisement went on to state:

> The chief thing that is aimed at in this college is to teach and engage the children to know God in Jesus Christ and to love and serve Him in all sobriety, godliness, and righteousness of life, with perfect heart and a willing mind, and to train them up in all virtuous habits and all such useful knowledge as may render them creditable to their families and friends, ornaments to their country, and useful to the public weal in their generations.[21]

The original shield of King's College (Columbia University) was adopted in 1755. The college's commitment to a biblical world order is evident the shield's figure and inscription. Over the head of the seated woman is the (Hebrew) Tetragrammaton, YHVH (*Jehovah*); the Latin motto around her head means "In Thy light we see light" (Psalm 36:10); the Hebrew phrase on the ribbon is *Uri El* ("God is my light"), an allusion to Psalm 27:1; and at the feet of the woman is the New Testament passage commanding Christians to desire the pure milk of God's word (1 Peter 2:1–2).[22]

Columbia long ago adopted a new seal. The only line remaining from the original shield is the Latin phrase "In Thy light we see light."

William and Mary (Virginia)

In 1662, the Assembly of Virginia passed an act to make permanent provision for the establishment of a college. The preamble of the act recites "that the want of able and faithful ministers in this country deprives us of those great blessings and mercies that always attend upon the service of God"; and the act itself declares "that for the advancement of learning, education of youth, supply of the ministry, and promotion of piety, there be land taken up and purchased for a college and free school, and that with all convenient speed there be buildings erected upon it for the entertainment of students and scholars."[23]

Although an act had passed for the establishment of a college, the College of William and Mary was not actually founded until 1693. But like all the colonial schools, William and Mary began with an evangelical purpose. The school would supply the church of Virginia "with a Seminary of Ministers" that the "Christian Faith may be propagated amongst the Western Indians, to the Glory of Almighty God."[24] These and other evangelical goals were reiterated in 1727.

Conclusion

The establishment of schools in the colonies maintained and advanced the Christian faith. Education, therefore, was a religious exercise: "The schools were intended to form Christian men, Christian citizens, and Christian ministers, not as a by-product but directly. They were instruments of the Church, which was, at least in the beginning, virtually coterminous with the community. Education was an enterprise undertaken primarily in the interests of religion, with religion of course defined in terms of the Calvinist orthodoxy then dominant in New England."[25]

In time a philosophical shift took place. Colleges and universities in the nineteenth century were built by wealthy entrepreneurs for decidedly secular purposes. "Ezra Cornell (telegraph, banking), Johns Hopkins (banking, railroads), Cornelius Vanderbilt (steamships, railroads), Leland Stanford (railroads), James Duke (tobacco), and James D. Rockefeller (oil) were only a few of the prominent businessmen who poured vast sums into the creation of modern universities."[26] Some institutions were more secular than others. For example, Andrew Dickson White, the founding president of Cornell University, promised that he would use the institution to "afford asylum for Science—where truth shall be sought for truth's sake, where it shall not be the main purpose of the Faculty to stretch or cut sciences exactly to fit 'Revealed Religion.'"[27]

Johns Hopkins (1795-1873) was a banker and financier who donated $7,000,000 to found Johns Hopkins University and Hospital.

America's institutions of higher learning have come a long way down the road of secularism, from Harvard's declaration that the main end of man's life is to "know God and Jesus Christ which is eternal life (John 17:3)" to viewing Darwinian evolution as "a scientifically credible theory of random and purposeless change."[28]

Andrew Dickson White stressed
"truth for truth's sake" as opposed to
"revealed religion."

Notes

1. Herbert Schlossberg, *Idols for Destruction: Christian Faith and Its Confrontation with American Society* (Wheaton, IL: Crossway Books, [1983] 1993), 209.
2. John T. McNeill, *The History and Character of Calvinism* (New York: Oxford University Press, 1954), 196.
3. Samuel L. Blumenfeld, *Is Public Education Necessary?* (Old Greenwich, CT: Devin-Adair, 1981), 10.
4. "Funds for a College at Henrico, Virginia (1619)," in Sol Cohen, ed., *Education in the United States: A Documentary History*, 5 vols. (New York: Random House, 1974), 1:336.
5. Henry F. May, *The Enlightenment in America* (New York: Oxford University Press, 1976), 32–33.
6. Quoted in George M. Marsden, *The Soul of the American University: From Protestant Establishment to Established Nonbelief* (New York: Oxford University Press, 1994), 322.
7. William C. Ringenberg, *The Christian College: A History of Protestant Higher Education in America* (Grand Rapids, MI: Eerdmans, 1984), 38.
8. Ringenberg, *The Christian College*, 42.
9. Reprinted in Richard Hofstadter and Wilson Smith, eds., *American Higher Education: A Documentary History* (Chicago, IL: University of Chicago Press, 1961), 1:9.

10. Marsden, *Soul of the American University*, 41. "Harvard, it is true, was more than a Seminary: in the seventeenth century only about half of its graduates entered the ministry. But secular learning too stood under the sign of the overriding religious purpose; the Harvard graduate who became a bookseller or a fur trader was expected to be as pious, and almost as knowledgeable in Scripture, as his classmate who entered the ministry. If, in the learned climate that New England's Puritans cherished, classicism and Christianity should conflict, or wrestle for precedence, it was never Christianity, always classicism, that must yield. This at least, in a life filled with uncertainty, was certain." (Peter Gay, *A Loss of Mastery: Puritan Historians in Colonial America* [Berkeley, CA: University of California Press, 1966], 23).

11. Hofstadter and Smith, "From the Beginnings to the Great Awakening," *American Higher Education*, 1:1.

12. Ari L. Goldman, *The Search for God at Harvard* (New York: Random House, 1991), 17.

13. Mark Silk, "Westminster feels more heat for non-Christian hiring ban," *Atlanta Journal/Constitution* (November 21, 1992), A1 and A16.

14. H. G. Good, *A History of American Education* (New York: Macmillan, 1956), 61.

15. Ringenberg, *The Christian College*, 38.

16. "Yale Laws (1745)" in Cohen, *Education in the United States*, 2:675.

17. Quoted in Hofstadter and Smith, *American Higher Education*, 1:49.

18. William F. Buckley, Jr., *God and Man at Yale: The Superstitions of "Academic Freedom"* (Chicago, IL: Henry Regnery Co., 1951).

19. Dinesh D'Souza, *Illiberal Education: The Politics of Race and Sex on Campus* (New York: The Free Press, 1991), 214.

20. "Advertisement on the Opening of Kings College," in Cohen, *Education in the United States*, 2:675.

21. "Advertisement on the Opening of Kings College," in Cohen, *Education in the United States*, 2:675.

22. See Gabriel Sivan, *The Bible and Civilization* (New York: Quadrangle/New York Times Book Co., 1973), 237.

23. B.F. Morris, *The Christian Life and Character of the Civil Institutions of the United States* (Philadelphia, PA: G.W. Childs, 1864), 94.

24. "Charter of William and Mary," in Cohen, *Education in the United States*, 2:645.

25. Will Herberg, "Religion and Education in America," *Religious Perspectives in American Culture*, eds. James Ward Smith and A. Leland Jamison (Princeton, NJ: Princeton University Press, 1961), 12.

26. Mark A. Noll, *A History of Christianity in the United States and Canada* (Grand Rapids, MI: Eerdmans, 1992), 365.
27. Cited in Noll, *A History of Christianity in the United States and Canada*, 366.
28. Cited in Noll, *A History of Christianity in the United States and Canada*, 366.

CHAPTER 7

GOD IN
OUR NATION'S CAPITOL

THE OFFICIAL MINUTES OF THE FIRST SESSION OF THE CONTINENTAL CONGRESS in 1774 show that Sam Adams made a proposal that the sessions be opened with prayer. Not everyone agreed. John Jay and John Rutledge opposed the recommendation claiming that the diversity of religious opinion precluded such an action. Their minority opinion did not carry the day. At the end of the debate over the proposal, Adams said that it did not become "Christian men, who had come together for solemn deliberation in the hour of their extremity, to say there was so wide a difference in their religious belief that they could not, as one man, bow the knee in prayer to the Almighty, whose advice and assistance they hoped to obtain."[1]

Reverend Jacob Duché led the prayer at the first session of the Continental Congress.

After the appeal by Sam Adams, the disputation ceased and Reverend Jacob Duché led in prayer.[2] John Adams wrote home to his wife that the prayer by Duché "had an excellent effect upon everybody here…. Those men who were about to resort to force to obtain their rights were moved by tears" upon hearing it. The Continental Congress also issued four fast-day proclamations. The July 12, 1775, fast-day is especially significant. All the colonies were to participate. John Adams, writing to his wife from Philadelphia, said, "We have appointed a Continental fast. Millions will be upon their knees at once before the great Creator, imploring His forgiveness and blessing; His smiles on American Councils and arms."[3]

Declaration of Independence

With the drafting of the Declaration of Independence in July of 1776, the colonies moved into a new era of political independence with ties to its Christian past. The Declaration is a religious document, basing its argument for rights on theological grounds. Rights, the Declaration maintains, are a gift from the Creator: "We are endowed by our Creator with certain inalienable rights." The logic is simple. No Creator, no rights.

The moral state of our nation is directly tied to this single phrase in the Declaration. Today, while our nation clamors for rights, it rejects the standard by which those rights secure their moral anchor. "Nature's God," who is the "Supreme Judge of the world," makes rights a reality. While the Declaration is a theistic document, referring to "Divine Providence," it is not specifically a Christian document. Even so, the religious phrases found in the body of the Declaration were easily understood in terms of the prevailing Christian worldview of the time.[4] One Roman Catholic signer of the Declaration wrote: "When I signed the Declaration of Independence I had in view, not only our independence from England, but the toleration of all sects professing the Christian religion, and communicating to them all equal rights."[5]

The Congressional Bible

In 1777 Congress issued a proclamation for a day of thanksgiving for November of that year. December 18 was also to be set aside for "solemn thanksgiving and praise." The proclamation called upon all citizens to "join the penitent confession of their manifold sins," and to offer "their humble and earnest supplication that it may please God through the merits of Jesus Christ, mercifully to forgive and blot them out of remembrance."[6]

The same year Congress issued an official resolution instructing the Committee on Commerce to import 20,000 copies of the Bible. With the outbreak of war with England, the sea lanes had been cut off to the colonies. This meant that goods that were once common in the colonies were no longer being imported—including Bibles printed in England. Congress decided to act. Historian B. F. Morris states the following:

The Declaration of Independence bases all human rights upon the Creator.

The legislation of Congress on the Bible is a suggestive Christian fact, and one which evinces the faith of the statesmen of that period in its divinity, as well as their purpose to place it as the corner-stone in our republican institutions. The breaking out of the Revolution cut off the supply of "books printed in London." The scarcity of Bibles also came soon to be felt. Dr. PATRICK ALLISON, one of the chaplains to Congress, and other gentlemen, brought the subject before that body in a memorial, in which they urged the printing of an edition of the Scriptures.[7]

The committee approved the importing of 20,000 copies of the Bible from Scotland, Holland, and elsewhere. Congressmen resolved to pass this proposal because they believed that "the use of the Bible is so universal, and its importance so great."[8] Even though the resolution passed, action was never taken to import the Bibles. Instead, Congress began to put emphasis on the printing of Bibles within the United States. In 1777 Robert Aitken of Philadelphia published a New Testament. Three additional editions were published in 1789, 1779, and 1781. The edition of 1779 was used in schools. Aitken's efforts proved so popular that he announced his desire to publish the whole Bible; he then petitioned Congress for support. Congress adopted the following resolution in 1782:

> *Resolved*, That the United States in Congress assembled, highly approve the pious and laudable undertaking of Mr. Aitken, subservient to the interest of religion as well as the progress of the arts in this country, and being satisfied from the above report, of his care and accuracy in the execution of the work, they commend this edition of the Bible to the inhabitants of the United States, and hereby authorize him to publish this recommendation in the manner he shall think proper.[9]

The Continental Congress's records show that it was not neutral to religion. "Its records are full of references to 'God,' under many titles, to 'Jesus Christ,' the 'Christian Religion,' 'God and the Constitution,' and the 'Free Protestant Colonies.'"[10]

The First United States Congress

The first order of business of the first United States Congress in 1789 was to appoint chaplains. The Right Reverend Bishop Samuel Provost and the Reverend William Linn became publicly paid chaplains of the Senate and House respectively. Since then, both the Senate and the House have continued regularly to open their sessions with prayer. Nearly all of the fifty states make some provision in their meetings for opening prayers or devotions from guest chaplains. Few if any saw this as a violation of the First Amendment.

On April 30, 1789, George Washington took the oath of office with his hand on a Bible. After taking the oath in Federal Hall, New York, he added, "I swear, so help me God"—words that were not part of the oath. Every president since Washington has invoked God's name in this way.[11] The inauguration was followed by "divine services" that were held in St. Paul's Chapel, "performed by the Chaplain of Congress."[12] The first Congress that convened after the adoption of the Constitution requested of the President that the people of the United States observe a day of thanksgiving and prayer:

> That a joint committee of both Houses be directed to wait upon the President of the United States to request that he would recommend to the people of the United States a day of public thanksgiving and prayer, to be observed by acknowledging, with grateful hearts, the many signal favors of Almighty God, especially by affording them an opportunity peaceably to establish a Constitution of government for their safety and happiness.

George Washington taking the oath of office as first president of the United States, on the balcony of the Old City Hall, New York.

This resolution was opposed by some as an infringement on the authority of the states: "It is a business with which Congress has nothing to do; it is a religious matter, and as such is proscribed to us."[13] Nevertheless, the resolution was adopted. Washington then issued a proclamation setting aside November 26, 1789, as a national day of thanksgiving, calling everyone to "unite in most humbly offering our prayers and supplications to the great Lord and Ruler of Nations, and beseech him to pardon our national and other transgressions."[14] Washington called for days of prayer and thanksgiving on January 1 and February 19, 1795.

Good Government and Religion

Prayers in Congress, the appointment of chaplains, and the call for days of prayers and thanksgiving do not stand alone in the historical record. The evidence is overwhelming that America has in the past always linked good government to religion—and, in particular, to Christianity. Historians and constitutional scholars Anson Stokes and Leo Pfeffer summarize the role that the Christian religion played in the founding of this nation and the lofty position it has retained:

> Throughout its history our governments, national and state, have co-operated with religion and shown friendliness to it. God is invoked in the Declaration of Independence and in practically every state constitution. Sunday, the Christian Sabbath, is universally observed as a day of rest. The sessions of Congress and of the state legislatures are invariably opened with prayer, in Congress by chaplains who are employed by the Federal government. We have chaplains in our armed forces and in our penal institutions. Oaths in courts of law are administered through use of the Bible. Public officials take an oath of office ending with "so help me God." Religious institutions are tax exempt throughout the nation. Our pledge of allegiance declares that we are a nation "under God." Our national motto is "In God We Trust" and is inscribed on our currency and on some of our postage stamps.[15]

After only a cursory study of the years leading up to and including the drafting of the Constitution and the inauguration of the first president, it becomes obvious that Christianity played a foundational role in shaping our nation. It is not surprising that when courts had to define religion, they linked it to the Christian religion. In 1930 the Supreme Court declared, "We are a Christian people, according to one another the equal right of religious freedom, and acknowledging with reverence the duty of obedience to the will of God."[16] Further evidence of the role that the Christian religion played in the maintenance of our nation can be found in national pronouncements and inscriptions in our nation's capital.

Official Acts of Congress and the President

1. Our nation's coins have not always had "In God We Trust" stamped on them. In 1862 many people began to request that our coinage make reference to God. A sermon by the Reverend Henry Augustus Boardman of Philadelphia declared that "The coinage of the United States is without a God."[17] Some suggested "God our Trust." In 1863 the motto "God and our Country" was proposed. The motto "In God We Trust" appeared for the first time in 1864; it did not receive formal Congressional approval until the following year. In 1865 Congress enacted the following:

> *And be it further enacted*, That, in addition to the devices and legends upon the gold, silver, and other coins of the United States, it shall be lawful for the director of the mint, with the approval of the Secretary of the Treasury, to cause the motto "In God we trust" to be placed upon such coins hereafter to be issued as shall admit of such legend thereon.[18]

The interest to secure a place for the motto was so high because of the events of the civil war. Repentance and trust in God were themes that echoed through the nation after blood of so many had been shed.

The motto was dropped in 1907 when President Theodore Roosevelt commissioned the American sculpture Augustus Saint-Gaudens to design new coins. Saint-Gaudens's design did not include the "In God We Trust" motto. As one might imagine, many people were upset at the change. In November of 1907, the president wrote a letter to a minister who objected to the omission. In it Roosevelt claimed that there was "no legal warrant for putting the motto on the coins." Of course, the president was mistaken, since the motto had been authorized by Congress. The matter came before Congress again on May 18, 1908, and an act was passed to restore the motto. "In 1955 Congress extended the act by requiring the phrase to appear not only on all coins but on all paper money thereafter minted or printed. The next year, 1956, Congress enacted a law making the phrase 'In God We Trust' officially the national motto."[19]

Theodore Roosevelt wrongly claimed that there was "no legal warrant for putting the motto ['In God We Trust'] on the coins."

2. The president is authorized to proclaim at least two National Days of Prayer each year. Public Law 82–324 requires the president to proclaim a National Day of Prayer on a day other than a Sunday. Under Public Law 77–379 the president proclaims the fourth Thursday of November each year as a National Day of Thanksgiving.

3. The words "under God" were inserted into the pledge of allegiance by an act of Congress in 1954. The House and Senate adopted the measure without a dissenting vote. On June 14 of that same year President Dwight D. Eisenhower stood on the steps of the Capitol Building and, for the first time, recited the revised pledge to the flag that included the phrase "one nation under God."[20]

4. On April 30, 1863, President Abraham Lincoln appointed a "National Fast Day." It reads in part: "It is the duty of nations as well as of men to own their dependence upon the overruling power of God, to confess their sins and transgressions in humble sorrow yet with assured hope that genuine repentance will lead to mercy and pardon, and to recognize the sublime truth, announced in the Holy Scriptures and proven by all history: that those nations only are blessed whose God is the Lord."[21]

Abraham Lincoln stated, "Those nations only are blessed whose God is the Lord."

5. Congress declared 1983 to be the "Year of the Bible": "The Bible, the Word of God, has made a unique contribution in shaping the United States as a distinctive and blessed nation.... Deeply held religious convictions springing from the Holy Scriptures led to the early settlement of our Nation.... Biblical teaching inspired concepts of civil government that are contained in our Declaration of Independence and the Constitution of the United States" (Public Law 97–280, 96 Stat. 1211, approved October 4, 1982).

6. When the Supreme Court convenes and the chief justice and associate justices stand before their desks, the marshal makes an ascription to Almighty God in the Court Call saying, "God save the United States and this honorable court."

7. The same year that Congress approved adding the phrase "one nation under God" to the Pledge of Allegiance, both houses passed a resolution directing the Capitol architect to make available "a room, with facilities for prayer and meditation, for the use of members of the Senate and House of Representatives."[22] The seventh edition of *The Capitol*, an official publication of the United States Congress, gives the following description:

> The history that gives this room its inspirational lift is centered in the stained glass window. George Washington kneeling in prayer...is the focus of the composition.... Behind Washington a prayer is etched:

"Preserve me, O God, for in Thee do I put my trust," the first verse of the sixteenth Psalm. There are upper and lower medallions representing the two sides of the Great Seal of the United States. On these are inscribed the phrases: *annuit coeptis*—"God has favored our undertakings"—and *novus ordo seclorum*—"A new order of the ages is born." Under the upper medallion is the phrase from Lincoln's immortal Gettysburg Address, "This Nation under God."…The two lower corners of the window each show the Holy Scriptures, an open book and a candle, signifying the light from God's law, "Thy Word is a lamp unto my feet and a light unto my path" [Psalm 119:105].[23]

The prayer room is decidedly Christian in character. The Bible is featured, not the Book of Mormon. Religious citations are taken from the Bible, not the Koran.

Government Buildings and Inscriptions

1. The words "In God We Trust" are inscribed in the House and Senate chambers.

2. On the walls of the Capitol dome, these words appear: "The New Testament according to the Lord and Savior Jesus Christ."

3. In the Rotunda of the Capitol is the figure of the crucified Christ.

4. The painting "The Baptism of Pocahontas at Jamestown" hangs in the Capitol Rotunda.[24]

The prayer room in the U.S. Capitol building features a stained glass window that bears this prayer from Psalms 16:1: "Preserve me, O God, for in Thee do I put my trust."

5. The painting "Embarkation of the Pilgrims" shows Elder William Brewster holding a Bible opened to the title page which reads "The New Testament of Our Lord and Savior Jesus Christ." The words "God With Us" are inscribed on the sail of the ship. This painting also hangs in the Rotunda of the Capitol.[25]

This painting portrays the Pilgrims' obvious devotion to God and submission to His providential care.

6. A relief of Moses hangs in the House Chamber. Moses is surrounded by twenty-two other lawgivers.[26]

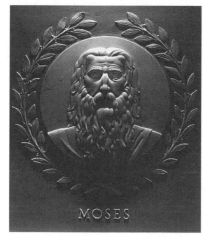

This relief of Moses is described by the Architect of the Capitol as a depiction of the *"unexcelled* Hebrew prophet and lawgiver."

7. The Latin phrase *Annuit Coeptis*, "[God] has smiled on our undertaking," is inscribed on the Great Seal of the United States.

8. Under the Seal is the phrase from Lincoln's Gettysburg address: "This nation under God."

9. The Liberty Bell has Leviticus 25:10 prominently displayed in a band around its top: "Proclaim liberty throughout all the land, unto the inhabitants thereof."

The Liberty Bell is inscribed with the words of Leviticus 25:10: "Proclaim liberty throughout all the land, unto the inhabitants thereof."

10. President Eliot of Harvard chose Micah 6:8 for the walls of the Library of Congress: "He hath showed thee, O man, what is good; and what doth God require of thee, but to do justly, and to love mercy, and to walk humbly with thy God."

11. The lawmaker's library quotes the Psalmist's acknowledgment of the beauty and order of creation: "The heavens declare the glory of God, and the firmament showeth His handiwork" (Psalm 19:1).

12. Engraved on the metal cap on the top of the Washington Monument are the words: "Praise be to God." Lining the walls of the stairwell are numerous Bible verses: "Search the Scriptures" (John 5:39), "Holiness to the Lord," and "Train up a child in the way he should go, and when he is old he will not depart from it" (Proverbs 22:6).

13. The crier who opens each session of the Supreme Court closes with the words, "God save the United States and the Honorable Court."

14. At the opposite end of the Lincoln Memorial, words and phrases from Lincoln's Second Inaugural Address allude to "God," the "Bible," "providence," "the Almighty," and "divine attributes."

15. A plaque in the Dirksen Office Building has the words "IN GOD WE TRUST" in bronze relief.

16. The Jefferson Memorial includes these words of Jefferson: "God who gave us life gave us liberty. Can the liberties of a nation be secure when we have removed a conviction that these liberties are the gift of God? Indeed I tremble for my country when I reflect that God is just, that his justice cannot sleep forever."

17. Each president takes his oath of office with his left hand placed on an open Bible and concludes the oath with these words: "So help me God." The Senate Doors (bronze) show George Washington taking the presidential oath with his hands on a Bible.[27]

18. Several bas-relief sculptures adorn the Supreme Court building. One which hangs directly over the bench shows two allegorical figures, "The Power of Government" (left) and "The Majesty of Law" (right), flanking a tablet with two rows of Roman numerals, I–V and VI–X, an obvious symbol of God's moral law. The Curator confirms that the tablets refer to "ancient law," and the only ancient law which is clearly represented by ten laws is the Ten Commandments. Behind the two allegorical figures and directly above the tablet, the American eagle spreads its wings, a universal symbol of protection.

The second bas-relief sculpture, "Justice, the Guardian of Liberty," portrays Moses holding the tablets of God's law. The shape of these tablets is similar to the shape of the tablet found in the "Majesty of Law" sculpture with its ten Roman numerals. In both sculptures, the tablets correspond to the universal depiction of the Ten Commandments; furthermore, Moses is almost always depicted holding the tablets which were given to him by God. Even though Confucius and Hammurabi are also portrayed in this sculpture, and even though each holds a copy of his law code, the carving clearly depicts these other figures standing in the background behind a central, elevated Moses.

Another sculpture is displayed on the south wall of the courtroom itself; this carving shows Moses, along with other noted law givers, holding a copy of the Ten Commandments inscribed in Hebrew.

Conclusion

It makes a difference that our coins are stamped with "In God We Trust" instead of "In Allah We Trust." It's important to note that the Library of Congress has a quotation from a Psalm, instead of a quotation from the Koran. In addition, it's significant to note that "every foreigner attests his renunciation of allegiance to his former sovereign and his acceptance of citizenship in this republic by an appeal to God"[28] and not to the Buddha. "But as true as these symbols may be, and as important as our structures may be, they are not, in and of themselves, evidence or assurance of America's greatness—past, present, or future. National greatness does not spring from an accumulation of archival antiquities and architectural details, or from symbols and slogans. It does not spring from documents, precedents, constitutions, or legislation. National greatness springs from righteousness, goodness, character, and true spirituality!"[29] As Scripture declares: "Righteousness exalts a nation, but sin is a reproach to any people" (Prov. 14:34) and "A throne is established by righteousness" (6:12).

Notes

1. Quoted in Key Paton, "Notable Chaplains," *Eternity* (November 1986), 28.
2. Two years later Duché "was later elected chaplain of Congress. This initiation of Congressional chaplaincies was somewhat inauspicious in that Duché resigned shortly after his election, having, in the words of John Adams, 'turned out an apostate and traitor' who urged Washington to call for recision of 'the hasty and ill-advised Declaration of Independence.'" (Anson Phelps Stokes and Leo Pfeffer, *Church and State in the United States* [New York: Harper & Row, 1964], 83).
3. Quoted in Stokes and Pfeffer, *Church and State in the United States*, 83.
4. See Gary T. Amos in *Defending the Declaration: How the Bible and Christianity Influenced the Writing of the Declaration of Independence* (Brentwood, TN: Wolgemuth and Hyatt, 1989). Also see "Is the Declaration of Independence 'Christian'?," *World* (December 9, 1989), 19–20.
5. Quoted in Stokes and Pfeffer, *Church and State in the United States*, 85.
6. Quoted in Stokes and Pfeffer, *Church and State in the United States*, 83–84.
7. B. F. Morris, *The Christian Life and Character of the Civil Institutions of the United States* (Philadelphia, PA: G.W. Childs, 1864), 215.
8. From a report submitted to Congress, quoted in John Wright, *Early Bibles in America*, 3rd rev. ed. (New York: Thomas Whittaker, 1894), 55.
9. Quoted in Wright, *Early Bibles in America*, 58.

10. Stokes and Pfeffer, *Church and State in the United States*, 86.

11. Richard G. Hutcheson, Jr., *God in the White House: How Religion Has Changed the Modern Presidency* (New York: Macmillan, 1988), 37.

12. Stokes and Pfeffer, *Church and State in the United States*, 87.

13. Quoted in Stokes and Pfeffer, *Church and State in the United States*, 87.

14. Quoted in Stokes and Pfeffer, *Church and State in the United States*, 87.

15. Stokes and Pfeffer, *Church and State in the United States*, 102–103.

16. *United States vs. Macintosh*, 283 U.S. 625 (1930).

17. Quoted in Stokes and Pfeffer, *Church and State in the United States*, 568.

18. Quoted in Stokes and Pfeffer, *Church and State in the United States*, 568.

19. Stokes and Pfeffer, *Church and State in the United States*, 570.

20. Much of the material in this section was taken from the seventh edition (1979) of *The Capitol* (Washington DC: United States Government Printing Office, 1979), 24–25.

21. Abraham Lincoln, "Proclamation Appointing a National Fast Day," April 30, 1863, *The Collected Works of Abraham Lincoln*, ed. Roy P. Bassler (New Brunswick, NJ: Rutgers University Press, 1953), 6:155–56.

22. "The Prayer Room of the United States Capitol," booklet published by the U.S. Printing Office, 1956.

23. *The Capitol*, 25. The eighth edition of *The Capitol* (1981) has removed the material on the congressional prayer room found in the seventh edition. While there is a picture of the room in the eighth edition (22), a description of its religious features is absent.

24. *Art in the United States Capitol* (Washington, DC: United States Government Printing Office, 1978), 130.

25. *Art in the United States Capitol*, 136.

26. *Art in the United States Capitol*, 283, 287.

27. *Art in the United States Capitol*, 349.

28. David J. Brewer, *The United States: A Christian Nation* (Philadelphia, PA: The John C. Winston Co., 1905), 31.

29. Peter J. Leithart and George Grant, *In Defense of Greatness: How Biblical Character Shapes a Nation's Destiny* (Ft. Lauderdale, FL: Coral Ridge Ministries, 1990), 4.

CHAPTER 8

THE TREATY OF TRIPOLI

T HE OPENING LINES OF THE "MARINES' HYMN"—"FROM THE HALLS OF
Montezuma, To the shores of Tripoli"—commemorate the Mexican
War (1846–48) and the war with Tripoli when Marines took part in the
capture of Derna on April 27, 1805. It seems that we're fighting Tripoli
again, but this new battle is over the facts of history. A single line in
the first Treaty of Tripoli (ratified June 10, 1797) is continually cited as
incontrovertible evidence that our founders self-consciously denied any
attachment to the Christian religion, and that there is a radical separation
between religion and civil government. This conclusion is based upon
Article 11 of the 1797 Treaty of Tripoli which reads:

> As the government of the United States of America *is not in any sense
> founded on the Christian religion*,—as it has in itself no character of enmi-
> ty against the law, religion or tranquility of Musselmen [Muslims],—and
> as the said States [of America] never have entered into any war or act
> of hostility against any Mehomitan nation, it is declared by the parties
> that no pretext arising from religious opinions shall ever produce an
> interruption of the harmony existing between the two countries.[1]

Who would have thought that a long-forgotten treaty would play
such an important role in the debate over religious freedom, justice, and
Christian involvement in politics?

Several anti-Christian groups have used the 1797 Treaty of Tripoli—which was drawn up to put an end to raids on American ships by
Barbary Coast pirates—to drive a provocative wedge into our culture and
disrupt the idea that religion played a major role in the founding of our
nation. The only way the debate can be settled is to survey the historical
record. When surveyed, the record will show that the Treaty of Tripoli
does nothing to disturb the proposition that America was founded as a
Christian nation.

The Washington Connection

The phrase "the government of the United States of America is not in
any sense founded on the Christian religion" has been attributed to

George Washington numerous times. A portion of the above quotation found its way in the September/October 1980 issue of *Liberty Magazine*, a publication of Review and Herald Publishing Company. The full page reproduction of Article XI gives the impression that George Washington wrote the words. Washington's signature follows the excerpted line that reads, "The United States of America is not in any sense founded on the Christian religion." As we will see, Washington never signed the treaty.

Washington has been wrongly attributed as saying that America is not a Christian nation.

The Encyclopedia of Philosophy concocts a story of how Washington "acquiesced" to the radical deistic views of Joel Barlow, the American consul in Algiers, by maintaining that America was not a Christian nation. Here is how the story is reported:

> In answer to a direct question from a Muslim potentate in Tripoli, Washington acquiesced in the declaration of Joel Barlow, then American Consul in Algiers, that "the government of the United States of America is not in any sense founded on the Christian religion."[2]

This excerpt gives the impression that Washington went to Tripoli and had a conversation with the Muslim potentate where Washington answered a question relating to America's religious foundation. This is pure fiction. Washington had no direct involvement with the Treaty. He had left office before the Treaty was signed and had no opportunity to review it.

Norman Geisler, author of *Is Man the Measure* and many other books on Christian apologetics, uncritically accepts the *Encyclopedia of Philosophy*'s conclusion concerning the Treaty of Tripoli and George

Washington's part in it. Geisler states that "our nation's founders were largely humanistic (or deistic).... There were few evangelical Christians among the signers of the Declaration of Independence, John Witherspoon being a notable exception. And when George Washington was asked if the United States was a Christian country, he replied that 'the government of the United States of America is not in any sense founded on the Christian religion.'"[3] Geisler offers no evidence that Washington was ever asked this question. As subsequent study will demonstrate, Washington never made a statement even remotely resembling the one being attributed to him by these scarcely researched articles.

During the 1984 presidential election, People for the American Way (PAW) aired a commercial entitled "Founding Fathers/Separation of Church and State." Noted actor Martin Sheen narrated the propagandistic segment. Sheen said: "Today the voices evoking religious dogma have invaded the highest places of government, challenging the ideas of our Founding Fathers and the separation of church and state." What did People for the American Way use to support this claim of the views of the founding fathers? PAW turned to a chopped quotation from the Treaty of Tripoli and maintained that they were the words of George Washington. Sheen continued: "'The government of the United States,' insisted Washington, 'is not in any sense founded on the Christian religion or any other religion.'"[4] PAW cannot even misquote with integrity. Nowhere does the Treaty of Tripoli contain the words "or any other religion."

The issue regarding whether Washington ever said or wrote that the government of the United States was not founded on the Christian religion is an old debate. Others more honest than today's critics of the Christian America position have called the story of Washington's denouncement what it really is—a myth.

> There is a myth (and it was revived in 1962 during the discussion following the Supreme Court's decision against the constitutionality of state-sponsored prayers in public schools) to the effect that Washington once declared while he was President that the government of the United States was not a Christian nation.[5]

A book dispelling hundreds of similar false quotations and misleading attributions states that "the statement was not Washington's" and that diplomats had used that particular phraseology because they were "eager to make it clear that Christianity was not an American state religion, and that therefore the U.S. government bore no official hostility toward Islam."[6] The key fact in this debate about Washington's alleged disavowal of a Christian America is that Washington was not even in office at the time the Treaty of Tripoli was signed. John Adams had been inaugurated as president in March of 1797, three months before the treaty was ratified.

The evidence supporting America's Christian founding is overwhelming. Those who dispute the claim cannot do it honestly. They must play fast and loose with the facts because the historical evidence is so against them. In an address to the Delaware Chiefs on May 12, 1797, Washington stated: "You do well to wish to learn our arts and ways of life, and above all, the religion of Jesus Christ."[7]

George Washington also stated that "it is the duty of all *nations* to acknowledge the providence of Almighty God, to obey His will, to be grateful for His benefits, and humbly to implore His protection and favor." He went on in his Thanksgiving Proclamation of October 3, 1789, to write, that as a nation "we may then unite in most humbly offering our prayers and supplications to the great *Lord and Ruler of Nations*, and beseech Him to pardon our national and other transgressions."[8]

The Adams Connection

Jim Castelli, in an article titled "'Christian America': A Myth Keeps Living On,"[9] attaches the name of John Adams to the infamous phrase. President Adams did sign the treaty on June 10, 1797, three days after it was passed by the Senate. However, a study of Adams's private and public statements show that he believed that Christianity must be rooted within the nation's culture in order for the nation to survive. Adams expressed his religious views on numerous occasions, but his call for a National Fast Day on March 6, 1799, is the most expressive:

> As no truth is more clearly taught in the Volume of Inspiration, nor any more fully demonstrated by the experience of all ages, than that a deep sense and a due acknowledgment of the growing providence of a Supreme Being and of the accountableness of men to Him as the searcher of hearts and righteous distributer of rewards and punishments are conducive equally to the happiness of individuals and to the well-being of communities.... I have thought proper to recommend, and I hereby recommend accordingly, that Thursday, the twenty-fifth day of April next, be observed throughout the United States of America as a day of solemn humiliation, fasting, and prayer; that the citizens on that day abstain, as far as may be, from their secular occupation, and devote the time to the sacred duties of religion, in public

and in private; that they call to mind our numerous offenses against the most high God, confess them before Him with the sincerest penitence, implore his pardoning mercy, through the Great Mediator and Redeemer, for our past transgressions, and that through the grace of His Holy Spirit, we may be disposed and enabled to yield a more suitable obedience to his righteous requisitions in time to come; that He would interpose to arrest the progress of that impiety and licentiousness in principle and practice so offensive to Himself and so ruinous to mankind; that He would make us deeply sensible that "righteousness exalteth a nation, but sin is a reproach to any people" [Proverbs 14:34].[10]

John Adams wrote that "The general principles on which the Fathers achieved independence, were . . . the general principles of Christianity."

On another occasion, John Adams wrote to Thomas Jefferson stating that "The general principles, on which the Fathers achieved independence, were...the general principles of Christianity."[11] A few years later Adams wrote a letter to Jefferson in which he stated that "Without religion this world would be something not fit to be mentioned in polite society, I mean hell."[12]

A Question of Diplomacy

How then do we reconcile the 1797 Treaty of Tripoli with Adams's favorable public remarks about Christianity? Why put a statement regarding religion in a treaty? There must have been a *diplomatic* reason for its inclusion. The treaty is nothing more than a pronouncement "that 'the Christian religion' as a formal institution was not a part of the American government in the same way that the religious structures of Islam are a part of Islamic governments. From many things that Adams and his contemporaries wrote it is clear that they did not use the word *religion* to exclude Christian ideas or principles as some do today. True, the founders did not make institutional religion a part of the government. But they never thought of excluding Christian principles."[13]

In surveying all the evidence, and taking into account the circumstances surrounding the necessity for such a treaty, it is not hard to explain the disputed phrase. The statement in question was nothing more than an assurance to a deeply religious (Muslim) government that America would not depose that government and impose Christianity by force. A single phrase ripped from its historical context does nothing to nullify the volumes of historical evidence that Christianity was foundational to the building and maintenance of this nation.

Muslim Nations versus Christian Nations

In order to understand the statement "As the government of the United States of America is not in any sense founded on the Christian religion," it must be read in context and with background knowledge of the religion of Islam. It is obvious by reading the original treaty that Tripoli considered America to be a Christian nation. In writing an annotated translation of the treaty in 1930, Dr. C. Snouck Hurgronje of Leiden, Netherlands, reviewed the original treaty and found numerous statements that clearly show that Tripoli considered America to be a Christian nation. Here is just one example:

> Glory be to God! Declaration of the third article. We have agreed that if American Christians are traveling with a nation that is at war with the well-preserved Tripoli, and he [evidently the Tripolitan] takes [prisoners] from the Christian enemies and from the American Christians with whom we are at peace, then sets them free; neither he nor his goods shall be taken.

The treaty constantly contrasts "Christian nations" (*e.g.*, Article VI) and "Tripoli," a Muslim stronghold that was used as a base of operations for Barbary pirates. Muslim nations were hostile to "Christian nations." The Barbary pirates habitually preyed on ships from "Christian nations," enslaving "Christian" seamen. "Barbary was Christendom's Gulag Archipelago."[14] In drafting the treaty, the United States had to assure the Dey (ruler) of Tripoli that in its struggle with the pirates "it has in itself no character of enmity against the laws, religion or tranquility of Musselmen," that "the said states never have entered into any war or act of hostility against any Mehomitan [Muslim] nation" due to religious considerations.

A survey of the state constitutions, charters, national pronouncements, and official declarations of the thirteen state governments would convince any representative from Tripoli that America was a Christian nation by law. The American consul in Algiers, Joel Barlow, had to construct a treaty that would assure the Dey of Tripoli that troops would not be used to impose Christianity on a Muslim people.

What was Mr. Barlow trying to say? Representing a nation whose laws do not make heresy a crime, and which has no established church or official religion, was he not trying to reassure those of a different religious and cultural tradition that we, for our part, had worked out an arrangement between the prevailing religion in America and our government that did not commit the destiny of that faith into the keeping of the state? Our government, therefore, could enter into amicable relationships with nations whose religion differs from our own.

History supports such an interpretation.[15]

The Barbary pirates regularly preyed on ships from other countries, enslaving and torturing Christians.

Tripoli may have feared a crusade-like invasion from the American navy. (Muslims well remembered the Crusades and the expulsion of Muslims from Grenada by Ferdinand and Isabella.) America was not founded as a Christian nation in the same way that Libya was founded as a Muslim nation. "Christianity was not an American state religion and therefore the United States government bore no official hostility toward Mohammadanism."[16] The Dey of Tripoli had to be convinced that America would not impose its Christianity on the Muslim people by force. "Could it have been that in Article 11, America was assuring Tripoli and all of the Barbary States that the United States did not have a state church system and would therefore not attack Tripoli for religious reasons of forced conversion?"[17] This seems to be the best explanation of the phrase found in Article 11 of the Treaty.

A study of later treaties with Muslim nations seems to support this conclusion. The 1816 "Treaty of Peace and Amity with Algiers" follows the language of the 1805 treaty made with Tripoli and adds the following: "It is declared by the contracting parties, that no pretext arising from religious opinions shall ever produce an interruption of the harmony between the two nations; and the Consuls and the Agents of both nations shall have liberty to celebrate the rights of their prospective religions in their own houses."[18]

A Question of Authenticity

There is some question, however, concerning the authenticity of much of the Treaty of Tripoli, especially Article 11. Constitutional lawyer John W. Whitehead maintains "that the Treaty of Tripoli is a mysterious, confusing and often misinterpreted document. Since the records of the Treaty negotiations of 1796–1797 are incomplete, many of the questions surrounding the treaty appear to be unanswerable."[19]

Joel Barlow oversaw the original translation process from Arabic to English. In 1930 the original Arabic version was retranslated into English by Dr. Hurgronje. Barlow's translation and Dr. Hurgronje's retranslation bear faint resemblance to each other. For example, in Article 12 of Barlow's version, all religious references have been removed: "Praise be to God!"; "May God strengthen [the Pasha of Tripoli], and the Americans"; "May God make it all permanent love and a good conclusion between us"; and, "by His grace and favor, amen!"

It seems that Barlow's translation deceptively altered the treaty. The deception does not stop with Article 12. There was even more tampering with the document in its translation process. In fact, the controversial Article 11 simply does not exist in the original Arabic text.

Most extraordinary (and wholly unexplained) is the fact that Article 11 of the Barlow translation with its famous phrase, "the government of the United States of America is not in any sense founded on the Christian religion," does not exist at all. There is no Article 11. The Arabic text which is between Articles 10 and 12 is in form of a letter, crude and flamboyant and withal quite unimportant, from the Dey [ruler] of Algiers to the Pasha [leader] of Tripoli. How that script came to be written and to be regarded, as in the Barlow translation, as Article 11 of the treaty as there written, is a mystery and seemingly must remain so. Nothing in the diplomatic correspondence of the time throws any light whatever on the point.[20]

Joel Barlow oversaw the original translation process from Arabic to English. His translation differs greatly from a more literal translation made in 1930.

A number of explanations have been put forth as to how Article 11 became part of the Treaty. "One explanation is that the Dey of Algiers wrote this note on the Treaty to mollify certain concerns of the Pasha [leader] of Tripoli about entering into a Treaty with an 'infidel' (non-Islamic) nation. The Algerian court official translating the document translated everything on the page without regard to its nature or source."[21] Another explanation is that the wording is that of the Barbary officials who believed they had the Americans over a diplomatic barrel. Either the Americans signed it with the offensive phrase or there would be no Treaty. The Treaty was signed. The fragile peace, however, did not last long.

The 1805 Treaty

Piracy remained a problem despite the 1797 Treaty. In addition, Tripoli demanded increased tribute payments in 1801. When President Jefferson refused to increase the tribute, Tripoli declared war on the United States. A United States navy squadron, under Commander Edward Preble, blockaded Tripoli from 1803 to 1805. After rebel soldiers from Tripoli, led by United States Marines, captured the city of Derna, the Pasha of Tripoli signed a treaty promising to exact no more tribute.

It is important to note that the 1805 Treaty with Tripoli differs considerably from the 1797 Treaty. The most important difference is this: In the 1805 version the phrase "as the Government of the United States of America is not in any sense founded on the Christian Religion" is conspicuously absent. The first treaty was terminated by war. A new treaty was drafted in 1805 (ratified April 12, 1806) during Jefferson's administration. Article 14 of the new treaty corresponds to Article 11 of the first treaty. It reads in part: "[T]he government of the United States of America has in itself no character of enmity against the laws, religion, or tranquility of Musselmen." The phrase declaring that the "government of the United States of America is not in any sense founded on the Christian Religion" does not appear. Assurances are still offered that the United States will not interfere with Tripoli's religion or laws.

Bombardment of Tripoli, August 1804.

It's obvious that by 1805 the United States had greater bargaining power and did not have to knuckle under to the demands of this Muslim stronghold. A strong navy and a contingent of Marines also helped. Robert Boston, a critic of the "Christian nation" thesis, gives scant attention to the revised 1805 Treaty. He concludes, "Perhaps by then U.S. officials felt the Muslims had been convinced of the new country's secular nature."[22] Boston assumes that the purpose of the article in the original Treaty was designed to make a philosophical statement rather than a diplomatic one. Boston assumes to be true what he has failed to prove.

The Trinitarian Treaties of 1783 and 1822

If the critics of a Christian America are going to be honest, then they must give an adequate reason why the 1805 treaty does not contain the

The Treaty of Paris of 1783 begins with these words: "In the name of the Most Holy and Undivided Trinity."

words that seem to denounce the Christian religion in the 1797 Treaty. They also must answer why the revised Treaty occurred during Thomas Jefferson's term as president, since Jefferson, when compared to Washington and Adams, was the most hostile to organized Christianity!

If treaties are going to be used to establish the religious commitment of the nation, then it's essential that we look at all of the treaties. In 1783, at the close of the war with Great Britain, a peace treaty was ratified that began with these words: "In the name of the Most Holy and Undivided Trinity. It having pleased the Divine Providence to dispose the hearts of the most serene and most potent Prince George the Third, by the Grace of God King of Great Britain, France, and Ireland, Defender of the Faith,...and of the United States of America, to forget all past misunderstandings and differences...."[23] The treaty was signed by John Adams, Benjamin Franklin, and John Jay. Keep in mind that the 1797 treaty with Tripoli was ratified under the administration of John Adams.

In 1822, the United States, along with Great Britain and Ireland, ratified a "Convention for Indemnity Under Award of Emperor of Russia as to the True Construction of the First Article of the Treaty of December 24, 1814."[24] It begins with the same words found in the Preamble to the 1783 treaty: "In the name of the Most Holy and Indivisible Trinity." Only Christianity teaches a Trinitarian view of God. If the 1797 Treaty of Tripoli turns America into a secular State (which it does not), the Treaty of 1822 reestablishes Trinitarian Christianity.

Notes

1. William M. Malloy, *Treaties, Conventions, International Acts, Protocols and Agreements between the United States of America and Other Powers, 1776–1909*, 4 vols. (New York: Greenwood Press, [1910] 1968), 2:1786.

2. Ernest Campbell Mossner, "Deism," *The Encyclopedia of Philosophy*, ed. Paul Edwards, 8 vols. (New York: Macmillan, 1967), 2:334.

3. Norman L. Geisler, *Is Man the Measure: An Evaluation of Contemporary Humanism* (Grand Rapids, MI: Baker Book House, 1983), 124–25.

4. Press release from People for the American Way: "Founding Fathers/ Separation of Church and State," (September 20, 1984), 1.

5. Paul F. Boller, Jr., *George Washington and Religion* (Dallas, TX: Methodist University Press, 1962), 87. Quoted in M. Kimberly Roberts, *The Tripoli Treaty of 1797: Its Use as a Precedent for Separation of Church*

and State, submitted in partial fulfillment of the requirements for the degree of Master of Arts in Public Policy, CBN University, Virginia Beach, VA, 1986, 7.

6. Paul F. Boller, Jr., and John George, *They Never Said It: A Book of Fake Quotes, Misquotes, and Misleading Attributions* (New York: Oxford University Press, 1989), 129.

7. George Washington, "Address to Delaware Chiefs," *The Writings of George Washington from the Original Manuscript Sources: 1749–1799*, ed. John C. Fitzpatrick (Washington, DC: United States Government Printing Office, 1936), 15:55.

8. George Washington, "Proclamation: A National Thanksgiving," *A Compilation of the Messages and Papers of the Presidents, 1789–1902*, ed. John D. Richardson, 11 vols. (Washington, DC: Bureau of National Literature and Art, 1907), 1:64.

9. This article appeared in newspapers across the country on July 4, 1984.

10. John Adams, "National Fast Day," *A Compilation of the Messages and Papers of the Presidents*, 1:284–86.

11. John Adams to Thomas Jefferson, June 28, 1813, in Lester J. Cappon, ed., *The Adams-Jefferson Letters*, 2 vols. (Chapel Hill, NC: University of North Carolina Press, 1959), 2:339–40.

12. John Adams to Thomas Jefferson (April 19, 1817) in Thomas Jefferson, *The Writings of Thomas Jefferson* (Washington, DC: The Thomas Jefferson Memorial Association, 1904), 15:105.

13. Gary T. Amos, *Defending the Declaration* (Brentwood, TN: Wolgemuth and Hyatt, 1989), 9.

14. Stephen Clissold, *The Barbary Slaves* (New York: Barnes & Noble, [1977] 1992), 4. The 1815 Treaty of Peace and Amity with Algiers includes the following in Article XV: "On a vessel or vessels of war belonging to the United States anchoring before the city of Algiers, the Consul is to inform the Dey of her arrival, when she shall receive the salutes which are, by treat or custom, given to the ships of war of the most favored nations on similar occasions, and which shall be returned gun for gun; and if, after such arrival, so announced, any Christians whatsoever, captives in Algiers, make their escape and take refuge on board any of the ships of war, they shall not be required back again, nor shall the Consul of the United States or commanders of said ships be required to pay anything for the said Christians." (Malloy, *Treaties, Conventions, International Acts, Protocols and Agreements between the United States of America and Other Powers*, 1:7).

15. *The Remnant*, "Memorandum No. XXXIII," Irvington-on-Hudson, NY: Foundation for Economic Education (September 22, 1965), 2.
16. Boller, *George Washington and Religion*, 87. Quoted in Roberts, *The Tripoli Treaty of 1797*, 23.
17. John W. Whitehead, "The Treaty of Tripoli," *The Rutherford Institute* (January/February 1985), 11.
18. Malloy, *Treaties, Conventions, International Acts, Protocols and Agreements Between the United States of America and Other Powers*, 1:15.
19. Whitehead, "The Treaty of Tripoli," 10.
20. Cited in Charles Bevans, *Treaties and Other International Agreements of the United States of America 1776–1959* (Washington, DC: Department of State, 1974), 11:1070.
21. John Eidsmoe, "Appendix 1: Treaty of Tripoli," *Christianity and the Constitution: The Faith of Our Founding Fathers* (Grand Rapids, MI: Baker Book House, 1987), 415.
22. Robert Boston, *Why the Religious Right is Wrong About Separation of Church and State* (Buffalo, NY: Prometheus Books, 1993), 79.
23. Malloy, *Treaties, Conventions, International Acts, Protocols and Agreements between the United States of America and Other Powers*, 1:586.
24. Malloy, *Treaties, Conventions, International Acts, Protocols and Agreements between the United States of America and Other Powers*, 1:634.

CHAPTER 9

THE SEPARATION MIRAGE

OES THE FIRST AMENDMENT REQUIRE A SECULAR GOVERNMENT? IS THE First Amendment violated when Christians apply biblical principles to public policy issues? In the simplest terms, separating Church and State means that the *institution* and the ecclesiastical *jurisdiction* of the Church is separate from the *institution* and the civil *jurisdiction* of the State. The Church as an institution cannot mingle in the institutional affairs of civil government. Neither can its officers. In the same way, civil government cannot disturb the ministry and operation of the Church by tampering with the Church's doctrines or courts.

Nowhere, however, does the First Amendment prohibit individuals from applying religious precepts to the legislative and judicial agenda of the State. For example, biblical laws against theft, murder, polygamy, abortion, homosexuality, rape, and perjury have been accepted by civil governments as having a civil application with no transgression of the First Amendment. At the same time, the State does not have the jurisdictional right to compel people to believe the gospel, confess the Christian religion, pay tithes, or attend church. Neither can the civil magistrate declare any single Christian denomination to be the nationally established Church.

Many people incorrectly maintain that the First Amendment was designed to remove any and all religious precepts and considerations from civil affairs. For example, the *Congressional Quarterly's Guide to the U.S. Supreme Court* provides the following definition of the establishment clause of the First Amendment.

> The two men most responsible for its inclusion in the Bill of Rights constructed the clause *absolutely*. Thomas Jefferson and James Madison thought that the prohibition of establishment meant that a presidential proclamation of Thanksgiving Day was just as improper as a tax exemption for churches.[1]

The historical facts dispute this seemingly authoritative interpretation of the First Amendment. James Madison issued at least four Thanksgiving Day proclamations.[2] If the *Congressional Quarterly's Guide to the U.S.*

Supreme Court has accurately captured the meaning of the establishment clause of the First Amendment, then Madison "violated both his oath of office and the very instruments of government that he helped write and labored to have ratified."[3] In the same way, if Jefferson "construed the establishment clause absolutely, he also violated his oath of office, his principles, and the Constitution when, in 1802, he signed into federal law tax exemption for the churches in Alexandria County Virginia."[4] Of course, neither Madison nor Jefferson violated the First Amendment by these official State acts. It is the modern day secularist interpreter of Madison and Jefferson who has misread, misinterpreted, and misapplied the First Amendment. This misreading of the First Amendment has come about through "the change in the intellectual climate of the universities, and consequently in the media and the courts. It is these opinion-making centers that have influenced common thinking about law, morality, and religion. These centers have thrown the credibility of religious witness into doubt."[5]

James Madison evidently did not believe that presidential proclamations of thanksgiving and prayer were unconstitutional. He issued at least four Thanksgiving Day proclamations.

Most of the misunderstanding surrounding Church-State issues arises from relying on secondary sources and misinformation. Most of this accepted misinformation is developed through the academic procedure which constitutional scholar Robert L. Cord calls "history by omission,"[6] that is, the failure to deal with historical facts that run counter to a strict separationist interpretation of the First Amendment.

What Does It Say?

Too many debates over the meaning and implementation of the First Amendment are confused by a failure to cite it accurately or comprehensively: "Congress shall make no law respecting an establishment of religion, or prohibiting the free exercise thereof; or abridging the freedom of speech or of the press; or the right of the people peaceably to assemble, and to petition the Government for a redress of grievances."

When the Founding Fathers signed the Constitution they had no intention of separating religion from civil life.

An accurate interpretation of the amendment must refer to the following points:

- There is no mention of the words Church, State or separation in the First Amendment or in the body of the Constitution.

- Included in the amendment are additional items which relate to the free exercise of religion. Usually these constitutional protections are narrowly applied so they are not a part of the freedom of religion provision: the right to talk about religion (freedom of speech), the right to publish religious works (freedom of the press), the right of people to worship publicly, either individually or in groups (freedom of assembly), and the right to petition the government when it goes beyond its delegated constitutional authority in these areas (the right of political involvement).

- The prohibition is addressed to *Congress*. Individual states and governmental institutions (e.g., public schools, capitol building steps, national parks, etc.) are not included in the amendment's prohibition. As clear as this is, some try to rewrite the First Amendment in order to fit their misconceptions about its meaning and implementation: "The First Amendment to the U.S. Constitution is the direct descendant of Jefferson's Virginia resolution, and its words are quite clear. Congress, *and by extension the states*, 'shall make no law respecting an establishment of religion.'"[7] If the constitutional framers wanted to include the phrase "and by extension the states," they would have done so.

- There is no mention of a freedom *from* religion. The First Amendment offers no support of a position that would outlaw religion just because it offends those of a different religion or those who have no religion at all (agnostics or atheists).

An interpreter of any written document must also consider historical circumstances, the author's purpose in writing, and the intended audience. With these considerations in mind, it would be wise, therefore, to follow the method suggested by Thomas Jefferson in understanding the *meaning* of the First Amendment: "On every question of construction, carry ourselves back to the time when the Constitution was adopted, recollect the spirit manifested in the debates, and instead of trying what meaning may be squeezed out of the text, or invented against it, conform to the probable one in which it was passed."[8]

The Amendment's History

With this brief introduction, let's look into the history behind this much referred to but often misquoted, misunderstood, and misapplied amendment. When the Constitution was sent to the states for ratification, there was fear that the new national government had too much power. It was then proposed that additional prohibitions should be listed in the Constitution to restrict further the national government's power and jurisdiction.

The area of religion was important since a number of the states had established churches. Some of the framers were concerned that the federal government would establish a *national* Church (e.g., Anglican, Presbyterian, or Congregational) to be funded by tax dollars. The concern was that this national Church would disestablish the existing state churches. So then, the First Amendment was designed to protect the *states* against the national (federal) government. The amendment was not designed to disestablish the Christian religion as it found expression in the state constitutions. Justice Joseph Story, a Supreme Court justice of the nineteenth century, offers the following commentary on the amendment's original meaning:

The real object of the First Amendment was not to countenance, much less to advance Mohammedanism, or Judaism, or infidelity, by prostrating Christianity, but to exclude all rivalry among Christian sects [denominations] and to prevent any national ecclesiastical establishment which would give to an hierarchy the exclusive patronage of the national government.[9]

Joseph Story stated that the purpose of the First Amendment was not to debase Christianity "but to exclude all rivalry among Christian [denominations]."

Story's comments are important. He states that the amendment's purpose was "to exclude all rivalry among *Christian* sects." This presupposes that Christianity was the accepted religion of the colonies but that no single denomination should be supported by the national government. The amendment was not designed to make all religions equal, only to make all *Christian* denominations (sects) equal.

The word "establishment," as used in the First Amendment, means recognition by civil government of a single denomination as the official Church. The amendment does not prohibit *the* establishment of religion in general, but rather *an* establishment of a particular Christian denomination, which our founders called a "sect." Furthermore, there is nothing in the First Amendment restricting the states. The restriction resides solely with Congress. Writing the minority opinion in the *Wallace vs. Jaffree* case (1985), Supreme Court Justice William Rehnquist stated, "The Framers intended the Establishment Clause to prohibit the designation of any church as a 'national' one. The clause was also designed to stop the Federal government from asserting a preference for one religious denomination or sect over others."[10]

If the amendment were constructed to prevent religion from having an impact on civil governmental issues, then it would seem rather strange that on September 24, 1789, the same day that it approved the First Amendment, Congress called on President Washington to proclaim a national day of prayer and thanksgiving. The first Congress resolved:

> That a joint committee of both Houses be directed to wait upon the President of the United States to request that he would recommend to the people of the United States a day of public thanksgiving and prayer, to be observed by acknowledging, with grateful hearts, the many signal favors of Almighty God, especially by affording them an opportunity peaceably to establish a Constitution of government for their safety and happiness.[11]

This proclamation acknowledges "the many signal favors of Almighty God, especially by *affording them an opportunity peaceably to establish a Constitution of government for their safety and happiness.*" This is odd language for a group of men who supposedly just separated religion from government at all levels. In fact, this resolution uses devoutly religious language to acknowledge that they would not even have a government without God's blessing.

The first Congress also established the congressional chaplain system by which official daily prayers to God are still offered. During the initial debate on the First Amendment, not one word was said by any congressman about a "wall of separation between Church and State." In addition, as was stated above, at the time of the drafting of the First Amendment, a number of the states had established churches. This arrangement was not seen as a violation of the First Amendment. State churches and the First Amendment coexisted for some time with no perceived violation of the Constitution.

> At the beginning of the Revolution established churches existed in nine of the colonies.... The first amendment in large part was a guarantee to the states which insured that the states would be able to continue whatever church-state relationship existed in 1791. Maryland, Virginia, North Carolina, South Carolina, and Georgia all shared Anglicanism as the established religion common to those colonies. Congregationalism was the established religion in Massachusetts, New Hampshire, and Connecticut. New York, on the other hand, allowed for the establishment of Protestant religions. Only in Rhode Island and Virginia were all religious sects disestablished. But all of the States still retained the Christian religion as the foundation stone of their social, civil, and political institutions. Not even Rhode Island and Virginia renounced

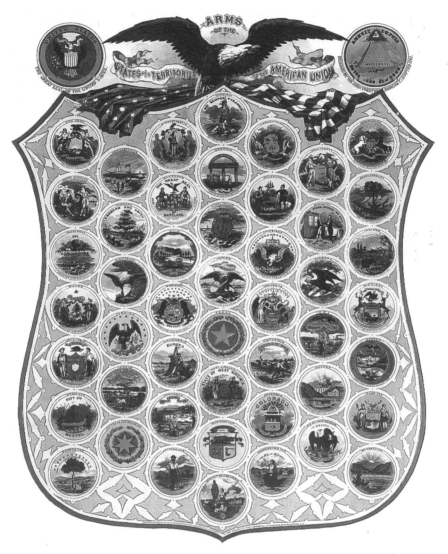

The United States Constitution was never intended to usurp authority from the states. The establishment of churches was left the prerogative of the individual state governments.

Christianity, and both states continued to respect and acknowledge the Christian religion in their system of law.[12]

The pluralism of the colonies was a pluralism among the numerous *Christian* sects. They shared a fundamental agreement on the basics of the Christian faith and the ethical system outlined in Scripture.

Historical Fiction

The "separation between Church and State" phrase has two sources. The first is in the writings of Roger Williams, founder of Rhode Island. The most noted reference, however, is a letter Thomas Jefferson wrote to a group of Baptist pastors in Danbury, Connecticut, in 1802. In that letter Jefferson wrote:

> Believing with you that religion is a matter which lies solely between man and his God, that he owes account to none other for faith or his worship, that the legislative powers of government reach actions only, and not opinions, I contemplate with sovereign reverence that act of the whole American people which declared that their legislature should "make no law respecting an establishment of religion, or prohibiting the free exercise thereof," thus building a wall of separation between church and state.[13]

Jefferson had no hand in the drafting of the Constitution or the Bill of Rights. He was in France at the time. While Jefferson's opinions are instructive, they remain opinions. His personal correspondence, even as president, has no legal standing. In addition, Jefferson's use of the phrase "separation between church and state" is "a mere metaphor too vague to support any theory of the Establishment Clause."[14] Yet, it is Jefferson's vague "metaphor" that has been adopted as the standard interpretation of the First Amendment.

But what did Jefferson mean? His doctrine of separation cannot be compared to today's absolutist position. According to Jefferson, "opinions" and what a person believes about God—"faith or worship"—are outside the jurisdiction of the State. The State, however, does have jurisdiction over what a person does. As Jefferson wrote to the Danbury Baptists, "The legislative powers of government reach actions only." Can civil governments appeal to religious precepts in the governance of actions? According to Jefferson's *official* acts as governor of Virginia and as president of the United States, civil government must have a religious basis.

When he was governor of Virginia, Jefferson readily issued procla-mations declaring days of "public and solemn thanksgiving and prayer to Almighty God."[15] Jefferson's Virginia "Bill for Punishing Disturbers of Religious Worship and Sabbath Breakers," was introduced by James Madison in the Virginia Assembly in 1785 and became law in 1786. The section on Sabbath desecration reads:

> If any person on Sunday shall himself be found labouring at his own or any other trade or calling, or shall employ his apprentices, servants or slaves in labour, or other business, except it be in the ordinary house-hold offices of daily necessity, or other work of necessity or charity, he shall forfeit the sum of ten shillings for every such offence, deeming every apprentice, servant, or slave so employed, and every day he shall be so employed as constituting a distinct offence.[16]

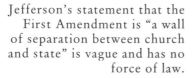

Jefferson's statement that the First Amendment is "a wall of separation between church and state" is vague and has no force of law.

As president, Jefferson included a prayer in each of his two inau-gural addresses. He signed bills appropriating money for chaplains in Congress and the armed services, and signed the Articles of War, which not only provided for chaplains but also "earnestly recommended to all officers and soldiers, diligently to attend divine services."[17] In 1803, Jefferson signed an appropriation of funds to be paid to the Kaskaskia Indians who "in part, called for the United States to build them a Roman Catholic Church and pay their priest."[18]

Jefferson advocated that the tax-supported College of William and Mary maintain "a perpetual mission among the Indian tribes" which included the instruction of "the principles of Christianity." Jefferson's proposed curriculum for the University of Virginia included a provision for a "professor of ethics" who would present "the Proofs of the being of God, the Creator, Preserver, and Supreme Ruler of the universe, the Author of all the relations of morality, and of the laws and obligations these infer."[19] While Jefferson was against ecclesiastical control of education, he was not against the teaching of religion.

In his Second Inaugural Address (1805), Jefferson stated, "In matters of religion I have considered that its free exercise is placed by the Constitution independent of the powers of the General Government. I have therefore undertaken on no occasion to prescribe the religious exercises suited to it, but have left them, as the Constitution found them, under the direction and discipline of the church or state authorities acknowledged by the several religious societies."[20] According to Jefferson, the federal ("General") Government has no jurisdiction over churches or state governments. "Many contemporary writers attempt to read back into the past a 'wall of separation' between church and state which in fact never has existed in the United States."[21]

The Northwest Ordinance

The meaning of the First Amendment, as history will attest, has nothing to do with separating the moral aspects of the Christian religion from civil affairs. The Northwest Ordinance of 1787, enacted by the Continental Congress and reenacted by the newly formed federal government in 1789 after it had agreed on the final wording of the First Amendment, stated that "good government" must be based on some moral foundation: "Religion, morality and knowledge, being necessary to good government and the happiness of mankind, schools and the means of education shall be forever encouraged."

> The First Congress did not expect the Bill of Rights to be inconsistent with the Northwest Ordinance of 1787, which the Congress reenacted in 1789. One key clause in the Ordinance explained why Congress chose to set aside some of the federal lands in the territory for schools: "Religion, morality, and knowledge," the clause read, "being necessary to good government and the happiness of mankind, schools and the means of learning shall forever be encouraged." This clause clearly implies that schools, which were to be built on federal lands with federal assistance, were expected to promote religion as well as morality. In fact, most schools at this time were church-run sectarian schools.[22]

Constitutional scholar Leo Pfeffer writes, "[F]or all practical purposes Christianity and religion were synonymous."[23] It is clear that our founders never supposed that moral precepts founded on the Christian religion should be excluded from policy making even though they worked diligently to keep the institutions and jurisdictions of Church and State separate.

The Founding Fathers believed that without the precepts of the Christian religion there could be no morality — for individuals as well as for nations.

Strict separationists do not see the Northwest Ordinance as convincing evidence that the constitutional framers regarded religion, politics, and morality as an acceptable mix. Robert Boston, an absolute separationist, asserts that if the founders had wanted to support religion the Northwest Ordinance would have ended, "...schools *and churches* shall forever be encouraged."[24] Boston assumes that since the delegates did not call for the support of churches that this meant they were opposed to mixing religion and politics. The source of Boston's confusion comes from the "tendency to employ the words 'Church' and 'religion' as synonyms. To maintain that there must be a separation between Church and State does not necessarily mean that there must be a separation between religion and State."[25] I wonder how the ACLU would react to the Northwest Ordinance if its principles were applied to today's public schools? Lawyers would be immediately dispatched to assert that the Ordinance was unconstitutional because it mixes religion and morality with public education. Those in Jefferson's day did not find a problem with this combination, either constitutionally or practically.

Today's Christian political activists are not calling on the State to establish churches. They are simply maintaining that we cannot have good government without religion, the very principle the Northwest Ordinance declares.

Conclusion

The First Amendment "provides a *legal* separation between Church and State: *not a moral nor a spiritual* separation.... There is no reason, under the Constitution of the United States, why the principles of Christianity cannot pervade the laws and institutions of the United States of America."[26] Indeed, without the principles of Christianity, these United States will fall.

Notes

1. *Congressional Quarterly's Guide to the United States Supreme Court* (Washington, DC: Congressional Quarterly, Inc., 1979), 461. Quoted in Robert L. Cord, "Church-State Separation and the Public Schools: A Re-evaluation," *Educational Leadership* (May 1987), 28.
2. The four proclamations in their entirely are published in Robert L. Cord, *Separation of Church and State: Historical Fact and Current Fiction* (Grand Rapids, MI: Baker Book House, [1982] 1988), 257–60.
3. Cord, "Church-State Separation and the Public Schools," 26.
4. 2 *Statutes at Large* 194, Seventh Congress, Sess. 1, Chap. 52. Quoted in Cord, "Church-State Separation and the Public Schools," 28.
5. Jude P. Dougherty, "Separating Church and State," *The World & I* (December 1987), 683.
6. Cord, "Church-State Separation and the Public Schools," 28.
7. Editorial Page, *Atlanta Constitution* (November 15, 1994), A18.
8. Jefferson in a letter to William Johnson (June 12, 1823). In Merrill D. Peterson, ed., *Thomas Jefferson: Writings* (New York: The Library of America, 1984), 1475.
9. Quoted by Judge Brevard Hand, in *Jaffree vs. Board of School Commissioners of Mobile County*, 544 F. Supp. 1104 (S. D. Ala. 1983) in Russell Kirk, ed., *The Assault on Religion: Commentaries on the Decline of Religious Liberty* (Lanham, NY: University Press of America, 1986), 84.
10. *Wallace v. Jaffree*, 472 U.S., 113. Quoted in Dougherty, "Separating Church and State," 686.
11. *The Annals of the Congress, The Debates and Proceedings in the Congress of the United States*, Compiled From Authentic Materials by Joseph Gales, Senior (Washington, DC: Gales and Seaton, 1834), 1:949–50.
12. Quoted by Hand in Kirk, *The Assault on Religion*, 22–23.
13. Quoted in Charles E. Rice, *The Supreme Court and Public Prayer: The Need for Restraint* (New York: Fordham University Press, 1964), 63.
14. Peter J. Ferrara, *Religion and the Constitution: A Reinterpretation* (Washington, DC: Free Congress Foundation, 1983), 34–35.
15. Quoted in Rice, *The Supreme Court and Public Prayer*, 63.

16. "A Bill for Punishing Disturbers of Religious Worship and Sabbath Breakers," in Julian P. Boyd, ed., *The Papers of Thomas Jefferson* (Princeton, NJ: Princeton University Press, 1950), Vol. 2, 1777 to June 18, 1779, Including the Revisal of the Laws, 1776–1786, 555. Quoted in Cord, *Separation of Church and State*, 217.

17. Act of April 10, 1806, C. 20, 2 Stat. 359, 360. Quoted in Rice, *The Supreme Court and Public Prayer*, 63–64.

18. Cord, "Church-State Separation and the Public Schools," 28.

19. "Bill for the Establishment of District Colleges and University" (1817). Quoted in Charles Wesley Lowry, *To Pray or Not to Pray!: A Handbook for Study of Recent Supreme Court Decisions and American Church-State Doctrine* (Washington, DC: University Press of Washington D.C., 1963), 38–39.

20. Thomas Jefferson, "Second Inaugural Address," in James D. Richardson, ed., *A Compilation of the Messages and Papers of the Presidents, 1789–1902*, 12 vols. (Washington, DC: Bureau of National Literature and Art, 1907), 1:379–80.

21. Franklin Hamlin Littell, *From State Church to Pluralism: A Protestant Interpretation of Religion in American History* (Chicago, IL: Aldine Publishing Co., 1962), 99.

22. Michael J. Malbin, *Religion and Politics: The Intentions of the Authors of the First Amendment* (Washington, DC: American Enterprise Institute for Public Policy Research, 1978), 14–15.

23. Leo Pfeffer, *Church, State and Freedom* (Boston, MA: Beacon Press, 1953), 98.

24. Robert Boston, *Why the Religious Right is Wrong about Separation of Church and State* (Buffalo, NY: Prometheus Books, 1993), 80.

25. J. Marcellus Kik, *Church and State: The Story of Two Kingdoms* (New York: Thomas Nelson & Sons, 1963), 124.

26. Kik, *Church and State*, 116.

CHAPTER 10

WHITEWASHING HISTORY:

THOMAS JEFFERSON AND GEORGE WASHINGTON

DURING THE HEIGHT OF THE 1992 PRESIDENTIAL ELECTION, REPORTER Barbara Ehrenreich wrote an essay for *Time* magazine entitled "Why the Religious Right is Wrong."[1] Ehrenreich calls forth long-dead witnesses to support her contention that the Religious Right is wrong in its insistence that religious values as they relate to moral choices have a role to play in politics. She believes that Washington, Jefferson, Adams, and Lincoln would shun such an idea.

If Ehrenreich had simply claimed that a number of the founders were not as orthodox as the general Christian population, she would have had ample historical support for her position. In fact, attacking politicians on their religious views is an old political strategy. Thomas Jefferson, for example, was accused by his opponents "of many things—cowardice, adultery, sympathy for the French Revolution, 'want of personal firmness,' and—most devastating of all—that he was an atheist."[2]

There is no doubt that on many doctrinal issues the founders were not orthodox. They did, however, believe in God and providence and the necessary relationship between religious values and good government. Ehrenreich incorrectly insists that these men, and others like them, would not have made religious values a primary point of discussion in the realm of politics. At the same time, she is correct in pointing out that these same men are not the pillars of Christian orthodoxy that many Christians make them out to be.

"No Religious Test"

Ehrenreich begins her attack on the "Christian Right" by appealing to the Constitution's "ban on 'religious test[s]' for public office." She is right. The Constitution forbids a government mandated religious test.[3] A *constitutional* test-ban does not prohibit citizens from applying a religious test of their own in evaluating the candidates. If voters want a president who believes in God, then there is nothing in the Constitution that would prohibit them from lobbying those of like mind to work for such a candidate.

All voters attach certain extra-constitutional requirements to candidates. For example, the Constitution states that a presidential candidate must be at least thirty-five years old (Art. II, sec. 1). Would it be wrong to make a campaign issue out of the fact that a forty-year-old candidate might be too young for the nation's highest political office? Some believed that Ronald Reagan was too old even though the Constitution does not set an upper age limit. The electorate apply any number of extra-constitutional criteria to those running for political office, including a candidate's religious views.

The Constitution states that religious tests are not to be required for public office. The Founders knew that the voters would issue their own tests.

Unfortunately, the "no religious test" requirement was only opposed by a few who knew that the nation would suffer dire consequences for taking a more secular course. "[I]f there be no religious test required," Henry Abbot of North Carolina suggested, "pagans, deists, and Mahometans might obtain office among us, and the senators and representatives might all be pagans."[4] The most base pagan practices—child killing and sodomy—are now accepted in our nation's capital as fundamental constitutional rights. Massachusetts voters have sent two acknowledged sodomites to Congress every two years. Abbot knew what he was talking about.

Even with a ban on a religious test, every president since Washington (except Jefferson) has taken the oath of office with his hand on a Bible, promising to keep that oath by uttering "So help me God." Even during the hurried swearing-in ceremony of Lyndon B. Johnson on Air Force One after the assassination of John F. Kennedy, the soon-to-be president took the oath with his hand on "the slain President's own leather-bound Bible."[5]

The effects of the Constitution's secularized interpretation have reached the local governmental levels. For example, South Carolina eliminated the word "God" and substituted the word "affirm" for "swear" in the state's Notary's oath.[6] Similarly, the words "so help me God" have been stricken from the written oath of office that Notaries must take in order to serve in the state of Florida. This phrase was deleted because a South Florida atheist said it violated the separation of Church and State. "Those words never should have been there to begin with," Ken Rouse, general counsel for the Florida Department of State, said. Religious leaders from Miami to Jacksonville were shocked. "This is frightening, that one person could sway the state to change things like that," said Glen Owens, assistant executive director of the Florida Baptist Convention in Jacksonville. "How can they completely abolish a system of doing things for one person?" The Reverend Gerard LaCerra, chancellor of the Archdiocese of Miami understands the implications of the ruling. "What are we supposed to base our commitments on if something like this is removed? The state?"[7]

Thomas Jefferson

Jefferson kept his religious views private because he believed that "once one started talking about one's religion openly the public quickly concluded that it had a right to know—everything!"[8] On the subject of religion, Jefferson had a lot to hide.[9]

Early in his campaign for president Jefferson was accused of being an atheist by many prominent clergymen. One of Jefferson's most vocal early critics was Timothy Dwight, president of Yale. On July 4, 1798, Dwight delivered a speech urging the voters to defeat the Jeffersonians—"the illuminati, the philosophers, the atheists, and the deists." Dwight predicted dire consequences if Jefferson and his party were to be elected to office: "We may see the Bible cast into a bonfire, the vessels of the sacramental supper borne by an ass in public procession, and our children, either wheedled or terrified, uniting in chanting mockeries against God."[10] Dwight was overly pessimistic at the time. The effects he predicted took nearly two hundred years to be realized.

Timothy Dwight, president of
Yale University, was one of
Jefferson's most vocal critics.

Rev. William Linn of New York voiced similar concerns over
a Jefferson presidency when he proclaimed that "the election of any
man avowing the principles of Mr. Jefferson would...destroy religion,
introduce immorality, and loosen all the bonds of society." He further
warned that "the voice of the nation in calling a deist to the first office
must be construed into no less than a rebellion against God."[11] The
New England clergy especially vilified Jefferson, "whom they hated
for 'disbelief in the deluge and his opposition to Bible reading in the
schools.'"[12] Even the press got into the act. The Federalist *Gazette of
the United States* (September 10, 1800) framed the key question of the
election, "to be asked by every American, laying his hand on his heart,
as: 'Shall I continue in allegiance to God—and a Religious President;
Or impiously declare for Jefferson—and No God!!!'"[13]

While Jefferson was no atheist, he was no evangelical Christian either.
He would only tolerate a religion that fit his conception of reasonableness.
Jefferson nearly abandoned any appreciation for Christianity until he read
Joseph Priestly's *An History of the Corruptions of Christianity* (1793).
Through this work and Priestly's *Socrates and Jesus Compared* Jefferson
no longer rejected Christianity, only what he believed were its "corrup-
tions." He alleged that the core of Christianity had been obscured by
Jesus' disciples, the apostle Paul being the first to conceal Jesus' "genuine
precepts." By stripping away the corruptions, Jefferson contended, the true
Christian would rediscover the "genuine precepts of Jesus himself."[14]

With respect to the "genuine precepts of Jesus," Jefferson wrote
to Benjamin Rush, "I am a real Christian...sincerely attached to his
doctrines, in preference to all others." While the ancients offered much
that was noteworthy, their ethics "were not only imperfect, but often

irreconcilable with the sound dictates of reason."[15] This dismissal of the "ancients" included those of the Hebraic writers. Jefferson believed that a better system of ethics was needed and regarded Jesus as an ethical innovator. He surmised that since Jesus left nothing from His own pen, "his sublime teachings fell into the hands of 'the most unlettered, and ignorant of men.' Thus, his teachings have reached us in a form that is 'mutilated, misstated, and often unintelligible.'"[16]

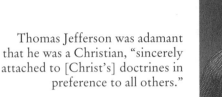

Thomas Jefferson was adamant that he was a Christian, "sincerely attached to [Christ's] doctrines in preference to all others."

Jefferson demonstrated his high regard for the ethics of Jesus while maintaining his anti-supernatural worldview by producing *The Life and Morals of Jesus of Nazareth*, a book which is often published as *The Jefferson Bible*. Jefferson studied the gospel accounts to extract from them what he believed to be the uncorrupted sublime moral teachings of Jesus without the supernatural "additions." While Jefferson included Luke's account of the birth of Jesus, he omitted references to angels and heavenly announcements pertaining to the event. In addition, "when Jesus performed a miracle in connection with some teaching, the teaching survived, the miracle did not…. Jefferson included verses detailing the death of Jesus but not the resurrection. No Easter morning sun rises in Jefferson's 'Bible.'"[17] His expurgated edition of the gospels ends this way: "There laid they Jesus, and rolled a great stone to the door of the sepulchre, and departed."

Jefferson hoped to present a "reasonable Christianity, a religion that ennobled the human race and in no way degraded or deluded it."[18] For all of his anti-biblical statements and beliefs, Jefferson understood that "no system of morality would work for the common man or woman 'without the sanction of divine authority stampt upon it.'"[19] But Jefferson's claim that "divine authority" was necessary to sanction a system of moral dogma is problematic because he had stripped Jesus of His divine authority. Why should anyone pay attention to the ethical precepts of an itinerant carpenter whose followers supposedly corrupted His teachings? What criteria could Jefferson use to determine what constituted a universal moral precept? Certainly reason could not be the final arbiter. Reasonable men disagree on what's reasonable.

Jefferson demonstrated his anti-supernatural worldview by deleting from the gospels all references to miracles.

Aware of the anti-religious climate that was directed at him, Jefferson wrote to Benjamin Rush that he would not publish *The Life and Morals of Jesus*. Did he fear public retribution?

[I am] averse to the communication of my religious tenets to the public, because it would countenance the presumption of those who have endeavored to draw them before that tribunal, and to seduce public opinion to erect itself into that inquest over the rights of conscience, which the laws have so justly proscribed.[20]

Jefferson knew that his unorthodox views, especially his rejection of the belief that Jesus is God in human flesh and the promised redeemer of mankind, would prove difficult for him and his party.

Here is one of the great ironies of history: The patron saint of absolutist Church-State separation, Thomas Jefferson, produced a volume that extracts the morals of Jesus, a system of ethics he describes as "the most sublime and benevolent code of morals which has ever been offered to man."[21] He decided to suppress the volume's publication because his unorthodox beliefs would not have been accepted by the generally orthodox public. He feared "public opinion." And yet Jefferson's "wee little book," as he called *The Life and Morals of Jesus*, was later published by an order of Congress in 1904.[22] If a contemporary conservative president had produced a similar work and had its publication financed by Congress, he would have been vilified by the liberal left for mixing religion and politics and violating the First Amendment to the Constitution! While Jefferson was unorthodox in his beliefs about the divinity of Christ and the revelatory character of the Bible, he was not opposed to applying religious precepts to morality.

Benjamin Rush was in constant communication with Jefferson regarding Jefferson's unorthodox religious views.

Thomas Jefferson had a hand in a draft document that proposed *A Bill for Proportioning Crimes and Punishments* for the state of Virginia. Jefferson's revision was a bold attempt to remedy a number of inequities in the common law, which James Madison described as "Our old bloody code." With an attempt to modify the list of crimes that merited capital punishment, Jefferson set about "to relax the severity of punishments, and to make them at the same time more humane and more rational."[23] While Jefferson had one foot firmly placed in the world of the Enlightenment, his other foot remained in the world of the Bible, the basis of much of English Common Law. Moreover, Jefferson's Enlightenment worldview did not cloud his judgment as a realistic observer of human nature. In Section I of the proposed bill, Jefferson wrote:

> Whereas it frequently happens that wicked and dissolute men, resigning themselves to the dominion of inordinate passions, commit violations on the lives, liberties, and property of others, and the secure enjoyment of these having principally induced men to enter into society, government would be defective in its principal purpose, were it not to restrain such criminal acts by inflicting due punishments of those who perpetuate them.[24]

Note that Jefferson believes that people can be "wicked." In addition, notice that Jefferson outlines what can be defined as a biblical model for civil government—"to restrain such criminal acts by inflicting punishments"—based on Romans 13:1–4. He goes on to revive the biblical ideal of "an eye for an eye," meting out punishment "in proportion to [the] offence." For example, theft was punished by hard labor and two-fold restitution (e.g., Exodus 22:4, 7; Luke 19:8–9) instead of "deprivation of...limb" (Sec. II). In Section XV of the bill Jefferson actually applied the *lex talionis* literally: "Whosoever on purpose, shall disfigure another, by cutting out or disabling the tongue, slitting or cutting off a nose, lip, or ear, branding, or otherwise, shall be maimed, or disfigured in like sort."

The law codes of many states demanded the death penalty for crimes such as murder, rape, and treason.

The modern-day image of Jefferson as a social and political liberal would be shattered after a single reading of his proposed bill. Capital punishment is maintained for murder and treason while rescinded for all other crimes. Even so, other crimes receive some rather harsh and politically incorrect penalties. Consider these examples:

- "If any person commit petty treason, or a husband murder his wife, a parent his child, or a child his parent, he shall suffer death, by hanging, and his body be delivered to Anatomists to be dissected" (Sec. IV).

- "Whosoever committith murder by poisoning, shall suffer death by poison" (Sec. V).

- "Whosoever shall be guilty of rape, *polygamy*, or sodomy with man or woman, shall be punished; if a man, by castration, a woman, by boring through the cartilage of her nose a hole of one half inch in diameter at the least" (Sec. XIV).

- "Whosoever committith a robbery, shall be condemned to hard labour four years in the public works, and shall make double reparation to the persons injured" (Sec. XX).

- "All attempts to delude the people, or to abuse their understanding by exercise of the pretended arts of witchcraft, conjuration, enchantment, or sorcery, or by pretended prophecies, shall be punished by ducking and whipping, at the discretion of a jury, not exceeding fifteen stripes" (Sec. XXIX).

Jefferson would be attacked by the left for his assessment, which coincides with that of the Bible, that sodomy is a crime. He would also be rightly criticized for calling for some rather medieval punishments that go far beyond what the Bible calls for.

George Washington

In her *Time* article, Ehrenreich cites an undocumented quotation in which Washington supposedly writes, "We have abundant reason to rejoice that in this Land...every person may here worship God according to the dictates of his own heart." Ehrenreich and her revisionist colleagues rebuke religious conservatives for ignoring this principle of religious liberty.

Washington's praise of religious liberty is not an argument for social anarchy.

However, no one from the Christian Right is telling anyone how to worship or suggesting that the State should make laws forcing people to go to church or become Christians.

The issue is "values"—how people act. The idea that people may worship as their consciences dictate does not negate the fact that some rule of morality must judge the actions of men.

For example, abortion and homosexuality—two hotly contested political issues—are what people do. They cannot be compared to race and gender, what people *are*. Colin Powell, former chairman of the Joint Chiefs of Staff, writes of the inappropriate linking of homosexual *behavior* with the civil rights movement: "Skin color is a benign, non-behavioral characteristic. Sexual orientation is perhaps the most profound of human behavioral characteristics. Comparison of the two is a convenient but invalid argument."[25] Since abortion and sodomy are what people *do*, the State has legitimate jurisdiction in these issues. In an October 1878 Supreme Court decision outlawing polygamy, Chief Justice Morrison R. Waite stated the following: "Laws are made for the government of actions, and while they cannot interfere with mere religious belief and opinions, they may with practices."

Supreme Court Justice Morrison Waite (seated, middle) stated, "Laws are made for the government of actions, and while they cannot interfere with mere religious belief and opinions, they may with practices."

The libertines on the Left assert that the State has no jurisdiction in these issues, because civil government may not intrude into the domain of the bedroom. Abortions, however, do not take place in bedrooms. They are performed in highly (government) regulated medical facilities. Furthermore, liberals only use this bedroom privacy argument as long as it fits their agenda. In fact, homosexuals want laws written to force employers to hire them based on what they do in the bedroom. Moreover, homosexuals want their sexually deviant behavior taught in schools. In both cases, the homosexual movement wants to use the power of the State to force the general public to accept what they *do* sexually.

Carrying the libertine logic through, are we to assume that if child abuse, incest, and assault occur in the sanctity of the home that the State has no jurisdiction? The retort by the moral anarchists is that *consensual* acts should not be outlawed. The pre-born baby has not consented. The libertines get around this fact simply by redefining the "fetus" as a bodily appendage. What if a ten-year-old boy consents to have sex with his stepfather? How about consensual murder? Why are we so distraught when someone kills himself if consent is the criterion for moral and legal legitimacy?

Homosexuals have always been with us. As long as they practiced their vile deeds in private there was little that the civil magistrate would or could do. While the act was still a crime, even when practiced behind closed doors, unlawful search and seizure kept the magistrate at bay. But now advocates of sodomy have come out of the closet and into the classroom. The homosexual now wants a once-closeted perversion sanctioned as legal behavior by the State on the same legal plane with heterosexual marriage. Now who is imposing morality on the rest of us? An employer would be forced not to consider such deviant behavior if a person was an admitted homosexual or was later found out to be a homosexual. No doubt we will soon be inundated by other deviants who want their secret sins and crimes protected by the long arm of the State. Anyone for pedophilia rights? How about rights for those who have sex with animals?[26]

A consistent evolutionist could maintain that laws prohibiting theft, homosexuality, abortion, bigamy, polygamy, murder, and incest are remnants of restrictions that are found in the Judeo-Christian tradition.[27] Since an atheist makes no appeal to a transcendent deity, he is not, in terms of atheism, obligated to follow a theistic ethical system. He could then claim that since he worships no deity he can live as he pleases.

Was Washington proposing anarchism when he lauded freedom of worship? I don't believe so. My guess is that Washington would defend a person's right to believe and worship as he pleases, but would argue that this freedom does not give him the right to live as he pleases. Some actions are civil wrongs, and it is the duty of the State to punish those who break the law. A person can *believe* that it is permissible to kill at will, but this does not make the *act* justifiable and legal. Such a defense would not get the murderer very far in a court of law. In the final analysis, a single question remains: What standard does the court use to render its judgments?

Those who defend liberal causes on the basis of historical precedent are off base. For example, Ehrenreich claims that the "fear of governmental tyranny kept the Founding Fathers from proscribing anything like 'family values.' Homosexuality was not unknown 200 years ago; nor was abortion. But these were matters, like religion, that the founders left to individual conscience." This is a remarkable assertion since the thirteen colonies that became our nation's first thirteen states had laws on the books making sodomy a crime. In some cases sodomy was punished by death![28] In *Bowers vs. Hardwick*, the court remarked:

> Sodomy was a criminal offense at common law and was forbidden by the laws of the original 13 States when they ratified the Bill of Rights. In 1868, when the Fourteenth Amendment was ratified, all but 5 of the 37 States in the Union had criminal sodomy laws. In fact, until 1961, all 50 States outlawed sodomy, and today [1986], 25 States and the District of Columbia continue to provide criminal penalties for sodomy performed in private and between consenting adults.[29]

Sodomy has never been tolerated in our nation's history. The law codes of fifty states prove it.

At a General Court Marshall, on March 10, 1778, a Lieutenant Enslin was "tried for attempting to commit sodomy with John Monhort." He was also tried for "Perjury in swearing to false Accounts." Enslin was "found guilty of the charges exhibited against him, being breaches of 5th. Article 18th. Section of the Articles of War." He was dismissed from the service "with infamy. His Excellency the Commander in Chief [George Washington] approve[d] the sentence and with Abhorrence and Detestation of such infamous Crimes order[ed] Lieutt. Enslin to be drummed out of the Camp...by all the Drummers and Fifers in the Army never to return."[30]

Ehrenreich also wants us to believe that there were no laws prohibiting abortion until the Christian Right came along. This is nonsense. She needs to be reminded that abortion was legalized in 1973—nearly two-hundred years after the ratification of the Constitution. Prior to the *Roe vs. Wade* decision, abortion was outlawed in all fifty states and the District of Columbia, with exceptions only for life endangerment of the mother.[31] Isn't this a perfect example of the "family values" which Ehrenreich tells us were not legislated?

George Washington believed that while the civil government cannot control people's beliefs, it must control people's actions.

Conclusion

Ehrenreich and her liberal peers are determined to ignore the historical record and to remake the founders in their own image. Both Jefferson and Washington believed that without religion, America's civil life would be chaotic. The legal decisions and public pronouncements of this nation attest to this fact: the "family values" that the liberal left disdain are rooted deeply in our heritage and are based on nothing other than principles of God's Word.

On the other hand, Christians must be careful not to sanitize the historical record and gloss over the truth as it relates to the belief patterns of America's most famous founders.

Notes

1. Barbara Ehrenreich, "Why the Religious Right Is Wrong," *Time* (September 7, 1992), 72.
2. Tim Hackler, "Jefferson and the Religious Right: New England Clergy Led America's First Negative Campaign," *Tulsa World* (September 24, 1994), Opinion Section, 1.
3. In response to the first edition of *America's Christian History*, Fred Clarkson objected to my assertion that the Constitution only banned "government mandated tests" as they relate to religious beliefs. He claims that non-government mandates do not exist ("Christian Reconstruction: Religious Right Extremism Gains Influence—Part One," *The Public Eye* [March 1994], 3). Clarkson's claim is off the mark. After the Republican Party secured leadership of the Senate and House of Representatives in the November 8, 1994 election, Rep. Newt Gingrich of Georgia said: "If this is not a mandate to move in a particular direction, I would like somebody to explain to me what a mandate is" (Quoted in *Atlanta Constitution* [November 10, 1994], A1). Also see Joseph Perkins, "The GOP gets mandate to govern," *Atlanta Constitution* (November 16, 1994), A13.
4. Henry Abbot, North Carolina ratifying convention: Elliot's *Debates*, 4:192. Quoted in Gary North, *Political Polytheism: The Myth of Pluralism* (Tyler, TX: Institute for Christian Economics, 1989), 390–91.
5. Nathan O. Hatch and Mark A. Noll, "Introduction," *The Bible in America: Essays in Cultural History*, eds. Nathan O. Hatch and Mark A. Noll (New York: Oxford University Press, 1982), 5.
6. "South Carolina: Compromise on atheist notary," *Atlanta Constitution* (March 5, 1993), A3.
7. "'God' Removed from Notaries' Oath," *Kansas City Star* (February 18, 1992), 2A.

8. Edwin S. Gaustad, *Neither King Nor Prelate: Religion and the New Nation, 1776–1826*, rev. ed. (Grand Rapids, MI: Eerdmans, [1987] 1993), 100.

9. Garry Wills, *Under God: Religion and American Politics* (New York: Simon and Schuster, 1990), 354–55.

10. Quoted in Hackler, "Jefferson and the Religious Right," 1.

11. Noble E. Cunningham, Jr., *In Pursuit of Reason: The Life of Thomas Jefferson* (Baton Rouge, LA: Louisiana State University Press, 1987), 225.

12. Hackler, "Jefferson and the Religious Right," 1.

13. Cunningham, *In Pursuit of Reason*, 225.

14. Thomas Jefferson to Benjamin Rush (April 21, 1803). Quoted in Gaustad, *Neither King Nor Prelate*, 100.

15. Jefferson to Rush. Quoted in Gaustad, *Neither King Nor Prelate*, 100.

16. Gaustad, *Neither King Nor Prelate*, 101.

17. Gaustad, *Neither King Nor Prelate*, 103.

18. Gaustad, *Neither King Nor Prelate*, 103.

19. Gaustad, *Neither King Nor Prelate*, 105.

20. Quoted in Russell Kirk, *The Roots of American Order*, 3rd ed. (Washington, DC: Regnery/Gateway, 1992), 343.

21. A letter to John Adams in 1813. Quoted in Douglas Lurton, "Foreword," *The Jefferson Bible* (Cleveland, OH: The World Publishing Company, 1942), ix.

22. Dumas Malone, *Jefferson and His Time*, 6 vols., *Jefferson the President: First Term, 1801–1805* (Boston, MA: Little, Brown and Company, 1970), 4:205.

23. Malone, *Jefferson and His Time: Jefferson the Virginian*, 1:270.

24. Thomas Jefferson, *A Bill for Proportioning Crimes and Punishments* in Merrill D. Peterson, ed., *Thomas Jefferson: Writings* (New York: The Library of America, 1984), 349.

25. Quoted in *World* (September 26, 1992), 5.

26. In 1994 the San Francisco board of supervisors unanimously approved an ordinance granting civil rights protections to members of the city's "transgender" community. The two most common subgroups are transsexuals and transvestites. The ordinance will give "transgender" people protection under the city's anti-discrimination law, which bans bias in the work place, public accommodations, educational institutions, and housing. It also covers all city contracts, whether or not the contractor is based in San Francisco. See Maria Goodavage, "San Francisco tough on transgender protection," *USA Today* (December 19, 1994), 7A.

27. In 1890 the Supreme Court narrowly defined the legal protections of the First Amendment to exclude polygamy on the grounds that the practice was out of accord with the basic tenets of Christianity: "It is contrary to the spirit of Christianity and the civilization which Christianity has produced in the Western world" (*Church of Latter Day Saints v. United States*, 136 U.S. 1 [1890]). In the same year, the Court declared that "Bigamy and polygamy are crimes by the laws of all civilized and Christian countries.... To call their advocacy a tenet of religion is to offend the common sense of mankind" (*Davis v. Beason*, 133 U.S. 333, 341–342 [1890]).

28. "Trials for sex crimes [in early Massachusetts] were occasionally noted but there was only one recorded execution." (Edwin Powers, *Crime and Punishment in Early Massachusetts, 1620–1692: A Documentary History* [Boston, MA: Beacon Press, 1966], 300).

29. *Bowers vs. Hardwick*, 478 US 186, 92 L Ed 2d 140, 106 S Ct 2841, reh den (US) 92 L Ed 2d 779, 107 S. Ct 29., 147–48. The plaintiff in the Hardwick case was caught engaging in the act of sodomy only after the police entered the house on an unrelated case.

30. *The Writings of George Washington, Bicentennial Edition* (Washington, DC: U.S. Government Printing Office, 1934), (March 1 through May 31, 1778), 11:83–84.

31. David Granfield, *The Abortion Decision* (Garden City, NY: Doubleday, 1969), 78–80.

CHAPTER 11

WHITEWASHING HISTORY:

JOHN ADAMS
AND ABRAHAM LINCOLN

B ARBARA EHRENREICH'S *TIME* ARTICLE FURTHER BLASTS CHRISTIAN
involvement in shaping American culture by discussing other founders, notably John Adams and Abraham Lincoln.

John Adams

Of Adams she writes: "Adams once described the Judeo-Christian tradition as 'the most bloody religion that ever existed.'"[1] Conveniently,
Ehrenreich never references a source. How do we explain this quotation,
if indeed it belongs to John Adams, when we read the following in his
Diary dated July 26, 1796?

> The Christian religion is, above all the Religions that ever prevailed or
> existed in ancient or modern Times, the Religion of Wisdom, Virtue,
> Equity, and humanity, let the Blackguard [Thomas] Paine say what he
> will; it is Resignation to God, it is Goodness itself to Man.[2]

There is no need to reconcile these two quotations because Ehrenreich misquotes Adams. The first "quotation" is pulled out of context
from a series of letters which Adams wrote to Judge F. A. Van der Kemp
on issues relating to religion and politics. Adams actually stated, "As I
understand the Christian religion, it was, and is, a revelation. But how
has it happened that millions of fables, tales, legends, have been blended
with both Jewish and Christian revelation *that have made them the most
bloody religion that ever existed*?"[3] In this letter Adams defended biblical
revelation against its many corruptions, certainly a worthy and needed
enterprise. Jesus made a similar point in his denouncement of the Pharisees: "Neglecting the commandment of God, you hold to the tradition of
men.... You nicely set aside the commandment of God in order to keep

your tradition" (Mark 7:8–9). As Jesus points out, the effect of adding to the Word of God can have disastrous results: "Woe to you, scribes and Pharisees, hypocrites, because you travel about on sea and land to make one proselyte; and when he becomes one, you make him twice as much a son of hell as yourselves" (Matthew 23:15). Norman Cousins, in introducing the religious views of Adams, writes that Adams "could be as eloquent and rhapsodic about the principles of Christianity as he could be scathing about the abuses carried on in its name."[4]

John Adams wrote, "The Christian religion is, above all the Religions that ever prevailed or existed in ancient or modern Times, the Religion of Wisdom, Virtue, Equity, and humanity."

Adams was not able to peer far enough into the future to see what political regimes would accomplish in the name of atheism, but he certainly had his suspicions. He believed that "the Hebrews have done more to civilize men than any other nation" and that God "ordered the Jews to preserve and propagate to all mankind the doctrine of a supreme, intelligent, wise, almighty sovereign of the universe," which he believed "to be the great essential principle of morality, and consequently all civilization."[5] Adams understood that the legal system of Israel was a model for the nations. Those nations that throw off the laws of the Bible are doomed.

Adams believed that republican governments could be supported only "by pure Religion or Austere Morals. Public Virtue cannot exist in a Nation without private [virtue], and public Virtue is the only Foundation of Republics." As for his sons, he told his wife to "Let them revere nothing but religion, Morality and Liberty."[6] And what about clergymen who spoke out on "social issues," an anathema to Ehrenreich and similar social commentators? What was Adams's opinion? While Adams believed in liberty, he also recognized that only a moral people can live in a condition of liberty.

The effect of adding to, or deleting from, the Word of God is destructive
for individuals as well as for nations.

It is the duty of the clergy to accommodate their discourses to the times, to preach against such sins as are most prevalent, and recommend such virtues as are most wanted. For example,—if exorbitant ambition and venality are predominant, ought they not to warn their hearers against those vices? If public spirit is much wanted, should they not inculcate this great virtue? If the rights and duties of Christian magistrates and subjects are disputed, should they not explain them, show their nature, ends, limitations, and restrictions?[7]

Adams chides those who laud and praise a clergyman "as an excellent man and a wonderful preacher" when he supports their cause, "[b]ut if a clergyman preaches Christianity, and tells the magistrate" something that the magistrate does not want to hear, then the clergyman is castigated for his views. Not much has changed in two-hundred years. The critics of the Right never seem to condemn those clergymen on the Left who support liberal causes. A double standard exists, and the Left refuses to admit it.[8]

A culture based on the precepts of the Christian religion will prosper in all spheres of life, including politics.

Why is it that the Rev. Jesse Jackson can quote the Bible in support of his pet causes, but conservative ministers and lay people must argue purely on secular grounds for their social and political agenda? For example, at the U.S. Conference of Mayors on June 23, 1992, in Houston, Texas, Jackson tried to depict Mary as an unwed mother and Dan Quayle as Herod. Where was the outrage in the press, not just for the absurd analogy, twisted history, and ludicrous exegesis, but simply for the fact that Jackson injected religion into the political debate? It seems that mixing religion and politics is acceptable as long as the road turns to the left.

In 1994 President Bill Clinton appealed to the members of the Full Gospel AME Zion Church in Temple Hills, Maryland, to help him pass a piece of legislation. Considering the overt Christian language Clinton employed, his appeal sounded surprisingly similar to the political petitions of conservative Christian leaders. Clinton requested the help of the congregation to help him pass the 1994 Crime Bill: "I ask you this whole week to pray for me and pray for the members of Congress. Ask us to not turn away from our ministry."[9] Did the president not clothe politics in religious garb?

On September 25, 1994, President Clinton returned to the pulpit to stump for the then Democratic governor of New York, Mario Cuomo. One reporter described it this way: "Rocking to resounding gospel strains, President Clinton went to a black church in the heart of Harlem today to rouse a vital constituency to turn out its vote for Gov. Mario M. Cuomo."[10] Clinton went to the Bible in his appeal to the members of Bethel AME Church to reelect the embattled Democratic governor. Clinton told the congregation: "Do not lose heart. Show up, talk to the people in your neighborhood, tell them to show up. Scripture says we're supposed to be good citizens, too. Mario Cuomo is the heart that you must not lose."[11] An Associated Press report called the President's antics "Bible-thumping politics."[12] Clinton's message was decidedly religious and partisan, as was Governor's Cuomo's remarks as he "also cited religious themes and maxims."[13]

Why didn't the press, the ACLU, and People for the American Way cry foul? Weren't the president and the governor of New York, along with other Democratic attendees, engaged in mixing religion and politics? Where were the trumpeting cries of "separation of Church and State"? For example, why didn't Michael Gartner, who wrote a column for *USA Today* on why religion and politics do not mix, criticize Bill Clinton for mixing religion and politics?[14] A perceptive letter writer noted the oversight: "Where is the outrage from the national media and the American Civil Liberties Union? Gartner's omission was just the latest example of the conspiracy of silence."[15]

On October 3, 1994, at a White House meeting with publishers, editors, and reporters representing different Baptist denominations, President Clinton stated that "he reads the Bible and other religious books for guidance and to cope with the isolation of the presidency."[16] Clinton went on to defend his administration's stand on abortion rights and homosexuals serving in the military. In fact, he supported his views on abortion and homosexuality by appealing to the Bible. The president said he studied those verses that have been used to condemn both abortion and homosexuality and claimed that those biblical arguments are not "free of ambiguity."[17]

Setting aside for the moment the ambiguity issue, can it not be said that President Clinton is following the lead of conservative Christians by appealing to the Bible for ethical direction? Why is it that Christian activists are regularly pilloried for basing social standards on biblical texts while liberals are actually praised for mixing religion and politics?

The president went on in his remarks to the Baptist ministers and told them, "The real issue, it seems to me, is not whether you think abortion is wrong or not; the issue is whether or not the government should criminalize the conduct in all cases."[18] One wonders how the president's remarks would have gone over in the mid-1960s if he had said, "The real issue, it seems to me, is not whether you think *segregation* is wrong or not; the issue is whether or not the government should criminalize the conduct in all cases." Why not turn back the clock a hundred years and plug in the word "slavery"?

Speaking at a religious rights conference at Emory University in Atlanta, South African Archbishop Desmond Tutu stated, "There's no political manifesto that is as radical as the Bible.... It's exciting, very exhilarating, to be a believer."[19] Jean Bethke Elshtain, one of the scholars attending the conference, "describes the classical Greek and Roman world as one in which the state made an absolute claim on human bodies—males as warriors, females as breeders. The Judeo-Christian dissent from this was a revolutionary claim of individual privacy, sacredness, choice."[20] For liberals, religion and politics mix as long as the results support their cause.

Like Jefferson, Adams held to an unorthodox faith. For example, he did not believe in the doctrines of original sin, the blood atonement, or the Trinity. He was not, however, an anti-supernaturalist. "Unlike Jefferson, Adams found materialism a thoroughly objectionable doctrine, because it made everything mechanical and fixed, without life or power or 'motion, action, thought, sensation, reflection, reason, and Sentiment.' A universe of that character Adams neither believed in nor cared to affirm."[21]

Like Jefferson and unlike many in our day, Adams stood for liberty and the inextricable bond of religion and morality. "Adams affirmed and reaffirmed the essential link between religion and morality. Not only were these two necessarily joined, but only in keeping the two together could the new nation survive."[22] In a letter to his clerical cousin, Zabdiel Adams, the future president wrote:

> Statesmen, my dear Sir, may plan and speculate for liberty, but it is religion and morality alone which can establish the principles upon which freedom can securely stand. The only foundation of a free constitution is pure virtue.[23]

Adams encouraged his cousin to pull "down the strong-holds of Satan…. This is…the real sentiment of my heart."

Abraham Lincoln

The liberal crowd also calls upon Abraham Lincoln to undermine today's Christian social activists. In her article, Barbara Ehrenreich claims that Lincoln did not believe in a "personal God, and refused to go to church." She bases this on the testimony of "his law partner of 22 years," William Herndon. This is at best hearsay evidence that is almost impossible to substantiate. Herndon does not produce any hard evidence to support his claim. His opinions are based on recollections and personal conversations. Herndon's evaluations are disputed by many of Lincoln's associates who have their own contrary recollections.[24]

Abraham Lincoln's public pronouncements and private letters demonstrate that he was not an atheist.

Both Lincoln's personal correspondence and speeches indicate that he had a strong belief in a personal God and the Bible. Of course, his published religious views could be, in the opinion of the anti-Christian bigot and homosexual author Gore Vidal, a superfluous veneer that Lincoln occasionally paraded for political purposes. Since we cannot personally question Lincoln or those who maintained he ridiculed the Christian religion and the Bible, we are left to evaluate his published works.

Even Herndon had to admit that Lincoln expressed very orthodox religious sentiments during his tenure with him. Consider the letter that Lincoln wrote to his stepbrother when Lincoln learned that his father was dying:

> I sincerely hope father may recover his health; but at all events tell him to remember to call upon and confide in our great and good and merciful maker, who will not turn away from him in any extremity. He notes the fall of a sparrow and numbers the hair of our head, and He will not forget the dying man who puts his trust in Him.[25]

William Herndon, Lincoln's law partner, biographer, and friend, stated that Lincoln was a skeptic of Christianity.

If Lincoln were an atheist, this event would have been an opportune time for him to demonstrate his opposition to Christianity by reassuring his father that only the grave awaited him. Lincoln quotes Jesus' words in Matthew 10:29–31 and Luke 12:6–7. A case can be made, as Ward Hill Lamon makes in his *Life of Lincoln*, that Lincoln's letter does not express the essentials of the Christian faith, especially blood atonement. This may be true. But Ehrenreich, with Herndon's biography as her source, claims that Lincoln was an atheist. This single letter refutes her claim. Moreover, Herndon was a bit muddled on what he thought of

Lincoln's religious beliefs. "For example, Herndon asserted the Lincoln *'was in short an infidel*—was a Universalist—was a Unitarian—a Theist'—four distinct propositions in the same sentence," some of which are contradictory.[26]

At the request of the Senate, Lincoln proclaimed April 30, 1863, "as a day of national humiliation, fasting and prayer." In the proclamation, Lincoln requested

> all the people to abstain on that day from their ordinary secular pursuits, and to unite in their several places of public worship and at their respective homes in keeping the day holy to the Lord and devoted to the humble discharge of the religious duties proper to the solemn occasion.
>
> All this being done in sincerity and truth, let us then rest humbly in the hope, authorized by the Divine teachings, that the united cry of the nation will be heard on high, and answered with blessings no less than the pardon of our national sins, and restoration of our now divided and suffering country to its former happy condition of unity and peace.

This proclamation clearly shows that Lincoln at least publicly claimed belief in a personal God. He also believed that a nation can sin and that God will punish a nation for its collective sins.

In his second inaugural address, delivered forty-two days before his death, Lincoln said, "Fondly do we hope, fervently do we pray, that this mighty scourge of war may speedily pass away. Yet, if God wills that it continue until all the wealth piled by the bondsman's 250 years of unrequited toil shall be sunk, and until every drop of blood drawn by the lash shall be paid by another drawn by the sword, as was said 3,000 years ago, so still it must be said, 'the judgments of the Lord are true and righteous altogether [Psalm 19:9].'"[27] These stirring words certainly indicate that Lincoln believed in God, the Bible, sin, and the need for repentance, even if he misunderstood the purpose of war.

It is ironic that Lincoln is an icon of the Left, the stalwart defender of civil liberties. Ehrenreich believes that the Republicans have something to learn from Lincoln and his alleged desire to keep religion out of politics. Yet it was Lincoln who used biblical rhetoric to declare a war that resulted in the death of nearly 600,000 Americans, more than the number of Americans killed in World War II. John Adams was right. When the Christian religion is blended with "millions of fables, tales, and legends"—as Lincoln did in the defense of the Civil War on

In his Gettysburg Address, Lincoln stated that only that "nation under God" will enjoy the blessings of true liberty.

religious grounds—you end up with a "bloody religion." True biblical Christianity operated in England with the abolition of the slave trade without a war long before abolitionists took up arms in America. Had the British government "not been in the hands of Christians there seems little reason to have expected it to mount its massive, expensive, and voluntary campaign against slavery."[28]

Had biblical law, instead of natural law, operated in America, chattel slavery would have been outlawed before it had ever reached our shores. The Bible is very clear on the slavery issue: "And he who kidnaps [lit., *steals*] a man, whether he sells him or he is found in his possession, shall surely be put to death" (Exodus 21:16). "By this law, every man-stealer, and every receiver of the stolen person, lost his life: whether the latter stole the man himself, or gave money to a *Slave-Captain* or *Negro Dealer* to steal for him. All kidnapping and slave-dealing are prohibited, whether practiced by individuals or the state."[29] Hanging a few slave-traders would have saved the lives of 600,000 Americans and stopped the slave trade dead in its tracks.

What about Lincoln's beliefs about the Bible? An atheist would have no cause to quote the Bible in support of any belief or cause. "Something of a skeptic as a young man, he came in maturity to defend the Bible as absolutely true—'God's best gift to man.' He possessed a rare command of biblical detail, searched its pages for personal strength, displayed its characters and settings in his humor, and, in time of national crisis, drew upon its themes to explain the meaning of slavery, civil war, and emancipation." Lincoln's views on religion were by no means conventional for the times. He "called for a Christianity exclusively biblical that had no place for clergy, denominations, confessions, or creeds. What he came to affirm was a faith drawn from the Scriptures without human mediation."[30]

In praise of Lincoln's supposed atheism, Ehrenreich informs us that Lincoln was not a member of a church and would only join a congregation upon one condition: "When you show me a church based on the Golden Rule as its only creed, then I will unite with it." During his bid for the U.S. House of Representatives in 1846, Lincoln was branded an infidel by his political opponent, Democrat Peter Cartwright, a circuit-riding Methodist minister. Lincoln answered the charge with a public statement printed in the *Illinois Gazette* on August 15, 1846:

> That I am not a member of any Christian Church, is true; but I have never denied the truth of the Scriptures; and I have never spoken with intentional disrespect of religion in general, or of any denomination

of Christians in particular. It is true that in early life I was inclined to believe in what I understand is called the "Doctrine of Necessity"—that is, that the human mind is impelled to action, or held in rest by some power, over which the mind itself has no control; and I have sometimes (with one, two or three, but never publicly) tried to maintain this opinion in argument. The habit of arguing thus, however, I have entirely left off for more than five years. And I add here, I have always understood this same opinion to be held by several of the Christian denominations. The foregoing is the whole truth, briefly stated, in relation to myself upon this subject.

I do not think I could myself, be brought to support a man for office, whom I knew to be an open enemy of, and scoffer at, religion.[31]

Peter Cartwright, a Methodist minister and Lincoln's political opponent, branded Lincoln as an infidel.

The death of Lincoln's children led him to question his faith, refusing "to be consoled by traditional Christian piety."[32] Some historians claim that "Abraham Lincoln was interested in necromancy, and his wife held seances in the White House (outdistancing Nancy Reagan's later consultation of an astrologer)."[33] The death of their twelve-year-old son took an unusually heavy toll on the Lincolns. But it is possible that, through this period of trial and civil conflict, the president may have come to Christ. "Many noticed that he was seen more frequently with a Bible in his hand and that he spent more time in prayer."[34]

Lincoln's faith may have matured when he had to look, possibly for the first time in his life, outside his own mind and heart for help to endure such personal grief and the burden of a war where often brother was pitted against brother. "From this time on, Lincoln regularly attended the New York Avenue Presbyterian Church on Sundays—often even going to the Wednesday evening prayer meeting—until his untimely death three years later."[35]

Barbara Ehrenreich is wrong about Lincoln being an atheist. Dr. Phineas Gurley, Lincoln's pastor at the New York Avenue Presbyterian Church, "claimed that the death of Willie Lincoln in 1862 and the visit to the Gettysburg battlefield in 1863 finally led Lincoln to personal faith in Christ. Gurley also indicated that Lincoln planned to make a public profession of his faith at some opportune time in the near future—a future which never came."[36]

Conclusion

The historical record shows that America's national leaders and founding fathers firmly believed that American society must be ordered by morality. Presidential proclamations—both public and private—attest to the stamp of Christianity on our culture. In fact, without the Christian values which the political left reject, any society will drift into moral anarchy.

Notes

1. Barbara Ehrenreich, "Why the Religious Right Is Wrong," *Time* (September 7, 1992), 72.
2. John Adams, *The Diary and Autobiography of John Adams*, ed. L.H. Butterfield (Cambridge, MA: The Belknap Press of Harvard University Press, 1962), 3:233–34.
3. Letter to F. A. Van der Kemp, December 27, 1816. See Norman Cousins, ed., *'In God We Trust': The Religious Beliefs and Ideas of the American Founding Fathers* (New York: Harper & Brothers, 1958), 104–105.
4. Cousins, *'In God We Trust,'* 74.
5. Letter to F. A. Van der Kemp, February 16, 1809. Quoted in Cousins, *'In God We Trust,'* 102–103.
6. Quoted in Philip Greven, *The Protestant Temperament: Patterns of Child-Rearing, Religious Experience, and Self in Early America* (New York: Alfred A. Knopf, 1977), 346.
7. John Adams, "Novanglus: A History of the Dispute with America, from its Origin, in 1754, to the Present Time (1774)." Reprinted in Cousins, *'In God We Trust,'* 89–90.
8. Gayle White, "Whatever Happened to God's Left Wing?," *Atlanta Journal/Constitution* (October 30, 1994), R1, 3.
9. Quoted in Bill Nichols, "White House regroups, comes out swinging," *USA Today* (August 15, 1994), 4A.

10. Todd S. Purdum, "At Harlem Church, Clinton Tells Cuomo to Keep Going," *New York Times* (September 26, 1994).
11. Purdum, "At Harlem Church, Clinton Tells Cuomo to Keep Going."
12. Barry Schweid, "Clinton defends U.S. mission in Haiti," *Marietta Daily Journal* (September 26, 1994), 2A.
13. Purdum, "At Harlem Church, Clinton Tells Cuomo to Keep Going."
14. Micael Gartner, "Religion and politics just don't mix," *USA Today* (October 4, 1994), 11A.
15. John K. Brubaker, "Clinton breaches religion wall," *USA Today* (October 7, 1994), 10A.
16. Gustav Niebuhr, "Presidential faith: Clinton turns to Bible for comfort, guidance," *Atlanta Constitution* (October 4, 1994), A14.
17. Niebuhr, "Presidential faith," A14.
18. Quoted in Niebuhr, "Presidential faith," A14.
19. Quoted in "The root of all human rights," *Atlanta Journal/Constitution* (October 9, 1994), R6.
20. "The root of all human rights," R6.
21. Edwin S. Gaustad, *Neither King Nor Prelate: Religion and the New Nation, 1776–1826*, rev. ed. (Grand Rapids, MI: Eerdmans, [1987] 1993), 93.
22. Gaustad, *Neither King Nor Prelate*, 92.
23. Letter to Zabdiel Adams (June 21, 1776) in Charles Francis Adams, ed., *The Works of John Adams* (Boston, 1850–56), 10:401. Quoted in Gaustad, *Neither King Nor Prelate*, 92.
24. For an account of the controversy, see David Donald, *Lincoln's Herndon* (New York: Alfred A. Knopf, 1948), 212–17, 236–38, 256–57, 271–82, 359.
25. *Abraham Lincoln, Complete Works*, eds. Nicolay and Hay, 2:574. Quoted in Clarence Edward Macartney, *Lincoln and the Bible* (Nashville, TN: Abingdon-Cokesbury Press, 1949), 35–36.
26. Herndon to Lamon, February 25, 1870. Quoted in Donald, *Lincoln's Herndon*, 359.
27. Quoted in Michael Barone, "Who Was Lincoln?," *U.S. News & World Report* (October 5, 1992), 71.
28. Otto J. Scott, *The Secret Six: John Brown and the Abolitionist Movement* (New York: Times Books, 1979), 85.

29. Adam Clarke, *Clarke's Commentary*. Quoted in George Bourne, *The Book and Slavery Irreconcilable with Animadversions upon Dr. Smith's Philosophy* (Philadelphia, PA: J.M. Sanderson & Co., 1816), 119. Bourne's work is reprinted in John W. Christie and Dwight L. Dumond, *George Bourne and The Book of Slavery Irreconcilable* (Wilmington, DE: The Historical Society of Delaware, 1969).

30. Nathan O. Hatch, "Sola Scriptura and Novus Ordo Seclorum," *The Bible in America: Essays in Cultural History*, eds. Nathan O. Hatch and Mark A. Noll (New York: Oxford University Press, 1982), 59.

31. Quoted in Benjamin P. Thomas, *Abraham Lincoln* (New York: Alfred A. Knopf, 1953), 108–109. Also see Donald, *Lincoln's Herndon*, 359.

32. Jon Butler, *Awash in a Sea of Faith: Christianizing the American People* (Cambridge, MA: Harvard University Press, 1990), 295.

33. Gary Wills, *Under God: Religion and American Politics* (New York: Simon and Schuster, 1990), 208.

34. Richard V. Pierard and Robert D. Linder, *Civil Religion and the Presidency* (Grand Rapids, MI: Zondervan/Academie, 1988), 96.

35. Pierard and Linder, *Civil Religion and the Presidency*, 97. For a helpful study of Lincoln's Christian pilgrimage, see D. James Kennedy, "Was Lincoln a Christian?," a publication of Coral Ridge Ministries, Ft. Lauderdale, Florida.

36. Pierard and Linder, *Civil Religion and the Presidency*, 316, note 24. The best material on Lincoln's faith is William J. Wolf, *The Almost Chosen People: A Study in the Religion of Abraham Lincoln* (Garden City, NY: Doubleday, 1959), chap. 7, "The Best Gift God Has Given to Man," 117–18. For a more accessible book on Lincoln's faith, see Mark A. Noll, *One Nation Under God: Christian Faith and Political Action in America* (San Francisco, CA: Harper & Row, 1988), chap. 6, "The Transcendent Faith of Abraham Lincoln," 90–104. Clarence Edward Macartney, *Lincoln and the Bible* (Nashville, TN: Abingdon-Cokesbury Press, 1949) is another helpful book.

The Remaking of America

Ａmerica's Christian heritage is a fading memory for most Americans. Decades of value-neutral public education have left our nation without a moral anchor. While the Bible is a perennial best seller, and Americans publish and purchase more Bibles than any other people on earth, "the Bible has virtually disappeared from American education. It is rarely studied, even as literature, in public classrooms."[1] And yet, it was the Bible that made America. The rejection of the Bible in our day is resulting in the unmaking of America. On May 28, 1849, Robert C. Winthrop (1809–1894), speaker of the Thirtieth Congress, addressed the Annual Meeting of the Massachusetts Bible Society in Boston and issued this warning:

Robert C. Winthrop stated, "Men must necessarily be controlled, either by a power within them, or by a power without them; either by the Word of God, or by the strong arm of man; either by the Bible, or by the bayonet."

The voice of experience and the voice of our own reason speak but one language.... Both unite in teaching us, that men may as well build their houses upon the sand and expect to see them stand, when the rains fall, and the winds blow, and the floods come, as to found free institutions upon any other basis than that morality and virtue, of which the Word of God is the only authoritative rule, and the only adequate sanction.

All societies of men must be governed in some way or other. The less they may have of stringent State Government, the more they must have of individual self-government. The less they rely on public law or physical force, the more they must rely on private moral restraint. Men, in a word, must necessarily be controlled, either by a power within them, or by a power without them; either by the word of God, or by the strong arm of man; either by the Bible, or by the bayonet. It may do for other countries and other governments to talk about the State supporting religion. Here, under our own free institutions, it is Religion which must support the State.[2]

The bayonet rules in those nations which reject the Bible. As the Bible ceases to govern in the hearts of the people, and those who rule reject the Bible as a moral standard, we will see more of the glistening steel of the sharpened bayonet govern in America.

How is it that a nation that seems to be in love with the Bible works so hard to reject its teachings? First, while Americans seem to hnor the Bible, they are ignorant of its contents. "Americans revere the Bible but by and large they don't read it. And because they don't read it, they have become a nation of biblical illiterates."[3] Six of ten adult Americans, George Gallup, Jr. and Jim Castelli report, have no idea who delivered the Sermon on the Mount. Fewer than half of those surveyed can name the first four gospels. If a majority of the people don't know what the Bible says, certainly we cannot expect them to know what it means and how it applies.

A similar deficiency exists in the area of American history and the record of men and women who knew, understood, and applied the Bible to every area of life.

One college teacher tells of a student who didn't understand why World War II was so named, since he'd never heard of World War I; another teacher tells of a student who was puzzled that George Washington is sometimes referred to as "General," since the student was unaware of Washington's role in the American Revolution. A recent survey of the general population done for the Hearst Corporation found that of those responding, 45 percent thought that the phrase, "from each according to his ability, to each according to his need," is from the U.S. Constitution.[4]

History is a teacher. "History," Thomas Jefferson wrote, "by apprising [people] of the past will enable them to judge...the future; it

Rejection of the moral foundations of the past will always result in the disintegration of a culture.

will avail them of the experience of other times and other nations; it will qualify them as judges of the actions and designs of men...."[5]

Second, in addition to rampant biblical and historical illiteracy, a prevailing belief persists that "religion" is strictly a private affair. On one level this is certainly true. Regeneration is a work done on the heart. But regeneration, as defined by Scripture, was never meant to stop at the heart. "What use is it," James asks, "if a man says he has faith, but he has no works? Can that faith save him?" (James 2:14). Works, that is, acts of righteousness, are evidence that regeneration has taken place. Things external are to confirm that something has happened internally. A religion that is solely a private affair is a false religion. Sadly, it seems that most Americans are comfortable with this type of religion. While they might be *personally* against abortion and special rights for homosexuals, they do not believe it is proper to impose such laws on society.

Ideas Have Consequences

Ideas, or the lack of them, have consequences. Ignorance of the Bible and the way it has been used by our forefathers is having disastrous results. To reject the Bible as the foundation upon which our nation rests is the rejection of America and its ideals, imperfect as they were. John Adams, an eyewitness to America's beginnings, in a letter to Thomas Jefferson, calls on us to remember the "general Principles" that made this nation great:

> The *general Principles*, on which the Fathers achieved Independence, were the only Principles in which that beautiful Assembly of young Gentlemen [representing the numerous religious denominations of the country at the time of the Revolution] could Unite.... And what were these *general Principles*? I answer, the general Principles of Christianity, in which all these Sects were United: And the *general Principles* of English and American Liberty, in which all those young Men United, and which had United all Parties in America, in Majorities sufficient to assert and maintain her Independence.
>
> Now I will avow, that I then believed, and now believe, that those general Principles of Christianity, are as eternal and immutable, as the Existence and Attributes of God; and that those Principles of Liberty, are as unalterable as human Nature and our terrestrial, mundane System.[6]

A similar observation was made by Franklin D. Roosevelt when he said: "We cannot read the history of our rise and development as a nation, without reckoning with the place the Bible has occupied in shaping the advances of the Republic…. [W]here we have been truest and most consistent in obeying its precepts, we have attained the greatest measure of contentment and prosperity."[7] The common ground of Christianity united the country.

Mark Hatfield, Republican Senator from the State of Oregon, disagrees. He said in a speech at Pepperdine University in Malibu, California, in January 1989, that "America is not a Christian nation. We as Christians must come to grips with this fact, and look to where our real struggle lies."[8] All of history is against Senator Hatfield, as this book has shown. President Woodrow Wilson, whom Hatfield quotes, declared that "America was born a Christian nation. America was born to exemplify that devotion to the elements of righteousness which are derived from the revelations of the Holy Scripture." Wilson knew his history.

The inscription over a raised platform in the House of Representatives reads, "IN GOD WE TRUST."

Hatfield maintains that "such things as prayer in the public school, the inscription of 'in God we trust' on our currency and pledges of allegiance to God and country do not make us a Christian nation." I agree. But Mr. Hatfield should be reminded that the prayers children prayed in public schools prior to 1963 were not to Allah or the Buddha. The book that was outlawed in 1962 as legally and constitutionally inappropriate for public school children was the Bible, not the Koran. A lot of historical revisionism has to take place to deny America's Christian origins.

It makes a big difference that the Ten Commandments are found in the Supreme Court building instead of selections from the code of Hammurabi and that our coins say "In God We Trust" instead of "In Baal We Trust." It makes a big difference that the Library of Congress has a quotation from a Psalm, instead of a quotation from the Koran.[9]

The God America trusted in is the God of biblical Christianity. Thomas Jefferson, who was by no means orthodox in his religious beliefs, still turned to the pages of the New Testament for ethical guidance. Jefferson reminds us in the Declaration of Independence that "we are endowed by our Creator with certain inalienable rights." Yes, Jefferson couched his meaning for morals in something called the "law of nature" or "natural law." Jefferson realized, however, that natural law needed a source of authority. Jefferson's "law of nature" needed "nature's God." "The point of the matter has always been that natural law itself needed divine sanction to become binding for men."[10]

The twentieth century has seen the results of shoving God out of the moral arena. Millions were slaughtered under Stalin and Hitler. Under these regimes, "morality" was defined by the State, an idea inherited from the Enlightenment. Charles Colson of Prison Fellowship shows its contemporary application and results:

> Nazism arose as a result of the Enlightenment and what it called the rights of man. Until that time, human rights in Western civilization rested on the Bible and the belief that all are equal before the creator.
>
> But as Christianity was rolled back, people tried to find a new basis for rights. Hannah Arendt, in her book *The Origins of Totalitarianism*, says the rights of man "meant nothing more nor less than that from then on man, and not God's command...should be the source of law."
>
> But what is man that he should possess all these wonderful rights by the bare facts of his existence? Apart from God, the rights of man dangle in the air without any basis.
>
> So into the vacuum rushed all sorts of ideologies. Nazism tried to lay a basis in race. Hitler's motto was that right and wrong are defined by what's good for the German people.
>
> Marxism tried to fill the vacuum with class structure. Lenin's motto was that right and wrong are defined by what's good for an individual's own race or gender group.[11]

America is now being defined in terms of "multiculturalism." An appreciation of diverse cultures is being used as a dodge to smuggle in aberrational moral standards that will have the effect of diluting the impact of biblical Christianity. Multiculturalism is a type of ethical polytheism: many moral law-orders based on many gods.

> Polytheism (all gods are equal) leads to relativism (all moral codes are equal); relativism leads to humanism (man makes his own laws); and humanism leads to statism (the State best represents mankind as the pinnacle of power). As Rushdoony remarks,[12] "because an absolute law is denied, it means that the only universal law possible is an *imperialistic law*, a law imposed by force and having no validity other than the coercive imposition."[13]

We are being driven back to the Tower of Babel on the theological bus of multicultural education: Multiculturalists want to make a name for *themselves* to displace the name of God. The multiculturalists are forcing the position, and the word is *forcing*, that all cultures are inherently equal, except, of course, Western culture which did not accept the view that all cultures are *ethically* equal. Christianity is what makes the difference.

The Remaking of America

Fundamentally, the real question is not whether America was or is a Christian nation. Rather, the question must be, Should America be a Christian nation? Senator Hatfield, as well as many others, says no! A careful reading of Wilson's quotation will show that Mr. Hatfield misunderstands and misapplies the notion of a "Cristian nation." Wilson affirmed that a Christian nation is not in its slogans but in the ethical system it chooses, the values that Wilson described as "elements of righteousness." What standard should be used to determine "righteousness"? Our earliest founders had the answer.

> Whether we look at the Puritans and their fellow colonists of the seventeenth century, or their descendants of the eighteenth century, or those who framed the Declaration of Independence and the Constitution, we see that their political programs were the rather clear reflection of a consciously held political philosophy, and that the various political philosophies which emerged among the American people were intimately related to the theological developments which were taking place. Political philosophies are not created in a vacuum, but are in turn the product of systems of thought which find their inspiration and nurture in theology. What is true of colonial and Revolutionary America is no less true of the America of the nineteenth and twentieth centuries.

Because of this there appeared in an early date in the colonies a kind of political orthodoxy, a way of looking at government and its functions and of the proper relationship which should exist between government and its citizens. *A Christian world and life view furnished the basis for this early political thought which guided the American people for nearly two centuries....* This Christian theism had so permeated the colonial mind that it continued to guide even those who had come to regard the Gospel with indifference or even hostility. The currents of this orthodoxy were too strong to be easily set aside by those who in their own thinking had come to a different conception of religion and hence of government also.[14]

Hatfield believes "that when you move from the parish to the city council, you enter a different arena." This implies a different standard—one for the parish (church) and another for the city council (civil government). This is why Hatfield is more comfortable with America as a "pluralistic nation."[15] Pluralism demands different ethical standards. No nation can survive under such a system of morality. If America is to survive, she will have to embrace the God of the Bible and the ethical system set forth therein.

There is, however, something even more fundamental. The law cannot save, no matter how righteously or vigorously it is embraced and applied. America was great because she was good. She was good because so many Americans embraced Jesus Christ as Lord and Savior. The leaven of the gospel was a force for good in America. If America is ever to regain her greatness, the churches of America must once again preach an authentic gospel—the gospel of free grace and biblical discipleship—not the gospel of works and superficial religiosity. Man must be told that he is a sinner, and he must also be told that Jesus is his only hope of redemption, two simple truths that are lost on most Americans, including many so-called "Christians." The remaking of America will come by way of the gospel and a love for God's commandments (John 14:15).

As Benjamin Franklin so eloquently stated at the Constitutional Convention: "God governs in the affairs of men." God governs because He is King, and this world is part of His universal kingdom-realm. While His kingdom is not "*of* this world," it certainly operates *in* and *over* this world. Franklin continued as he addressed the members of the constitutional convention: "And if a sparrow cannot fall to the ground without his notice [Matthew 10:29], is it probable that an empire can rise without his aid? We have been assured...in the sacred writings that 'except the Lord build the house, they labor in vain that build it' [Psalm 127:1]. I

This painting found in the United States Capitol building shows William Brewster holding the standard for society: the Bible.

firmly believe this, and I also believe that without his concurring aid we shall succeed in this political building no better than the builders of Babel." The kingdoms of men are dependent upon the operation of the Kingdom of God *in and over this world*. Birds do not fall and kingdoms do not rise without the overruling of God's providential hand.

A Christian Commonwealth

More than a century before the drafting of the Declaration of Independence, John Eliot, the Puritan missionary to the Indians, wrote in his *The Christian Commonwealth* (a document intended as a plan of government for the Natick Indian community), that it is not for man "to search humane Polities and Platformes of Government, contrived by the wisdom of man; but as the Lord hath carried on their works for them, so they ought to go unto the Lord, and enquire at the Word of his mouth, what Platforme of Government he hath therein commanded; and humble themselves to embrace that as the best.... [The] written Word of God is the perfect System or Frame of Laws, to guide all the Moral actions of man, either towards God or man."[16] Because we are living in God's kingdom, Eliot taught, it is our duty to follow the rules of the King and not to look at earthly rulers as saviors.

SAVIOURS OF OUR COUNTRY.

There are no political messiahs, but rather one Savior of society, King Jesus. All men—laymen and civil rulers alike—must bow the knee to Him.

Notes

1. Kenneth Woodward, "How the Bible Made America," *Newsweek* (December 27, 1982), 45.
2. Quoted in Verna M. Hall, ed., *The Christian History of the American Revolution* (San Francisco, CA: Foundation for American Christian Education, 1975), 20.
3. George Gallup, Jr. and Jim Castelli, *The People's Religion: American Faith in the Nineties* (New York: Macmillan, 1989), 60.
4. Lynne V. Cheney, "Foreword" in Diane Ravitch and Chester E. Finn, Jr., *What Do Our 17-Year-Olds Know?: A Report on the First National Assessment of History and Literature* (New York: Harper & Row, 1987), viii–ix.
5. Cheney, "Foreword," *What Do Our 17-Year-Olds Know?*, vii.
6. John Adams in a letter to Thomas Jefferson, June 28, 1813.
7. Taken from a 1935 radio broadcast. Quoted in Gabriel Sivan, *The Bible and Civilization* (New York: Quadrangle/The New York Times Book Co., 1973), 178.
8. Quoted in *New England Christian Life* (July/August 1990), 13.
9. Peter J. Leithart and George Grant, *In Defense of Greatness: How Biblical Character Shapes A Nation's Destiny* (Ft. Lauderdale, FL: Coral Ridge Ministries, 1990), 4–5.
10. Hannah Arendt, *On Revolution* (New York: The Viking Press, 1963), 191.
11. Charles Colson, "The Skinheads' Source of Law," *World* (December 26, 1992), 13.
12. Rousas J. Rushdoony, *The Institutes of Biblical Law* (Phillipsburg, NJ: The Craig Press, 1973), 17.
13. Gary North, *Political Polytheism: The Myth of Pluralism* (Tyler, TX: Institute for Christian Economics, 1989), 158.
14. C. Gregg Singer, *A Theological Interpretation of American History*, rev. ed. (Phillipsburg, NJ: Presbyterian and Reformed, [1964] 1981), 325–26.
15. Quoted in Judy Tarjanyi, "Still Seeking 'City upon A Hill,'" *The Blade* (Toledo, Ohio) (September 24, 1989), E1.
16. John Eliot, *The Christian Commonwealth: or, The Civil Policy of the Rising Kingdom of Jesus Christ* (1659). Quoted in John Eidsmoe, *Christianity and the Constitution: The Faith of Our Founding Fathers* (Grand Rapids, MI: Baker Book House, 1987), 33–34.

APPENDIX A

THANKSGIVING AND GOD

O N THURSDAY, SEPTEMBER 24, 1789, THE FIRST HOUSE OF REPRESENTA-tives voted to recommend—in its exact wording—the First Amendment to the states for ratification. The next day, Friday, September 25, Congressman Elias Boudinot from New Jersey proposed that the House and Senate jointly request of President Washington to proclaim a day of thanksgiving for "the many signal favors of Almighty God." Boudinot said that he "could not think of letting the session pass over without offering an opportunity to all the citizens of the United States of joining, with one voice, in returning to Almighty God their sincere thanks for the many blessings he had poured down upon them."[1]

Congressman Elias Boudinot proposed that the House and Senate jointly request President Washington to pronounce a Thanksgiving proclamation.

Roger Sherman spoke in favor of the proposal by reminding his colleagues that the practice of thanksgiving is "warranted by a number of precedents in holy writ: for instance, the solemn thanksgivings and rejoicings which took place in the time of Solomon, after the building of the temple.... This example, he thought, worthy of Christian imitation on the present occasion."[2]

A People Full of Thanksgiving
The colonists of another era were aware of the many instances of thanksgiving celebrations found in "holy writ." Thanksgiving, as it was

practiced by the colonists, was a religious celebration that shared the sentiments of their biblical forerunners, giving thanks to God for His faithful provision. For these devoutly religious people, thanksgiving would have come naturally. "Twice en route the passengers [aboard the *Arbella*] participated in a fast, and once (two days after sounding ground beneath the *Arbella*) a 'thanksgiving.' When the sailing season ended with all ships accounted for, 'we had a day of thanksgiving in all the plantations.'"[3]

The Puritans were fervent in their thanks to God for sustaining them during their turbulent voyage to the New World.

There are numerous claims to the first Thanksgiving. One of the earliest recorded celebrations occurred a half century before the Pilgrims landed at Plymouth in 1621. "A small colony of French Huguenots established a settlement near present-day Jacksonville, Florida. On June 30, 1564, their leader, René de Laudonnière, recorded that 'We sang a psalm of Thanksgiving unto God, beseeching Him that it would please Him to continue His accustomed goodness towards us.'"[4]

In 1610, after a hard winter called "the starving time," the colonists at Jamestown called for a time of thanksgiving. This was after the original company of 409 colonists had been reduced to 60 survivors. The colonists prayed for help that finally arrived by a ship filled with food and supplies from England. They held a prayer service to give thanks.

This thanksgiving celebration was not formerly commemorated yearly. An annual commemoration of thanks came nine years later in another part of Virginia. "On December 4, 1619, 38 colonists landed at a place they called Berkeley Hundred [in Virginia]. 'We ordain,' read an instruction in their charter, 'that the day of our ship's arrival...in the land of Virginia shall be yearly and perpetually kept holy as a day of Thanksgiving to Almighty God.'"[5]

While none of these Thanksgiving celebrations was an official national pronouncement (no nation existed at the time), they do support the claim that the celebrations were religious. "Thanksgiving began as a holy day, created by a community of God-fearing Puritans sincere in their desire to set aside one day each year especially to thank the Lord for His many blessings. The day they chose, coming after the harvest at a time of year when farm work was light, fit the natural rhythm of rural life."[6]

On October 3, 1863, Abraham Lincoln declared that the last Thursday of November 1863 would be set aside as a nationwide celebration of thanksgiving. His proclamation stated that

> No human counsel hath devised, nor hath any mortal hand worked out these great things. They are the gracious gifts of the most high God, who, while dealing with us in anger for our sins, hath nevertheless remembered mercy.... I do, therefore, invite my fellow citizens in every part of the United States, and those who are sojourning in foreign lands, to set apart and observe the last Thursday in November next as a day of Thanksgiving and praise to our beneficent father who dwelleth in heaven.

Starting with Lincoln, United States Presidents proclaimed the last Thursday in November for Thanksgiving. Franklin D. Roosevelt changed the celebration to the third Thursday in November "to give more shopping time between Thanksgiving and Christmas. At this point Congress enacted the 'fourth Thursday' compromise."[7] Ever since this pragmatic and commercial approach to Thanksgiving was promoted, its original meaning has steadily been lost.

Notes

1. *The Annals of the Congress, The Debates and Proceedings in the Congress of the United States*, Compiled From Authentic Materials by Joseph Gales, Senior (Washington, DC: Gales and Seaton, 1834), 1:949–50.
2. *Annals of the Congress*, 1:950.
3. David D. Hall, *Worlds of Wonder, Days of Judgment: Popular Religious Belief in Early New England* (New York: Alfred A. Knopf, 1989), 166.
4. Diana Karter Appelbaum, *Thanksgiving: An American Holiday, An American History* (New York: Facts on File Publications, 1984), 14–15.

5. Jim Dwyer, ed., *Strange Stories, Amazing Facts of America's Past* (Pleasantville, NY: The Reader's Digest Association, Inc., 1989), 198.

6. Appelbaum, *Thanksgiving*, 186. The celebration of Christmas, in addition to Thanksgiving, has become an ordeal in censorship. *Silent Night* and other sacred songs have been stripped from public school Christmas pageants and replaced with *Jingle Bells* and *Frosty the Snowman*. Public school officials and school teachers are made to substitute "winter holiday" for Christmas. In St. Paul Minnesota, an affirmative action officer for the state tax department, banned what she called the "unwelcome greeting of Merry Christmas" via the department's electronic mail. ("'Merry Christmas' offense, bureaucrat rules," *Atlanta Journal/Constitution* [December 11, 1994], A11).

7. Edmund H. Harvey, Jr., ed., *Readers Digest Book of Facts* (Pleasantville, NY: The Reader's Digest Association, [1985] 1987), 125.

APPENDIX B

THEOCRACY AND DEMOCRACY

IN THE MINDS OF MOST PEOPLE, A THEOCRACY IS WHAT IRAN IS EXPERIENC-
ing—religious leaders (Mullahs) who rule the nation and force religious
observance under penalty of law. For theocratic critics, "theocracy" is
defined as the institutional Church ruling over the State and every other
institution. This is an incorrect definition. The system of rule in which
the Church rules in society with religious leaders (ministers or priests) as
the governmental officials is called an "ecclesiocracy": *ekklesia* (church)
and *kratos* (power, strength, rule).

Jurisdictional Separation

An ecclesiocracy means that the Church (either a single local body or a
network of churches like a denomination or the Roman Catholic Church
ruled by a Pope) is the primary and absolute governing institution in
society. An ecclesiocracy does not allow for a jurisdictional separation
between Church and State. It means that the institutional Church rules
the State, and the State carries out the ecclesiastical objectives of the
Church. *This is not the biblical model.*

Scripture defines a very decentralized governmental system and a
jurisdictional separation between Church and State. In biblical terms,
government is defined in terms broader than the State or the institutional
Church. Government includes the family, Church, and various levels of
civil jurisdiction, all responsible to God's government and supported
by man's self-government.[1] Only God's government is defined in the
singular (Isaiah 9:6). R.J. Rushdoony writes:

> [W]e do not equate government with the state. To do so is totalitari-
> anism. Government is first of all the self-government of man; it is
> also the family, the church, the school, our vocation, society and its
> institutions, and finally, civil government. Our problem today is that
> government is equated with the state, an anti-Christian view.[2]

Defining Theocracy

What then is a "theocracy"? Like ecclesiocracy, theocracy is made up
of two Greek words: *theos* (God) and *kratos* (power, strength, rule). In

its simplest definition, theocracy means the "rule of God." The word is not found in the Bible, although the concept is certainly present. The word was coined by Josephus, the Jewish historian for the Romans in the first century, and appears in his writings only once in *Against Apion* (2.164–165): "placing all sovereignty and authority in the hands of God." Gabriel Sivan, a Jewish writer who has contributed articles to the *Encyclopedia Judaica*, offers the following as a helpful clarification of the term:

> To the modern ear the word "theocracy" has distinctly pejorative overtones, suggesting the rule of some oppressive priestly caste, "government by state by immediate Divine guidance or by officials regarded as divinely guided," to quote a standard definition. Yet, unlike certain other systems known in antiquity, "the 'Theocracy' of Moses was not a government of priests, as opposed to kings; it was a government by God Himself, as opposed to the government by priests or kings" (Dean Arthur Stanley, *A History of the Jewish Church*, 1862). The U.S. jurist and statesman Oscar Straus, a close associate of President Theodore Roosevelt, also stressed this point in his study of American culture's indebtedness to the Hebraic concept: "The very fact that…with the single exception of Eli, no priest was ever elected to the magistracy during the entire period of the Commonwealth, decidedly negatives [*sic*] any such interpretation" (*The Origin of the Republican form of Government in the United States of America*, 1887).[3]

"Theocracy" describes the rule of God over all His creation. Jesus is said to be "the ruler of the kings of the earth" (Revelation 1:5). God is "the only Sovereign, the King of kings and Lord of lords" (1 Timothy 6:15).

In a theocracy, civil law is not administered by priests or pastors acting as God's civil ministers. While the Church is under the rule of God in a theocracy, the Church is not the judicial agent of the theocracy. The civil rule of the Church is an ecclesiocracy, a Church-State. Theocracy, on the other hand, is God's government in, of, and over the universe. It is synonymous with the kingdom of God. The Church is not the kingdom of God. The State is not the kingdom of God. The Church is a part of God's kingdom. The State is also a part of God's kingdom, but it is not the sole agent used to advance the kingdom.

A person who believes in the lordship of Jesus Christ believes in theocracy as defined above. This does not mean a belief in a Church-State or a State-Church. Theocracy is not a form of government like aristocracy, democracy, oligarchy, monarchy, or a republic. Rather, theocracy tells us ultimately who rules over all creation and who is in charge of the governments of men (Isaiah 9:6–7; Daniel 4:17, 34–35).

John Knox instructs Mary, Queen of Scots, that all earthly rulers are subject to the laws of the King of kings.

Democracy "As Heresy"?

The word 'democracy' is derived from the Greek word *demokratia*, the root meanings of which are *demos* (people) and *kratein* (to rule). The word entered the vocabulary of Greece in ancient Athens in the fifth century B.C. In its simplest terms democracy is a form of government in which, in contradistinction to monarchies and aristocracies, the people rule.

How should Christians evaluate the ideals of democracy? Carl F. H. Henry claims that some Christians "view democracy as heresy."[4] But what does he, or anyone, mean by "democracy"? In one of his recent works, Henry remarks that "even in the United States, despite widespread belief in a God-of-the-gaps and in a blessed immortality come what may, the nationalism of democracy now frequently slips into a kind of political atheism that accommodates only the rituals of civil religion and in fact actually conceal the decline of faith in the schoolroom and in the inner city."[5] Wouldn't this type of democracy be heretical"?

"The nationalism of democracy," Henry writes, gave us "fascism and communism."[6] In fact, in another place, Henry laments that the inaction of Christians leads to a vacuum in the democratic process that is quickly filled by opponents of the democratic process.

Evangelical inactivity in political affairs contrasts so sharply with the subversive exploitation of democratic processes that it indirectly contributes a setting where left-wing strategists can more easily gain their political objectives. According to J. Edgar Hoover, astute director of the Federal Bureau of Investigation: "The Red Fascists have long followed the practice of making full use of democratic liberties: elections, lawful agitation, and propaganda, and free speech, press, assembly. Their basic premise: Reap every advantage possible."[7]

So then, when democratic means are used by the righteous, democracy is good for a nation. When democratic means are used by the unrighteous, democracy is a heresy.

The word "democracy" has as many definitions as there are people to define it. The definitions of *democracy* are so diverse that British philosopher John L. Austin "once dismissed the word as 'notoriously useless.'"[8] Is it any wonder that nearly everyone claims to embrace the ideals of democracy? It can mean anything and everything.

There are two striking historical facts. First, nearly everyone today says they are democrats no matter whether their views are on the left, centre or right. Political regimes of all kinds in, for instance, Western Europe, the Eastern bloc and Latin America claim to be democracies. Yet, what each of these regimes says and does is radically different. Democracy seems to bestow an 'aura of legitimacy' on modern political life: rules, laws, policies and decisions appear justified and appropriate when they are 'democratic'.[9]

Democracy is bandied about as an incantation. When "the people" express themselves in opposition to egregiously oppressive political regimes, this is claimed to be "democracy in action," as if public expression were somehow a magical spell that will make forty or fifty years of socialistic and communistic oppression go away.

Democracy: A Dark Definition

John Winthrop (1588–1649), first governor of Massachusetts Bay Colony, declared *direct* democracy to be "the meanest and worst of all forms of government."[10] John Cotton (1584–1652), seventeenth-century Puritan minister in Massachusetts, wrote in 1636: "Democracy, I do not conceive that ever God did ordain as a fit government either for church or commonwealth. If the people be governors, who shall be governed?"[11] In the *Federalist Papers* (No. 10), James Madison (1751–1836), fourth president of the United States who was recognized as the "father of the Constitution," writes that democracies are "spectacles of turbulence and contention." Pure democracies are "incompatible with personal security or the rights of property…. In general [they] have been as short in their lives as they have been violent in their deaths."[12] These more realistic descriptions of the effects of direct democracy are a far cry from today's modern appraisal.

John Cotton criticized the idea of pure democracy, saying that "if the people be governors, who shall be the governed?"

So, contrary to what is widely taught in the schools of the United States and bruited about in the news media and expressions of politicians, the United States is *not*—in the opinion of one its principle founders and interpreters—a democracy. The Constitution itself, Article IV, Section 4, says: "The United States shall guarantee to every State in this Union a Republican form of government…." Taken simply literally it is a guarantee of a republican government *in* the states and a republican government *outside* and *above* the states. There is no mention of the word democracy in the Constitution.[13]

What should we think of this dismissal of democracy? Did these men oppose the democratic process? Winthrop certainly did not. Although voting in the colonies was restricted compared to our nation's universal suffrage, assistants were chosen "by the general vote of the people" through the raising of hands.[14] Certainly Madison, as one of the architects of the Constitution, cannot be accused of rebuffing the democratic process since the Constitution mandates that representatives from the states be elected by popular vote.

These men feared that the whims of the majority cut off from an ethical base would prevail if direct democracy were ever accepted as a legitimate form of civil government. On the other hand, these men knew that only "the people" could keep a civil government in check. There was no divine right of kings (or a divine right of representatives or judges), and there must be no divine right of the people. Our founders strived for a system of checks and balances in civil government. But if at any time the character of the people changed, the effort would have been for nought.

There must be some consensus of opinion of what democracy is and what makes it work before it will function as an effective and stable aspect of government. Just to say the word does not make it a reality. As Christians there is one thing we should all agree upon, *Vox populari est non vox dei* (the voice of the people is *not* the voice of God), for we know that with a simple majority, evil as well as good can be implemented into law.

Pure democracy resulted in "mobocracy" during the French Revolution when the masses forced their way into the Tuileries in 1792.

One of the last accurate definitions of democracy was published in 1928 in a training manual developed by the U.S. War Department. In it democracy was described as "a government of the masses." Authority was said to be "derived through mass meeting or any other form of 'direct' expression." Direct democracy, according to the manual, would result in "mobocracy." The "attitude toward property is communistic—negating property rights. Attitude toward law is that the will of the majority shall regulate, whether it be based upon deliberation or governed passion, prejudice, and impulse, without restraint or regard to consequences."[15] In a word, direct democracy makes "we the people" the immediate sovereigns without any guarantee of external moral restraint. C. Gregg Singer, echoing this opinion, writes that "Modern political theory has replaced the doctrine of the sovereignty of God with that of the sovereignty of man."[16]

Is it any wonder, therefore, that John Adams, the second president of the United States, declared that "the voice of the people is 'sometimes the voice of Mahomet, of Caesar, of Catiline, the Pope, and the Devil.'"[17] The results can be devastating. Francis Schaeffer describes law by majority opinion, certainly a definition of direct democracy, as "the dictatorship of the 51%, with no controls and nothing with which to challenge the majority."[18] Schaeffer deduces a simple result of this definition of democracy: "It means that if Hitler was able to get a 51% vote of the Germans, he had a right to kill the Jews."[19] Winthrop understood that a standard had to be found to direct the life and morals of governors and the governed.

> The Fundamentals which God gave, to the [Commonwealth] of Israel, were a sufficient Rule to them, to guide all their affairs: We having the same, with all the Additions, explanations and deductions, which have followed: it is not possible, we should want a Rule in any case: if God give wisdom to discern it.[20]

Winthrop believed rightly that God gave us His law to check the totalitarian inclinations of the minority and the majority, the one and the many.

The Necessity of Values

William J. Bennett, editor of the highly popular *Book of Virtues* and former drug czar, believes that the drug war can be won by a return to what he describes as "democratic values."[21] John Dewey wrote, "The keynote of democracy as a way of life may be expressed as the necessity for the participation of every mature human being in formation of the values that regulate the living of men together."[22] Bennett and Dewey, on opposite ends of the political spectrum, talk about values and their regulation of life, but where do these values originate? Which ones are legitimate? Only those validated by the majority? The words of John Adams are to the point: "If the majority is 51 and the minority 49,...is it certainly the voice of God? If tomorrow one should change to 50 vs. 50, where is the voice of God? If two and the minority should become the majority, is the voice of God changed?"[23]

Nineteenth-century Americans affirmed, as the primary doctrine of their democratic faith, that beneath society, its customs and institutions, a law exists that men did not make. This law outlines the patterns of both individual and social life. For the individual it establishes principles on which to found a beneficent and constructive life. For society it institutes an order within which persons may grow in understanding and in virtue. The idea of the fundamental law as it existed in the thought of early nineteenth-century America had two different origins and, as a consequence, two different emphases. It came, on the one hand, from the idea of natural law as first formulated by Plato in ancient Athens and, on the other hand, from that belief in moral law that had been carried down from the time of Moses by the Judeo-Christian tradition.[24]

We get closer to understanding how democracy can and should work with the following: "A 'natural law,' or moral tenet, guarantees to every person both liberty and the right to property; and this natural law is morally superior to man-made law."[25] Democratic law, that is, a law that originates with the people cut off from a transcendental ethical norm, is morally *inferior*. The people can only serve as conduit to a "morally superior" law. That law does not reside in man. It is a "higher law."

Supreme Court Justice John Marshall stated that principles of justice are based on "the Creator of all things."

Chief Justice John Marshall (1755–1835), in an 1823 decision, gave the following opinion from the bench: "There are principles of abstract justice which the Creator of all things has impressed on the mind of his creature man and which are admitted to regulate, in great degree, the rights of civilized nations."[26] In 1828 Joseph Story (1779–1845) voiced similar sentiments when he wrote: "In ascending to the great principles upon which all society rests, it must be admitted that there are some which are of eternal obligation, and arise from our common dependence upon our Creator. Among these are the duty to do justice, to love mercy, and to walk humbly before God" [Micah 6:8]."[27]

But natural law has as many definitional ambiguities as does democracy. Natural law can mean almost anything. And in secular terms, it almost always means something in opposition to biblical law. Again, we are back to our original question: What standard will be used by both governors and the governed? During the early eighteenth century, natural law was equated with biblical law, but by the time of the Declaration of Independence the "rational nucleus of Christianity...was derived from the doctrines of 'natural religion' and 'deism.'"[28]

> The idea of natural religion suited the peculiar temper of the Enlightenment. It signified religion divested of mystery and dogmatism, as well as sectarian bigotry. Man's religious needs and problems, like every other exigency of life, were to be met by the exercise of his natural faculties.
>
> The more radical deism proposed to *reduce* positive religion to natural religion. Its exponents, such as John Toland, Anthony Collins, Matthew Tindal, Thomas Chubb, and Thomas Paine, were moved by a negative and revolutionary temper of mind. They were *anti*-clerical, *anti*-ecclesiastical, and *anti*-authoritarian. They found an adequate revelation of God in the constitution of nature.[29]

Natural law was viable as long as a vibrant Christianity functioned along side it. As Christianity became diluted and biblical law was exchanged for a reason-based substitute, natural law became more and more secularized. With the near rejection of the Christian faith in our day among the people, democracy has become a system of government with no ethical mooring. "The prevalent tendency among modern political theorists is to define democracy without reference to a transcendent ethical standard."[30]

Staunch defenders of democracy can rant and rave against those who assail undefined democracy, but they still must answer the fundamental question: What standard should be used in making our laws so that a legitimate democracy can work?

A writer for the *New York Times* depicted the rise of the New Christian Right and its war with entrenched liberalism as a battle between "'churches and church-allied groups' who favor freedom, democracy, and the rights of minorities, on the one hand, and a right-wing fringe interest in setting up a theocracy governed by a 'dictatorship of religious values,' on the other hand."[31] This writer is critical of "religious values," but he offers no substitute set of values. Laws against theft, murder and libel are "religious values." The enforcement of all laws are usually considered to be dictatorial by those who break them. What does he mean by "freedom, democracy, and the rights of minorities"?

After viewing a propaganda piece put out by People for the American Way depicting Christians who are involved in politics as those who "were conspiring to curb civil liberties for all," one viewer remarked that "if a majority of the people decided to take freedom of speech out of the Constitution, they had the right to do so."[32] Of course, no one has proposed such a measure. But the point is well made: If advocates of pure democracy are going to be consistent, then they must allow whatever democracy brings, even the overturning of democracy. Anything less is less than democratic.

The failure to distinguish between the democratic process and democracy as a system of government where the autonomous will of the people is law is a grievous error. The democratic process, as most historians would define it, is simply the right and freedom of the people to participate directly in the political and social operations of a nation. Without the democratic process, we are left with totalitarianism. But democracy needs an anchor. The people must appeal to a fixed, external law in order to defend their freedom. Otherwise, they face the prospects of despotism by an unrestrained national government or the unbridled desires of the majority.

The right that voters have to participate directly in the political and social operations of a nation guards that nation from totalitarianism.

Both State and Society (not to be equated) must agree on the same law. When the law no longer operates, the people are left with no appeal. The covenant has been broken. In the case of the United States, the loss of a higher law means that the Constitution is merely an empty shell with no principles behind its words. Democracy as a political system takes over. The will of a majority of the people becomes the voice of God. The law is what "the people" want. But "the people" rarely get a chance to speak in unison. Rather, special interests who claim to "represent the people" get the ear of lawmakers. The pro-abortionists appeal to "public opinion polls" to support their bloody business. We're told that this is "democracy in action." But this type of democracy rarely cuts both ways. Although similar polls show that most Americans (as high as 90%) want prayer in public schools, the courts and Congress are still opposed. Why? The leverage of some special interest groups is greater than others, and without the anchor of God's law, humanism will always be promoted.

Theocracy and Democracy

Theocracy and the democratic process are not mutually exclusive. In a theocracy, where the democratic process is retained, the people acknowledge that "God rules in the affairs of men" (Benjamin Franklin's exhortation to the Constitutional Convention). Our founding fathers spoke in theocratic terms. Benjamin Franklin expressed the theocratic/democratic ideal when he quoted Psalm 127:1 during the Convention: "Except the LORD build the house [theocracy], they labour in vain that build it [democratic process]." In the same speech, Franklin continued: "I firmly believe this and I also believe that, without His concurring aid, we shall succeed in this political building no better than the builders of Babel...."[33]

Abraham Lincoln expressed similar sentiments, when on April 30, 1863, he appointed a "National Fast Day."

[I]t is the duty of nations as well as of men to own their dependence upon the overruling power of God, to confess their sins and transgressions in humble sorrow yet with assured hope that genuine repentance will lead to mercy and pardon, and to recognize the sublime truth, announced in the Holy Scriptures and proven by all history: *that those nations only are blessed whose God is the Lord.*

And, insomuch as we know that, by His divine law, nations like individuals are subjected to punishments and chastisements in this world, may we not justly fear that the awful calamity of civil war, which now desolates the land may be but a punishment inflicted upon us for our presumptuous sins to the needful end of our national reformation as a whole people? We have been the recipients of the choicest bounties of Heaven. We have been preserved these many years in peace and prosperity. We have grown in numbers, wealth and power as no other nation has grown. But we have forgotten God. We have forgotten the gracious hand which has preserved us in peace, and multiplied and enriched and strengthened us; and we have vainly imagined, in the deceitfulness of our hearts, that all these blessings were produced by some superior wisdom and virtue of our own. Intoxicated with unbroken success, we have become too self-sufficient to feel the necessity of redeeming and preserving grace, too proud to pray to the God that made us![34]

Lincoln understood the relationship between theocratic and democratic concepts: (1) God rules over the nations; (2) man is responsible for his actions; and (3) "nations like individuals are subjected to punishments and chastisements in this world." Lincoln's message is the warp (theocracy) and woof (democratic process) of a blessed nation.

Notes

1. See Gary DeMar, *God and Government*, 3 vols. (Atlanta, GA: American Vision, 1990).
2. Response to Ed Dobson and Ed Hindson, "Apocalypse Now?: What Fundamentalists Believe About the End of the World," *Policy Review* (Fall 1986), 6, 17–22. Rushdoony's response appears in the Winter 1987 issue, 88. See Gary DeMar, *Ruler of the Nations: Biblical Principles for Civil Government* (Atlanta, GA: American Vision, 1987), 3–38.
3. Gabriel Sivan, *The Bible and Civilization* (New York: Quadrangle/The New York Times Book Co., 1973), 145.
4. Carl F. H. Henry, "The New Coalitions," *Christianity Today* (November 17, 1989), 26. For a similar appraisal, see Rodney Clapp, "Democracy as Heresy," *Christianity Today* (February 20, 1987), 17–23.
5. Carl F. H. Henry, *God Revelation and Authority*, 6 vols. (Waco, TX: Word Books, 1979), 4:8.
6. Henry, *God Revelation and Authority*, 4:8.
7. Carl F. H. Henry, *Aspects of Christian Social Ethics* (Grand Rapids, MI: Eerdmans, 1964), 127.
8. Greg L. Bahnsen, "The Theonomic Position on God and Politics," in Gary Scott Smith, ed., *God and Politics: Four Views on the Reformation of Civil Government* (Phillipsburg, NJ: Presbyterian and Reformed, 1989), 53, note 25.
9. David Held, *Models of Democracy* (Stanford, CA: Stanford University Press, 1987), 1.
10. Quoted in A. Marvyn Davies, *Foundation of American Freedom: Calvinism in the Development of Democratic Thought and Action* (Nashville, TN: Abingdon Press, 1955), 11.

11. Letter to Lord Say and Seal, quoted by Perry Miller and Thomas H. Johnson, eds., *The Puritans: A Sourcebook of Their Writings*, 2 vols. (New York: Harper and Row, [1938] 1963), 1:209–10. Also see Edwin Powers, *Crime and Punishment in Early Massachusetts: 1620–1692* (Boston, MA: Beacon Press, 1966), 55.

12. Alexander Hamilton, James Madison, and John Jay, *The Federalist*, Jacob E. Cooke, ed. (Middletown, CT: Wesleyan University Press, 1961), 61.

13. Ferdinand Lundberg, *The Myth of Democracy* (New York: Lyle Stuart, 1989), 12.

14. Edmund S. Morgan, *The Puritan Dilemma: The Story of John Winthrop* (Boston, MA: Little, Brown and Company, 1958), 90.

15. *Training Manual*, No. 2000–25 (Washington, DC: War Department, 1928), 91.

16. C. Gregg Singer, *John Calvin: His Roots and Fruits* (Nutley, NJ: Presbyterian and Reformed, 1977), 43.

17. John Adams, quoted by Gilbert Chinard, *Honest John Adams* (Boston, MA: Little, Brown and Co., [1933] 1961), 241 in John Eidsmoe, "The Christian America Response to National Confessionalism," in Gary Scott Smith, ed., *God and Politics: Four Views on the Reformation of Civil Government* (Phillipsburg, NJ: Presbyterian and Reformed, 1989), 227–28. C. Gregg Singer writes: "The coming of democracy, some fifty years later [after the drafting of the Constitution], began a process of secularization of American political thought, and that equality implied in the Reformed doctrine of the priesthood of the believers was transformed into the democratic concept of equalitarianism which came to America as a result of the French Revolution. It is pertinent to note that this secularized version of Presbyterianism must logically lead to a democratic despotism because its doctrine of 'the priesthood of the voter' is devoid of any Biblical foundation and denies that man is a sinner by nature" (*John Calvin*, 43).

18. Francis A. Schaeffer, *The Church at the End of the Twentieth Century* (1970) in *The Complete Works of Francis A. Schaeffer: A Christian Worldview*, 5 vols. (Westchester, IL: Crossway Books, 1982), 4:27.

19. Schaeffer, *The Church at the End of the Twentieth Century*, 4:27.

20. Winthrop, "Discourse on Arbitrary Government," *Winthrop Papers*, 5:473. Quoted in Powers, *Crime and Punishment in Early Massachusetts*, 253.

21. Clyde Wilson, "Cultural Revolutions," *Chronicles* (November 1989), 6.

22. John Dewey, "Democracy and Educational Administration," *School and Society* (April 3, 1937). Quoted in Thomas R. Dye and L. Harmon Zeigler, *The Irony of Democracy: An Uncommon Introduction to American Politics*, 4th ed. (North Scituate, MA: Duxbury Press, 1978), 7.

23. Quoted in Eidsmoe, "Christian America Response," 228, note 15.

24. Ralph Henry Gabriel, *The Course of American Democratic Thought*, 2nd ed. (New York: Ronald Press, [1940] 1956), 14.

25. Dye and Zeigler, *The Irony of Democracy*, 7.

26. *Johnson and Graham's Lessee v. William M'Intosh*, Wheaton, 543, 572. Quoted in Gabriel, *The Course of American Democratic Thought*, 16.

27. Joseph Story, *Miscellaneous Writings* (1835), 74. Quoted in Gabriel, *The Course of American Democratic Thought*, 17.

28. Ralph Barton Perry, *Puritanism and Democracy* (New York: Vanguard Press, 1944), 152.

29. Perry, *Puritanism and Democracy*, 152 and 153.

30. Claes G. Ryn, *Democracy and the Ethical Life: A Philosophy of Politics and Community* (Baton Rouge, LA: Louisiana State University Press, 1978), 3.

31. E.J. Dionne, Jr., "Religion and Politics," *New York Times*, (September 15, 1987). Quoted in Robert Wuthnow, *The Struggle for America's Soul: Evangelicals, Liberals, and Secularism* (Grand Rapids, MI: Eerdmans, 1989), 22.

32. Robert Wuthnow, *The Struggle for America's Soul*, x.

33. Benjamin Franklin, "Motion for Prayers in the Convention," *The Works of Benjamin Franklin*, Federal edition, ed. John Bigelow (New York and London: The Knickerbocker Press, 1904), 2:337–338.

34. Abraham Lincoln, "Proclamation Appointing a National Fast Day," April 30, 1863, *The Collected Works of Abraham Lincoln*, ed. Roy P. Bassler (New Brunswick, NJ: Rutgers University Press, 1953), 6:155–156.

CHRISTOPHER COLUMBUS AND THE FLAT EARTH MYTH

HOW MANY ELEMENTARY-SCHOOL STUDENTS ARE TAUGHT THAT PRIOR to the progressive thinking of Christopher Columbus any ship that journeyed beyond the horizon feared falling off the edge of the earth? Columbus supposedly stood firm against the religious and scientific leaders of his day proposing that the earth was round and not flat. History books tell the story that the learned men of the day ridiculed the explorer's theory of a round earth.

While a historical account of one man doing battle with the religious and academic establishment of his day makes interesting copy, none of it is true. "Columbus, like all educated people of his time, knew that the world was round...."[1] The shape of the earth was not even a topic for debate in Columbus's time; it was an established fact.

Real Myths

Daniel J. Boorstin, an accomplished historian, writes that "The greatest obstacle to discovering the shape of the earth, the continents, and the ocean was not ignorance but the illusion of knowledge."[2] Early observers of earth's landscape and the heavens that were beyond their grasp put forth theories of design that were picturesque but woefully inaccurate. A survey of ancient cultures, from Chaldean to Chinese, reveals a great number of mistaken assumptions about the structure of the cosmos. "All who leave the earth go to the moon," declared an Upanishad, an ancient Hindu text, "which is swallowed by their breath during the first half of the month."[3] The Bible, however, paints an altogether different cosmological picture. While ancient pagan astronomers believed that the sun and moon shared attributes of deity, the Bible describes them as created objects with no power over the destiny of man.

> The heavens were personified by the Mesopotamians as the god, Anu, and they were regarded by the Egyptians as the divine Mother; but to the Hebrews they were but one aspect of Yahweh's power and glory. The Mesopotamians, again, conceived of the sun as Shamash, the god

of justice; the Egyptians invested it with the properties of a divine creator; but the Hebrews merely accounted for it as one of the luminaries created by Yahweh. The moon was similarly worshipped by the Babylonians as the god Sin, and the stars were thought to determine the destiny of man; but to the Hebrews they were created by God.[4]

The Bible teaches that the universe had a beginning, that it was created by God *ex nihilo*, out of nothing. Such a belief system was a far cry from anything competing cosmologies had to offer. Not even Plato's demiurge is similar to the self-existent God of the Bible.

Boorstin and others have charged that Christian theologians, along with their pagan competitors, impeded the progress of exploration with their unscientific theories of astronomy and geography. No doubt there were some Christians who adopted theories that could not stand up to modern scientific scrutiny, but these were in the minority. Moreover, they had little or no following among the faithful.[5] The most influential of Christian writers, however, did not adopt mythological descriptions of the construction of the universe, including the myth of a flat earth.

Through Greek-Colored Glasses

Medieval science as practiced by Christians went astray when "the Bible was...read through 'Greek' spectacles."[6] Certainly the Greeks were right in many of their observations, but it was an almost religious attachment to Greek cosmology that was the West's greatest impediment to further discovery and scientific advance. The Greeks, specifically Aristotle, put forth the geocentric theory, the belief that the earth is the physical center of the universe.

Galileo Galilei's (1564–1642) struggle to get a hearing for his scientific views is often depicted as a war between religion and science, with the Christian religion being the chief antagonist. Like the Columbus myth, the facts surrounding the Galileo affair are not quite what they seem. Giorgio de Santillana, author of *The Crime of Galileo*, "argues that the Galileo affair was not a confrontation between 'the scientist' and a religious credo at all. Ironically 'the major part of the Church intellectuals were on the side of Galileo,' de Santillana notes, 'while the clearest opposition to him came from secular ideas' (i.e., from the academic philosophers."[7]

Galileo's "sin" was that he attacked "Aristotelian philosophy—and all the metaphysical, spiritual, and social consequences" the Church "associated with it."[8] For the most part, the formulation of religious and moral laws were based on Aristotelian philosophy, not the Bible.

The reason some churchmen resisted giving up Aristotelian physics and cosmology was because these were intimately tied to an overall vision of moral and social life. If that tie were broken, they feared morality itself would be destroyed. Hence Galileo seemed to promote doctrines that were not only wrong but dangerous.[9]

The Church in Galileo's day was reading the Bible and the world through the blurred vision of Aristotle (384–322 B.C.). Aristotle attempted to present a comprehensive explanation of reality without any reference to the Christian God. His "unmoved mover" or "first cause" was a principle of existence, not a personal being. For Aristotle the universe was eternal, without beginning or end, and man had no individual immortality, doctrines that contradicted biblical revelation. It was Thomas Aquinas (1224–1274) who hoped to teach Aristotle to "speak like a Christian,"[10] to harmonize Aristotelian philosophy with Christianity. By the time of Galileo, the views of Aristotle had become the views of the Church. So then, it was pagan Greece that led the Church astray, not a supposed flawed biblical cosmology.

Galileo opposed the prevailing cosmology adopted by the church, a cosmology that was shaped by Aristotle.

Flat or Round?

Ancient cosmologists conceived of the earth resting on some rather peculiar foundations. "Some pictured it as riding upon the back of four giant elephants, which perched atop a giant turtle that spent its day meandering about in a sea of milk."[11] The most famous depiction of ancient cosmology is that of Atlas supporting the earth on his shoulders. None of these cosmologies solved anything since they did not explain what was supporting the support. Atlas had to stand

Thomas Aquinas hoped to teach Aristotle to "speak like a Christian," to harmonize his philosophy with Christianity.

on something, and that something had to rest on something, and that something.... You get the picture.

The Bible, on the other hand, does not engage in speculative considerations of the earth's external foundations. It simply states that God "stretches out the north over empty space, and *hangs the earth on nothing*" (Job 26:7). Job was not influenced by the "naive view of his age about the universe, and conceived of the earth as a heavenly body floating in space, like the sun, moon, and stars."[12]

Those who accuse the Bible of teaching a flat earth point to how the Bible speaks of "four corners" (Isaiah 11:2 and Revelation 7:1) and "four winds" (Jeremiah 49:36 and Matthew 24:31). There is nothing unusual or unscientific about depicting the earth as having four corners. The modern compass works in terms of a linear perspective. The Bible references direction by north, east, south, and west (Genesis 28:14). Flat maps have always been used to plot direction.

This second-century map drawn by Claudius Ptolemy depicts Asia stretching much farther around the globe than is accurate. There was no question of a flat earth.

The Hebrew and Greek words translated "corner" are best understood as "directions" or "headings."

The division of all geography into four quadrants (northeast, northwest, southwest, and southeast), with the "origin of coordinates" at the location of the observer, is standard practice in all surveying and navigation.... The "four angles" of the earth means simply the four directions.[13]

The myth of Atlas supporting the earth on his shoulders ignores the demand for an ultimate foundation.

The Bible's description of four directional points is little different from modern-day usage. "Four corners" is used metaphorically, both in the Bible and in every day usage, because of the difficulty of describing linear movement on a globe. When is the last time you took a globe on a trip? Why should we expect the Bible to describe reality in a way different from the way we describe reality?

In addition, the Bible expresses theological concepts as interpretive models. For example the Bible pictures the earth as an altar, with four corners (Revelation 7:1; 9:13–21). The cherubim have four wings (Ezekiel 1). The Hebrew word for "corner" literally means "wings." The garment worn by each Hebrew male was to have four "wings" or "corners," so that his garment was analogous to a house or tent which he carried with him at all times (Numbers 15:38; Deuteronomy 22:12; Haggai 2:12). The Garden of Eden, which had four rivers flowing out to water the whole earth, pictures the Earth as having corners. Heaven is also described as a dwelling place, a house (John 14:2).

> So, when the Bible uses language that indicates that the earth is flat, that it has ends, and that it has corners, we are to understand such language in its Biblical context. And that Biblical context is the house-model of the world, seen in the glory cloud, the Garden of Eden, the Tabernacle, the Temple, the holy land, the entire earth, the human body, the clothing of the human body, the cherubim, etc. We are *not* to try to stretch this language to answer cosmological questions which it was not intended to address....[14]

If the earth is flat or box-shaped like a house, then Jesus is a door, vine, and temple with four corners (John 2:21). Similarly, a Christian is said to be "a temple of the Holy Spirit" (1 Corinthians 6:19).

The Flat-Earth Culprit

How and why did the flat-earth myth get started? The legend was popularized by Washington Irving in the three-volume *History of the Life and Voyages of Christopher Columbus* (1828). Irving, best known for "The Legend of Sleepy Hollow" and "Rip Van Winkle," applied his fiction-writing skills and fabricated a supposed confrontation that Columbus had with churchmen who maintained that the Bible taught that the earth was flat. No such encounter ever took place. Samuel Eliot Morison, a noted Columbus biographer, tells it this way:

The result is that wonderful chapter where [Irving describes Columbus as] "an obscure navigator, a member of no learned society, destitute of all the trappings and circumstances which sometimes give oracular authority to dullness, and depending on the mere force of natural genius," [who] sustains his thesis of a spherical globe against "pedantic bigotry" of flat-earth churchmen, fortified by texts from the Bible, Lactantius and Saint Augustine, until he began to feel nervous about the Inquisition.[15]

Morison describes the story as "misleading and mischievous nonsense,…one of the most popular Columbian myths."[16]

Washington Irving popularized the legend that the churchmen of Columbus's day believed in a flat earth.

Irving had a bad habit of fictionalizing history. His *History of New York from the Beginning of the World to the End of the Dutch Dynasty* (1809) was published under the pseudonym Diederich Knickerbocker. "He perpetrated a prolonged hoax in order to persuade the reading public that Knickerbocker was a real person."[17] In the 1848 edition of the *History of New York* Irving admitted that he had embellished "the few facts" he could collect "with fragments of [his] own brain."[18]

Irving's fictionalized account of Columbus's confrontation with the "foolish clergymen at the 'council of Salamanca'"[19] has anti-clericalism written all over it. I would venture a guess that the reason the flat-earth myth persists is that it gives the Church a drubbing and makes the Bible into a book of superstition and fantasy which should not consulted by "moderns."

Drawing from "fragments of his own brain," Irving's fictionalized account of Columbus describes him as being "assailed with citations from the Bible and the Testament: the book of Genesis, the psalms of

David, the orations of the Prophets, the epistles of the apostles, and the gospels of the Evangelists. To these were added expositions of various saints and reverend Commentators…. Such are specimens of the errors and prejudices, the mingled ignorance and erudition, and the pedantic bigotry, with which Columbus had to contend."[20] There is only one problem with Irving's account: "It is fabrication, and it is largely upon this fabric that the idea of a medieval flat earth was established."[21]

This painting by Nicolò Barabino depicts Columbus as exhausted from ar- guing with ridiculing clergymen.

Attacking the Church

The modern mind cannot bear the thought that people who lived far before the twentieth century could have gotten anything right relating to science. Even as late as 1961 the *Encyclopedia Britannica* perpetuated the myth of a round-earth solution for Columbus's voyages: "Before Columbus proved the world was round, people thought the horizon marked its edge. Today we know better." The people knew better in Columbus's day.

A 1983 textbook for fifth-graders misinformed students by report- ing that Columbus "felt he would eventually reach the Indies in the East. Many Europeans still believed that the world was flat. Columbus, they thought, would fall off the earth."[22] A 1982 text for eighth-graders said that Europeans "believed…that a ship could sail out to sea just so far before it fell off the edge of the sea…. The people of Europe a thousand years ago knew little about the world."[23]

In the 1988 edition of *Atlas of the World* we read, "In the Middle Ages the earth was thought to be a flat plain surrounded by waters, with

Jerusalem at its center and Paradise somewhere in the Far East. Then, in the late 15th and early 16th centuries, Europe's conquest of the sea revolutionized man's knowledge of his planet and helped to give Europe a new supremacy in world affairs."[24] In fact, the Pythagoreans of the sixth century B.C. taught that the world was spherical and Aristotle proved it by observing "during an eclipse that the earth casts a spherical shadow on the moon."[25] Boorstin asserts that from A.D. 300 to at least 1300 Europe suffered under what he describes as "scholarly amnesia" due to the rise of "Christian faith and dogma [that] suppressed the useful image of the world that had been so slowly, so painfully, and so scrupulously drawn by ancient geographers."[26] Boorstin claims that the scientific advances made by the Greeks were dismantled by Christians based on an appeal to the Bible. It is actually the Bible, independent of any competing cosmology, which supports the empirical data that the earth is a globe:

> Scientific demonstration of the earth's rotundity was enforced by religion; God made the earth a sphere because that was the most perfect form. In the Old Testament there is a reference to this in Isaiah xl.22: "It is he that sitteth upon the circle of the earth"—"circle" being the translation of the Hebrew *khug*, sphere.[27]

Of course, not all Christians made appeals to the Bible for their views of the shape of the earth. Actually, the Bible has little to say on the subject. Nothing in the Bible, however, contradicts the empirical data. For example, Bede (673–735), monk of Jarow and "the Father of English history," maintained "that the earth is a globe that can be called a perfect sphere because the surface irregularities of mountains and valleys are so small in comparison to its vast size." He specifies that the "earth is 'round' *not* in the sense of 'circular' but in the sense of a ball."[28] Historian Edwin Scott Gaustad confirms the historical and scientific record that the earth was believed to be ball-shaped: "Cartographers drew it so; astronomers reckoned it so; mariners intended to prove it so."[29] Proof is what was needed. Morison writes:

> That it was theoretically possible to reach the Orient by sailing west every educated man would admit, since every educated man knew the earth to be a sphere, but nobody had done anything to test the theory. In 1476, when Columbus reached Lisbon, the proposition of sailing west to reach the Orient was at about the same stage as man-made flight in 1900—theoretically possible but full of practical difficulties.[30]

In 1492 Columbus supplied the proof to substantiate the long-held propagated theory that the earth was indeed a globe.

Deep and Wide

The debate in Columbus's day was not over whether the earth was flat or round. Many scholars contend that the width of the ocean was the crucial factor; the distance between continents determined the cost and feasibility of an expedition. "The issue was the width of the ocean; and therein the opposition was right."[31] The common criticism of Columbus was that he underestimated the circumference of the earth and the width of the ocean by a significant number of miles. "In fact, the distance Columbus was planning to cover [based on accurate maps] was 10,600 miles by air."[32]

> Educated opinion in Columbus's day was that the earth was a sphere of about 24,000 miles in circumference. Therefore, since China was some 8,000 miles to the east, the conventional wisdom held it impractical to sail west for 16,000 miles to reach the Orient. That is why Columbus had such a hard time finding backers for his concept.
>
> Columbus calculated the earth's circumference at about 18,000 miles, and he also believed Ptolemy's too-large estimate of the eastward extent of Asia. Combining these two errors, he came to the conclusion Japan lay about 3,000 miles to the west of the Canary Islands.[33]

Many contend that Columbus's proposal to sail around the globe was flawed because he underestimated the circumference of the earth.

Others claim that Columbus made additional mistakes, for example, underestimating the length of a degree. Columbus may have been misled by relying on inaccurate information from Marco Polo's *Description of the World*, Cardinal D. Ailly's *Imago Mundi,* and a statement in the Apocryphal Second Book of Esdras, which stated that the Earth consisted of six parts land and one part sea, instead of the real 3:1 ratio. "To make matters worse, he made all his calculations in Italian miles, unaware that they were shorter than the Arabic miles used in many contemporary maps."[34]

It's possible that if Columbus had been correctly informed on the earth's circumference and the length of a degree, he might have stayed home! Ptolemy's mistaken calculations were "a happy mistake. For it encouraged navigators like Columbus and Cabot to believe that the Atlantic could be crossed in a reasonable time."[35]

Columbus would never have arrived in the Orient based on his calculations. Providentially, the Americas stood in his way.

Despite the charge that Columbus's measurements may have been flawed, "Columbus always rates the highest accolades from scholars when it comes to his seamanship. He was, without question, the finest sailor of his time."[36] Virtually every student of Columbus accepts the opinion of Bartolome de Las Casas who wrote in his *Historia de las Indias* that "Christopher Columbus surpassed all of his contemporaries in the art of navigation."[37]

Conclusion

The Columbus myth is another example of historical revisionism, the attempt by secularists to cast the Church in a negative light. Liberal historians relish the fact that schoolchildren all over the country are being taught that Christians are ignorant, flat-earth kooks who will not listen to reason and science. When the facts of history are accurately surveyed, however, we discover true science never conflicts with the Bible. Scientific misinformation is never promoted through an accurate understanding of the Bible. Instead, the manipulation of truth always occurs *outside* the biblical worldview.

Notes

1. Zvi Dor-Ner, *Columbus and the Age of Discovery* (New York: William Morrow and Company, Inc., 1991), 72.
2. Daniel J. Boorstin, *The Discoverers: A History of Man's Search to Know His World and Himself* (New York: Random House, 1983), 86.
3. Quoted in Boorstin, *The Discoverers*, 87.
4. C.F. Whitley, *The Genius of Ancient Israel* (Amsterdam: Philo Press, 1969), 61–62. Quoted in Kenny Barfield, *Why the Bible is Number 1: The World's Sacred Writings in the Light of Science* (Grand Rapids, MI: Baker Book House, 1988), 107.
5. Jeffrey Burton Russell, *Inventing the Flat Earth: Columbus and Modern Historians* (New York: Praeger Publishers, 1991), 4
6. R. Hooykaas, *Religion and the Rise of Modern Science* (Grand Rapids, MI: Eerdmans, 1972), xiii.
7. Nancy R. Pearcey and Charles B. Thaxton, *The Soul of Science: Christian Faith and Natural Philosophy* (Wheaton, IL: Crossway Books, 1994), 38.
8. Pearcey and Thaxton, *The Soul of Science*, 39.
9. Pearcey and Thaxton, *The Soul of Science*, 39.
10. Quoted in Mark A. Noll, *The Scandal of the Evangelical Mind* (Grand Rapids, MI: Eerdmans, 1994), 45.
11. Barfield, *Why the Bible is Number 1*, 107.
12. M. Buttenwieser, quoted in John E. Hartley, *The Book of Job* (NICOT) (Grand Rapids, MI: Eerdmans, 1988), 365.
13. Henry M. Morris, *The Biblical Basis for Modern Science* (Grand Rapids, MI: Baker Book House, 1984), 247.
14. James B. Jordan, "The Geocentricity Question" (1981) in Gary North "Geocentricity-Geostationism: The Flat Earth Temptation," Position Paper (November 1992), 7.
15. Samuel Eliot Morison, *Admiral of the Ocean Sea: A Life of Christopher Columbus* (Boston, MA: Little, Brown and Co., 1942), 89.

16. Morison, *Admiral of the Ocean Sea*, 89.
17. Russell, *Inventing the Flat Earth*, 52.
18. Washington Irving, *A History of New York*, ed. Michael L. Black and Nancy B. Black (Boston, 1994). Quoted in Russell, *Inventing the Flat Earth*, 52.
19. Russell, *Inventing the Flat Earth*, 52.
20. Quoted in Russell, *Inventing the Flat Earth*, 53.
21. Russell, *Inventing the Flat Earth*, 53.
22. *America Past and Present* (Scott Foresman, 1983), 98. Quoted in Russell, *Inventing the Flat Earth*, 3.
23. *We the People* (Heath, 1982), 28–29. Quoted in Russell, *Inventing the Flat Earth*, 3.
24. Joseph L. Gardner, ed., *Atlas of the World* (Pleasantville, NY: The Reader's Digest Association, 1988), 56.
25. Richard Shenkman, *Legends, Lies, and Cherished Myths of American History* (New York: William Morrow, 1988), 13.
26. Boorstin, *The Discoverers*, 100.
27. Samuel Eliot Morison, *The European Discovery of America: The Northern Voyages* (New York: Oxford University Press, 1971), 6.
28. Russell, *Inventing the Flat Earth*, 20.
29. Edwin S. Gaustad, *A Religious History of America* (New York: Harper & Row, 1966), 3.
30. Samuel Eliot Morison, *Christopher Columbus, Mariner* (New York: Mentor, 1954), 14.
31. Morison, *Admiral of the Ocean Sea*, 89.
32. Kenneth C. Davis, *Don't Know Much About History: Everything You Need to Know About American History but Never Learned* (New York: Crown Publishers, 1990), 6.
33. Sam Dargan, "Will the Real Christopher Columbus Please Stand Up," *World* (October 7, 1989), 20. Not everyone agrees that Columbus miscalculated the circumference of the earth. "Columbus made the statement—*in writing*—that the circumference of the earth at the equator was 20,400 miles." (Paul H. Chapman, *Discovering Columbus* [Columbus, GA: The Institute for the Study of American Cultures, 1992], 24.
34. "How Columbus Discovered the 'New World,'" *How in the World? A Fascinating Journey Through the World of Human Ingenuity* (Pleasantville, NY: The Reader's Digest Association, 1990), 357.
35. Morison, *The European Discovery of America*, 7.
36. Robert H. Fuson, *The Log of Christopher Columbus* (Camden, MN: International Marine Publishing Co., 1987), 29.
37. Quoted in Fuson, *The Log of Christopher Columbus*, 29.

APPENDIX D

GEORGE L'HOTE
V.
CITY OF NEW ORLEANS
(1900)

SINCE THE PUBLICATION OF AMERICA'S CHRISTIAN HISTORY, I RECEIVED a letter from Robert Boston, Assistant Director of Communications for Americans United for Separation of Church and State (AU) and author of *Why the Religious Right Is Wrong about Separation of Church and State.* Boston objected to the analysis I made in *America's Christian History* about the AU pamphlet that discusses a New Orleans prostitution case. AU claims that this case overruled the religious language and the conclusions of the *Holy Trinity* (1892) case that America was a "Christian nation." I claimed that "research shows that no such court case exists." In his letter to me, Boston wrote:

> Before assuming that we on the staff of Americans United fabricate court cases—in effect calling us liars—you might have wanted to pick up the phone and ask me for the citation of the case referred to in the AU pamphlet. I would have been happy to provide it. It is George L'Hote v. City of New Orleans, 177 U.S. 587 (1900).

The truth is that American Vision staff members did call AU repeatedly, asking for documentation to the New Orleans case and for information about the anonymously written pamphlet. AU offered no documentation. We were told that the case was "archaic and obscure" and that the only reference to it they could find was in a footnote in a doctoral dissertation. At no time were we told that Robert Boston was the author of the pamphlet.

In addition, since the AU pamphlet stated that this allusive case occurred five years after the *Trinity* ruling, we made a search of all 1897 Supreme Court cases having anything to do with New Orleans or prostitution. Nothing turned up. Americans United was mistaken in claiming that the New Orleans case came five years after the *Trinity* ruling. The New Orleans case was in fact decided in 1900, eight years after the *Holy Trinity* ruling.

Now that we have finally identified this "archaic and obscure" case, we can now analyze its contents and see if it comports with Boston's assertions. The AU pamphlet claims that David Brewer "seemed to step away" from his statement that America was a Christian nation when he ruled in favor of allowing prostitution in one zone of the city, ignoring religious arguments to the contrary. An expanded version of Boston's analysis of the New Orleans case appears in his *Why the Religious Right Is Wrong about Separation of Church and State.* Boston states it this way: "The New Orleans dispute arose when a Methodist church sought an injunction to bar implementation of a city ordinance allowing prostitution in one zone in the city. The Methodists argued the measure would 'destroy the morals, peace and good order of the neighborhood.'"[1]

Repeating the mistake of the AU pamphlet, Boston states that the case "came along five years after the *Holy Trinity* ruling." As in the pamphlet, the name of the case is not given. Are Boston and AU trying to hide something by this omission?

George L'Hote v. City of New Orleans is not about the legalization of prostitution or the dilution of religious principles. In fact, the court continually describes prostitutes as "notoriously abandoned," "lewd," and "immoral"—value judgments in keeping with the *Holy Trinity* case of 1892. While prostitution was illegal in New Orleans, it was still regulated. The Common Council set the boundaries of a red-light district by ordinance. No "'public prostitute or woman notoriously abandoned to lewdness' was allowed to 'occupy, inhabit, live or sleep in any house, room or closet' except within the district. The ordinance meticulously detailed where the district began and ended: 'South side of Custom House street from Basin to Robertson street...' and so on. Outside those boundaries, no one could lawfully rent space to such a woman; and it was illegal to 'establish or carry on a house of prostitution or assignation' except in the zone. Of course, to carry on inside the district was just as illegal, but the Common Council ignored that troublesome fact."[2]

Boston gives us the impression that the case concerned the legality of prostitution. However, Brewer's opinion clearly states that "the ordinance does not attempt to give to persons of such character license to carry on their business in any way they see fit, or, indeed, *to carry it on at all,* or to conduct themselves in such a manner as to disturb the public peace within the prescribed limits" (emphasis mine). He further concludes that the ordinance is "clearly designed to restrain any public manifestation of the vocation which these persons pursue, and to keep so far as possible unseen from public gaze the character of their lives." Brewer considered prostitution to be one "of the difficult social problems of the day" because it "minister[s] to and feed[s] upon human weaknesses, appetites, and passions." This, too, is a biblical value judgment.

Brewer, writing for a unanimous court, argued that such vice was best regulated by the local "police powers" since "they affect *directly* the public health and morals" (emphasis mine). Taking a "states rights" approach, Brewer reasoned, "It has been often said that the police power was not by the Federal Constitution transferred to the nation, but was reserved to the states, and that upon them rests the duty of so exercising it as to protect the public health and morals....*It is no part of the judicial function to determine the wisdom or folly of a regulation by the legislative body in respect to matters of a police nature*" (emphasis mine). Today's Supreme Court should learn from Brewer's federalism. These matters are best left to the states to adjudicate.

The plaintiff, George L'Hote, objected to the city ordinance that designated a part of the city for public prostitution because it devalued his property! "The ordinance, he felt, would attract 'lewd and abandoned women,' and people coming to the area 'to gratify their depraved appetites.' The ordinance thus amounted to a 'taking' of his property, for which he demanded compensation."[3] L'Hote claimed that the ordinance violated the Fifth Amendment to the Constitution which provides that private property shall not "be taken for public use, without *just compensation.*" L'Hote reasoned that since the city established a restricted zone for the "lewd and abandoned women," and since his property was adjacent to the restricted zone, his property would lose its monetary value because of the nature of the residents. The Methodist Episcopal Church reasoned similarly.

L'Hote believed that while he still retained all of his property, its value had so depreciated that he was justified in demanding compensation. The court disagreed. Using L'Hote's logic, all property owners who claim that their property has been adversely affected by the exercise of police powers could claim that their property has been "taken" and would have to be compensated by a county, city, state, or federal government.[4]

The Supreme Court ruled, citing several examples and cases, that in L'Hote's case a "taking" had not occurred. "The truth is," Brewer wrote, "that the exercise of the police power often works pecuniary injury, but the settled rule of this court is that the mere fact of pecuniary injury does not warrant the overthrow of legislation of a police character." Brewer's decision was an exercise in judicial restraint; it addressed the only the issues brought before the court, not the ethical issue of prostitution.

In addition, following the biblical model of decentralized government, Brewer recognized the realities of jurisdictional boundaries. *L'Hote v. City of New Orleans* does not support Robert Boston's assertion that Brewer "seemed to step away" from his 1892 decision that America was a Christian nation. In fact, Brewer's 1905 book, *The United States: A Christian Nation,* shows that Boston and AU are off-base in their understanding of Brewer and the way the Supreme Court should function in terms of its prescribed constitutional powers. While AU did not lie, they certainly shaved the truth.

Notes

1. Robert Boston, *Why the Religious Right Is Wrong about Separation of Church and State* (Buffalo, NY: Prometheus, 1993), 84.
2. Lawrence M. Friedman, *Crime and Punishment in American History* (New York: Basic Books 1993), 227.
3. Friedman, *Crime and Punishment in American History,* 228n.
4. "If the owner complains, seeking just compensation for a taking, government may reply that it has simply regulated under the police power, but has not 'taken' the property and thus need not compensate." Joseph L. Sax, "Taking of Property," *Encyclopedia of the American Constitution,* edited by Leonard W. Levy (New York: Macmillan, 1986), 1856.

APPENDIX E

DAVID BREWER UNDER REVIEW

ROBERT BOSTON, ASSISTANT DIRECTOR OF COMMUNICATIONS FOR AMERICANS United for Separation of Church and State, has taken another dig at David Brewer. Brewer was the Supreme Court Justice who proclaimed in *The Church of the Holy Trinity vs. United States* (1892) that America is a "Christian nation." Boston writes that Brewer's book titled *The United States: A Christian Nation* "is very interesting, and needless to say, never quoted by the Religious Right since it is completely at odds with their view."[1] I find it hard to believe that Boston has read everything that has ever been written by Religious Right authors. He cannot possibly know that Brewer's book has "never been quoted."

I was not aware of the book's existence until I saw it referenced in Stephen L. Carter's *The Culture of Disbelief*, and that only in a note.[2] Robert T. Handy also referred to Brewer's 1905 written work in *Undermined Establishment: Church-State Relations in America, 1880–1920*, also only in a note.[3] Once I knew of Brewer's book, I found a copy, read it, quoted extensively from it, and found that it supported what advocates of America's Christian history have been saying for years.

Boston gives us the impression that secular advocates of church-state separation are well aware of Brewer's book and interact with it. Such is not the case. For example, in "Suggestions for Further Reading Section," Boston lists Leo Pfeffer's *Church, State and Freedom* (1967) as a "classic volume" that "thoroughly examines the history behind the religion clause of the Constitution and looks at contemporary church-state issues."[4] This "classic volume" nowhere refers to Brewer's book, neither in the five-page "Selected Bibliography" (650–54) nor in its discussion of Brewer's *Church of the Holy Trinity vs. United States* ruling.

Anson Phelps Stokes and Leo Pfeffer co-authored *Church and State in the United States*, a revised and updated one-volume edition of the original three-volume work.[5] Like *Church, State and Freedom*, the nine-page bibliography of this book does not list Brewer's book. Even in Stokes and Pfeffer's discussion of the Christian nation thesis, Brewer's book is not referenced. How can Boston accuse "Religious Right" authors of never quoting Brewer's book when authors and books he recommends do not mention it, list it in their bibliographies, or interact with it?

Boston claims that Brewer's book "is completely at odds" with the views of the Christian Right, that is, with those who maintain that America was founded as a Christian nation. Boston writes, quoting Brewer:

"But in what sense can [the United States] be called a Christian nation?" asked Brewer. "Not in the sense that Christianity is the established religion or the people are compelled in any manner to support it. On the contrary, the Constitution specifically provides that 'Congress shall make no law respecting an establishment of religion or prohibiting the free exercise thereof.' Neither is it Christian in the sense that all its citizens are either in fact or in name Christians. On the contrary, all religions have free scope within its borders. Numbers of our people profess other religions, and many reject all."[6]

As far as I know, advocates of the Christian America thesis do not believe the State should either compel people to become Christians or have tax monies collected to support churches. Moreover, the Christian America thesis is not dependent upon the idea "that all its citizens are either in fact or in name Christians." Brewer is simply supporting the constitutional doctrine that *Congress*—America's only *national* legislative body—is prohibited from establishing Christianity as the nation's tax-supported religion. If Brewer doesn't mean this, then why does he, for example, list Maryland's 1776 constitution which states that "the legislature may, in their discretion, lay a general and equal tax, for the support of the Christian religion"?[7] Furthermore, why does Brewer recount that "in several colonies and states a profession of the Christian faith was made an indispensable condition to holding office"?[8] He even mentions North Carolina's constitution that remained in force until 1868, eighty years after the drafting of the United States Constitution and the First Amendment. It reads in part: "That no person who shall deny the being of God or the truth of the Christian religion, or the divine authority either of the Old or New Testaments, or who shall hold religious principles incompatible with the freedom and safety of the State, shall be capable of holding any office or place of trust or profit in the civil department within this State."[9] States were permitted to require a religious test for office holders, a stipulation that Brewer does not refute or take issue with.

Brewer states that the people are not compelled "in any manner to support" the Christian religion, and yet he asserts that the setting aside of Sunday "from the other days as a day of rest is enforced by the legislation of nearly all if not all the States of the Union."[10] Notice that the legislation is *enforced.* Enforcement is the prerogative of civil government and its courts. Brewer summarizes the historical record this way: "By these and other evidences I claim to have shown that the calling of this republic a Christian nation is not a mere pretence but a recognition of an historical, legal and social truth."[11]

Boston first uses Brewer against the "Religious Right" by incorrectly claiming that Brewer's position is "completely at odds with their view."[12] Then he turns around and maintains that the *Holy Trinity* case is "a legal anomaly," an "obscure ruling that has no bearing on the type of church-state relationship the Framers intended for this nation." He goes on to claim that it "cannot seriously be considered today as [an] appropriate guideline for American society."[13] So which is it? Does Brewer support or oppose the agenda of Americans United? Robert Boston has once again demonstrated that he plays fast and loose with the facts.

Notes

1. Robert Boston, *Why the Religious Right Is Wrong about Separation of Church and State* (Buffalo, NY: Prometheus Books, 1993), 84.
2. Stephen L. Carter, *The Culture of Disbelief: How American Law and Politics Trivialize Religious Devotion* (New York: Anchor/Doubleday, [1993] 1994), 292, note 8.
3. Robert T. Handy, *Undermined Establishment: Church-State Relations in America,* 1880–1920 (Lawrenceville, NJ: Princeton University Press, 1991), 13, note 11.
4. Boston, *The Religious Right,* 245.
5. Anson Phelps Stokes and Leo Pfeffer, *Church and State in the United States,* revised one-volume edition (New York: Harper and Row, [1950] 1964).
6. Boston, *Religious Right,* 245. Boston is quoting from David J. Brewer, *The United States: A Christian Nation,* (Philadelphia, PA: The John C. Winston Company, 1905), 12.
7. Brewer, *United States: A Christian Nation,* 22.
8. Brewer, *United States: A Christian Nation,* 22.
9. Brewer, *United States: A Christian Nation,* 24.
10. Brewer, *United States: A Christian Nation,* 56.
11. Brewer, *United States: A Christian Nation,* 46.
12. Boston, *Religious Right,* 85.
13. Boston, *Religious Right,* 85.

APPENDIX F

DEISM AND THE FOUNDING OF AMERICA

THE CLAIM IS OFTEN MADE THAT DEISM WAS THE PREVAILING RELIGIOUS worldview leading up to and including the Constitutional era. Unfortunately, many who make this claim rarely follow the classic definition of deism in making their assessment of the religious beliefs of those who qualify as the "founders of America" and the documents they drafted. Here's a typical definition of Deism:

> The primary leaders of the so-called founding fathers of our nation were not Bible-believing Christians; they were deists. Deism was a philosophical belief that was widely accepted by the colonial intelligentsia at the time of the American Revolution. Its major tenets included belief in human reason as a reliable means of solving social and political problems and belief in a supreme deity who created the universe to operate solely by natural laws.[1]
>
> Some Christians were of course involved in the shaping of our nation, but their influence was minor compared to the ideological contributions of the Deists who pressed for the formation of a secular nation.[2]

Thomas Paine authored *Common Sense* in 1776 in which he appealed to the Bible to support his anti-monarchy views.

The above quotation is representative of the current secular understanding of the founding of America, but is it an accurate definition of deism, and does it truly represent the views of the founders?

Thomas Paine and Common Sense

Deism is a philosophical belief system that claims that God exists but is not involved in the world. While God created all things and set the universe in motion, He is no longer involved in its operation. Given this definition of deism, which of the founding fathers were deists? Then there's the question of who is a "founding father." Thomas Paine is considered a founding father even though he had no hand in drafting the Declaration of Rights and Grievances, the Declaration of Independence, the Articles of Confederation, or the Constitution.

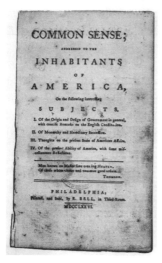

Common Sense made frequent references to the Bible rather than secular sources

Paine's *Common Sense* did put forth arguments for independence from Great Britain, but how did Paine argue his case? What were his sources? Did he follow deistic lines of argument similar to those of the French revolutionaries? "He constructed his arguments from materials that were familiar to the average colonist, favoring allusions to popular history, nature, and scripture rather than Montesquieu, Tacitus, and Cicero."[3] There is no hint of deism in *Common Sense*, but there is a substantial appeal to the Bible, something a deist would never do.

A. J. Ayer remarks that "the first argument that Paine brings against the institution of kingship is scriptural."[4] Paine declared that "government by kings was first introduced into the world by the Heathens, from which the children of Israel copied the custom.... As the exalting of one man so greatly above the rest cannot be justified on the equal rights of nature, so neither can it be defended on the authority of scripture; for the will of the Almighty, as declared by Gideon and the prophet Samuel, expressly disapproves of government by kings. All anti-monarchical parts of scripture have been smoothly glossed over in monarchical governments, but they undoubtedly merit the attention of countries which have their governments yet to form. 'Render unto Caesar the things which are Caesar's' is the scriptural doctrine of courts, yet it is no support of monarchical government, for the Jews at that time were without a king, and in a state of vassalage to the Romans."

Paine makes an often neglected point. Using Matthew 22:21 to support the claim that civil governments are not to be questioned or confronted by lesser magistrates or the people is misplaced and misunderstood. Israel was under the domination of Rome. We don't live under Caesar today, and the Americans didn't live under Caesar in the eighteenth century. Their dispute with the British monarchy and Parliament was over contractual issues. England had violated an agreement made by two sovereign powers and governments. Actually, in terms of the states, there had been multiple violations because there were 13 state governments.

Paine has an extended discussion of Judges 8:22–23 where he describes "the King of Heaven" to be Israel's "proper sovereign." He then spends several pages quoting, discussing, and making application of the importance of 1 Samuel 8 to the modern situation. He concludes this section of *Common Sense* with these words: "In short, monarchy and succession have laid (not this or that kingdom only) by the world in blood and ashes. 'Tis a form of government which the word of God bears testimony against, and blood will attend it."

The Later Paine

It's the later Paine, the author of *The Age of Reason*, that secularists turn to in support of their claim that he was a deist and an ardent critic of Christianity and organized religion in general. While *Common Sense* was written in 1776, *The Age of Reason* was published in the early 1790s, after the drafting of the Constitution. While Americans in general embraced *Common Sense*—"fifty-six editions had been printed and 150,000 copies sold by the end of 1776"[5]—there was little support for *The Age of Reason* by Thomas Jefferson, John Adams, Benjamin Rush, John Jay, and Benjamin Franklin:

As for the supposition that the other Founders embraced "The Age of Reason" or its mindset: Jefferson advised Paine never to publish the book. Benjamin Franklin, Paine's patron and friend, gave his protégé the same advice. After reading a draft, Franklin noted: "He who spits against the wind spits in his own face. If men are wicked with religion, what would they be without it?"

John Adams, once a fan of Paine, having received his copy, called Paine a "blackguard"[6] who wrote out of the depths of "a malignant heart." And Washington, previously one of Paine's fiercest advocates, attacked Paine's principles in his Farewell Address (without referring to his name)[7] as unpatriotic and subversive.[8]

John Adams, once a supporter of Paine, called him a "blackguard" after reading his book *The Age of Reason*

Paine's later views were so opposed by the public that he spent his last years in New York in relative obscurity. "Paine had expressed a wish to be buried in a Quaker cemetery, but the Society of Friends denied his request. In attendance at his graveside on his farm were his Quaker friend Wilbert Hicks, "Madame Bonneville, her son Benjamin, and two black men who wished to pay tribute to Paine for his efforts to put an end to slavery. It is probable that a few other persons were there but no one who officially represented either France or the United States."[9] Stokes and Pfeffer, writing in *Church and State in the United States*, state that "For a long time

"Who Wants Me"
A political cartoon depicting
Thomas Paine by
George Cruikshank

Paine, notwithstanding his great contributions to the Revolutionary cause, was held low in American public opinion."[10] Theodore Roosevelt's description of Thomas Paine "as a 'filthy little atheist' represented all too accurately the public estimate"[11] of him at the time. Although Paine was not an atheist—he believed in God and immortality—the expression of his religious views in *The Age of Reason* put him outside the religious mainstream which was generally Christian.

The Thomas Paine of *Common Sense* and the Thomas Paine of *The Age of Reason* must be kept separate, both by time and philosophy. The later Paine cannot be superimposed on the earlier Paine.

Theodore Roosevelt described Thomas Paine as a "filthy little atheist." In reality, Paine remained a theist to his dying day

Without Paine's biblical arguments in *Common Sense* the book would have been studied with great suspicion and might have sunk without a trace. Mark A. Noll, Professor of Christian Thought at Wheaton College, makes a similar argument:

> If Paine's *Age of Reason* (with its dismissive attitude toward the Old Testament) had been published before *Common Sense* (with its full deployment of Scripture in support of republican freedom), the quarrel with Britain may have taken a different course. It is also likely that the allegiance of traditional Christian believers to republican liberty might not have been so thoroughly cemented. And it is possible that the intimate relation between republican reasoning and trust in traditional Scripture, which became so important after the turn of the new century, would not have occurred as it did.[12]

The next time someone says that America was founded by deists, ask them to define deism and produce an official document from the founding era that explicitly uses deistic expressions. When Thomas Paine comes up in a discussion, ask if it's the early Paine or the later Paine. There is a big difference.

"Tom Paine's Nightly Pest" by James Gillray

Notes

1. www.infidels.org/library/modern/farrell_till/myth.html. Christians maintain that reason is reliable but limited. God Himself says, "Come, let us reason together" (Isa. 1:18). The NT tells us to love God with "all your mind" (Luke 10:27). The Bible recognizes that the mind is fallen. This is why we are told to renew the mind (Rom. 12:2).

2. www.infidels.org/library/modern/farrell_till/myth.html

3. Scott Liell, 46 Pages: *Thomas Paine, Common Sense, and the Turning Point to American Independence* (Philadelphia Press, 2003), 20.

4. A.J. Ayer, *Thomas Paine* (New York: Atheneum, 1988), 40. Ayer remarks that that his appeal to the Old Testament is curious "in view of the want of respect he was later to show for the Old Testament" (40).

5. Ayer, *Thomas Paine*, 35.

6. "The Christian religion is, above all the Religions that ever prevailed or existed in ancient or modern Times, the Religion of Wisdom, Virtue, Equity, and humanity, let the Blackguard [scoundrel] Paine say what he will; it is Resignation to God, it is Goodness itself to Man." (John Adams, *The Diary and Autobiography of John Adams*, ed. L.H. Butterfield [Cambridge, MA: The Belknap Press of Harvard University Press, 1962], 3:233–234).

7. "Of all the dispositions and habits which lead to political prosperity, religion and morality are indispensable supports . . . And let us indulge with caution the supposition that morality can be maintained without religion . . . . Reason and experience both forbid us to expect that national morality can prevail to the exclusion of religious principle." (Excerpted from George Washington's 1796 "Farewell Address").

8. Steve Farrell, "Paine's Christianity"—Part 1: www.newsmax.com/archives/articles/2003/9/4/212340.shtml

9. Ayer, *Thomas Paine*, 180.

10. Anson Phelps Stokes and Leo Pfeffer, *Church and State in the United States*, one-volume ed. (New York: Harper & Row, Publishers, 1964), 50.

11. Stokes and Pfeffer, *Church and State in the United States*, 50.

12. Mark A. Noll, *America's God: From Jonathan Edwards to Abraham Lincoln* (New York: Oxford University Press, 2002), 84.

APPENDIX G

JESUS CHRIST
AND THE
FOUNDING OF AMERICA

IF DEISM WAS SO PREVALENT IN THE FOUNDING OF AMERICA, THEN WHY don't the official documents reflect deistic beliefs? Congress proclaimed days of fasting and thanksgiving annually throughout the period when the War for Independence was fought. On March 16, 1776, Congress called for a "day of Humiliation, Fasting and Prayer" throughout the colonies. The Proclamation stated that it is the "indispensable duty of these hitherto free and happy colonies, with true penitence of heart, and the most reverent devotion, publicly to acknowledge the over ruling providence of God; to confess and deplore our offences against him; and to supplicate his interposition for averting the threatened danger, and prospering our strenuous efforts in the cause of freedom, virtue, and posterity." There was the recognition of "God's superintending providence." These statements alone are enough to dispel any notion of deism. But there's more. The people were called on to bewail their "manifold sins and transgressions, and, by a sincere repentance and amendment of life, appease his righteous displeasure, and, through the merits and mediation of Jesus Christ, obtain his pardon and forgiveness; humbly imploring his assistance to frustrate the cruel purposes of our unnatural enemies." James H. Hutson writes that "This document is characteristic of the numerous fasts and thanksgiving day proclamations issued by Congress throughout the Revolutionary War. All contained Christian language, though not in every case a specific invocation of the "merits and mediation of Jesus Christ." Massachusetts ordered that a "suitable Number" of these proclamations be printed so "that each of the religious Assemblies in this Colony, may be furnished with a Copy of the same" and added the motto "God Save This People" as a substitute for the usual "God Save the King."[1]

On November 1, 1777, the Continental Congress proclaimed a day of public thanksgiving for the recent victory at Saratoga. Congress

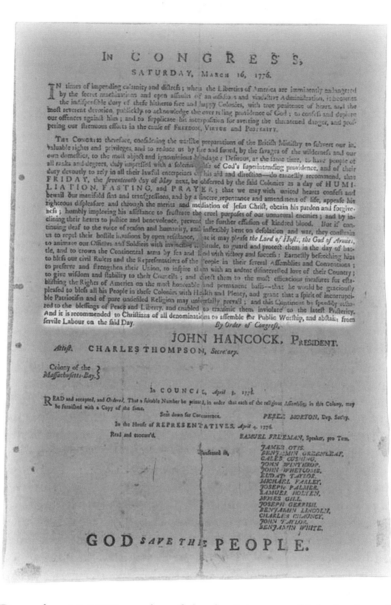

set December 18, 1777 as a day of thanksgiving on which the American people "may express the grateful feelings of their hearts and consecrate themselves to the service of their divine benefactor" and on which they might "join the penitent confession of their manifold sins . . . that it may please God, through the merits of Jesus Christ, mercifully to for-

STATE OF NEW-HAMPSHIRE.

THE COUNCIL and ASSEMBLY of said State, have ordered,-- that the following Proclamation of the Hon'ble Continental CONGRESS, for a General THANKSGIVING throughout the United States, be printed, and sent to the several religious Societies in this State, to be observed, agreeable to the Directions therein.

M. WEARE, (PRESIDENT OF THE COUNCIL.

E. THOMPSON, Secretary.

A PROCLAMATION
For a General THANKSGIVING,
Throughout the United-States of AMERICA.

In *CONGRESS, November 1, 1777.*

FORASMUCH as it is the indispensible Duty of all Men, to adore the superintending Providence of *Almighty GOD*, to acknowledge with Gratitude their Obligation to *Him* for Benefits received, and to implore such further Blessings as they stand in Need of ; and it having pleased Him, in his abundant Mercy, not only to continue to us the innumerable Bounties of his common Providence ; but also to smile upon us, in the Prosecution of a *just and necessary WAR*, for the Defence and Establishment of our unalienable Rights and Liberties ; particularly, in that he hath been pleased in so great a Measure to prosper the Means used for the Support of our Troops, and to crown our Arms with most signal Success :

IT is therefore recommended to the Legislative or executive Powers of these several *UNITED STATES*, to set apart *THURSDAY*, the eighteenth Day of December next, for solemn *THANKSGIVING* and *PRAISE* : That at one Time and with one Voice the good People may express the grateful Feelings of their Hearts, and consecrate themselves to the Service of their Divine Benefactor ; and that together with their sincere Acknowledgments and Offerings they may join the penitent Confession of their manifold Sins whereby they had forfeited every Favour, and their humble and earnest Supplication that *GOD*, thro' the Merits of *Jesus Christ*, would mercifully forgive and blot them out of Remembrance ; that it may please him graciously to afford his Blessing on the Government of these states respectively, and prosper the public Council of the whole ; to inspire our Commanders both by Land and Sea, and all under them, with that Wisdom & Fortitude which may render them fit Instruments, under the Providence of *Almighty GOD*, to secure for these *United-States*, the greatest of all human Blessings, *Independence* and *Peace* ; that it may please him to prosper the Trade and Manufactures of the People, and the Labour of the Husbandman, that our Land may yet yield its Increase ; to take Schools and Seminaries of Education, so necessary for cultivating the Principles of true Liberty, Virtue, and Piety, under his nurturing Hand ; and to prosper the Means of Religion for the Promotion and Enlargement of that Kingdom which consisteth in *Righteousness, Peace, and Joy in the Holy Ghost.*

And it is further recommended, that servile Labour and Recreation, altho' at other Times innocent, may be unbecoming the Purpose of this Appointment, be omitted on so solemn an Occasion.

Extract from the Minutes,

Attest,   CHA. THOMPSON, Secretary.

GOD save the UNITED-STATES of AMERICA.

EXETER; Printed by ZECHARIAH FOWLE, 1777.

give and blot them out of remembrance." Congress also recommended that Americans petition God "to prosper the means of religion for the promotion and enlargement of that kingdom which consisteth in righteousness, peace and joy in the Holy Ghost."[2]

Notes

1. James H. Hutson, *Religion and the Founding of the American Republic* (Washington, D.C.: The Library of Congress/University Press of New England, 1998), 52, note.
2. www.loc.gov/exhibits/religion/vc006494.jpg

APPENDIX H

The Baptism of Pocahontas at Jamestown, Virginia (1613)

(See next page for identification of subjects)

The Baptism of Pocahontas at Jamestown, Virginia (1613)

1. Pocahontas
2. John Rolfe
3. Alexander Whiteaker
4. Sir Thomas Dale
5. Sister of Pocahontas
6. Nantequaus, Brother of Pocahontas
7. Opechancanough
8. Opachisco, Uncle of Pocahontas
9. Richard Wyffin
10. Standard Bearer
11. Mr. and Mrs. Forrest, the lady being first gentlewoman to arrive in the colony
12. Henry Spilman
13. John and Anne Laydon, the first persons married in the colony
14. The Page

INDEX